PUNCH

PUNCH

The Delights (and Dangers)
of the Flowing Bowl

*An Anecdotal History of the Original Monarch of Mixed
Drinks, with More Than Forty Historic Recipes, Fully
Annotated, and a Complete Course in the Lost
Art of Compounding Punch*

David Wondrich

A PERIGEE BOOK

A PERIGEE BOOK
Published by the Penguin Group
Penguin Group (USA) Inc.
375 Hudson Street, New York, New York 10014, USA
Penguin Group (Canada), 90 Eglinton Avenue East, Suite 700, Toronto, Ontario M4P 2Y3, Canada
(a division of Pearson Penguin Canada Inc.)
Penguin Books Ltd., 80 Strand, London WC2R 0RL, England
Penguin Group Ireland, 25 St. Stephen's Green, Dublin 2, Ireland (a division of Penguin Books Ltd.)
Penguin Group (Australia), 250 Camberwell Road, Camberwell, Victoria 3124, Australia
(a division of Pearson Australia Group Pty. Ltd.)
Penguin Books India Pvt. Ltd., 11 Community Centre, Panchsheel Park, New Delhi—110 017, India
Penguin Group (NZ), 67 Apollo Drive, Rosedale, North Shore 0632, New Zealand
(a division of Pearson New Zealand Ltd.)
Penguin Books (South Africa) (Pty.) Ltd., 24 Sturdee Avenue, Rosebank, Johannesburg 2196,
South Africa
Penguin Books Ltd., Registered Offices: 80 Strand, London WC2R 0RL, England

While the author has made every effort to provide accurate telephone numbers and Internet addresses at the time of publication, neither the publisher nor the author assumes any responsibility for errors or for changes that occur after publication. Further, the publisher does not have any control over and does not assume any responsibility for author or third-party websites or their content.

First edition: November 2010

Library of Congress Cataloging-in-Publication Data

Wondrich, David.
    Punch : the delights (and dangers) of the flowing bowl : an anecdotal history of the original monarch of mixed drinks, with more than forty historic recipes, fully annotated, and a complete course in the lost art of compounding punch / David Wondrich.
        p. cm.
"A Perigee Book."
Includes bibliographical references and index.
ISBN 978-0-399-53616-8
1. Punches (Beverages)   2. Cocktails.   3. Fruit drinks.   I. Title.
TX951.W57   2010
641.8'74—dc22   2010030835

PRINTED IN THE UNITED STATES OF AMERICA

10 9 8 7 6 5

The recipes contained in this book are to be followed exactly as written. The publisher is not responsible for your specific health or allergy needs that may require medical supervision. The publisher is not responsible for any adverse reactions to the recipes contained in this book.

For Spence,

who would have dug it

CONTENTS

The Age of Punch as seen by its grandsons.

INVOCATION

In the Age of Chaos, long before the creation of the Cocktail, Spirituous and Aqueous, Thick and Thin, Sweet and Sharp and Unctuous were all tumbled together in One Undifferentiated Mass without Form or Order. Then from the East there rose a Sun to dry the Wet and distill the Light from the Heavy. And then all Drinks began to know their Proper Kinds and submit the Willfulness of their Doing to the Correction of Just Reason. That Sun had a Name, and that Name was Punch.

PREFACE

This book is about Punch. And by "Punch," I don't mean the stuff sluiced around at fraternity mixers—several 1.75-liter handles of whatever hooch is the cheapest, diluted with a random array of sodas and ersatz juices and ladled elegantly forth from a plastic trash can. Nor do I mean the creative concoctions proffered by feature articles on stylish entertaining—light, colorful things that are all fizz and fruit and are far too eager to please to be taken seriously as a delivery system for beverage alcohol.[1]

In short, there are lots of "punches" this book *isn't* about. But you wouldn't expect a serious book on the Martini (such things do

---

1 I have written the drink's name with a capital "P," both to distinguish it from the degenerate compounds that have usurped its name and to indicate that it is a specific class of drink. I have done the same throughout with other classes of drink. I don't know if this fits the canon of literary English, but it is done thus in drink-writing, and I am a drink-writer.

exist) to waste a lot of time on the so-called Chocolate Martini or, in fact, on anything not containing gin, vermouth and practically nothing else that tries to pass itself off as a Martini—to say nothing of the "x-tini," where $x \neq$ "Mar." And this is a serious book about Punch—well, as serious as a book can be that tells the story of a means of communal inebriation and its associated traditions, supported by a slew of sometimes rather fiddly formulae for re-creating drinks that haven't been tasted by humankind in at least a century and a half. In any case, it's the first of its kind, and as such, it's going to discriminate.

The fact that nobody's published a real book about Punch before is in and of itself a remarkable thing. Open just about any volume written in English between the late 1600s and the mid 1800s that deals with the details of day-to-day life and odds are sooner or later somebody's going to brew up a bowl of the stuff—Behn, Defoe, Addison and Steele, Swift, Pope, Fielding, Richardson, Smollett, Sheridan, Boswell, Burney, Edgeworth, Austen, Coleridge, Byron, Thackeray, Dickens, world without end. The rakes of the Restoration knew it, William and Mary's subjects drank it readily, the reigns of the three Georges were damp with it—very damp—and the Regency was well steeped indeed. George Washington enjoyed it, and Thomas Jefferson owed a part of his property to it. For some two hundred years, Punch—at base a simple combination of distilled spirits, citrus juice, sugar, water and a little spice—was the reigning monarch of the kingdom of mixed drinks. If nothing else, it has stories to tell.

Most of Punch's stories are of warm fellowship and conviviality and high-spirited gatherings afloat on oceans of witty talk. But it would be disingenuous to pretend that there aren't also plenty of battles and brawls and all the other products of the temporary madness that overtakes even the strongest-headed when they've consumed more distilled spirits than they can keep track of. For every cozy evening like the ones the settled Sussex townsman and diarist Thomas Turner used to spend, back in the days of George III, drinking Punch made from smuggled French brandy with his fellow tradesmen, there was one like Captain Drake's in early 1709, when he sat up guzzling Arrack Punch with three fashionable whores in his cell in London's Newgate Prison, where he was being held for treason under arms. "On a sudden some difference arose between the ladies," he later recalled, causing them to engage in "bloodshed and battery" until they were exhausted and their clothes and coiffures in tatters—at which point they patched themselves up as best they could, rearranged their hair, and called for another bowl.

But sufficient as it may be, the chance to retail a few drams of damp anecdotes is far from the only reason to write a book about Punch. Recent years have seen public interest in the fine art of mixing drinks fizz up to an almost alarming level, spawning a number of surprisingly sober books on the subject—books that focus almost obsessively on the craft and history of the Cocktail. (I myself have written three.) Almost without exception, these books have focused on the American part of the story—the part that begins with the Sling, the Cocktail, the Mint Julep and all the other ancestral "American sensations," progenitors of pretty much every mixed drink we lap up today save Vodka and Red Bull, and you could even squeeze that one in among the Slings if you were to rub it with a little Vaseline first.

We don't know who first came up with the Julep or the Cocktail or indeed almost any of the foundational American drinks. But somebody had to teach those anonymous folk geniuses how to mix drinks. Mixology might be simple enough, as far as crafts go, but it still has its secrets, its right ways and wrong ways, its tricks and traditions. Indeed, by 1806, when the Cocktail was first defined in print, concerned men and women had been grappling for two centuries and more with all the issues of balance, potency and proper service that mixing drinks with distilled spirits raises. Admittedly, in the larger scheme of things, these are pretty trivial—unless, that is, you've just laid down good coin for a drink, coin that was earned by the sweat of your brow (or whatever other part of your body you sweat with). In that case, it has real meaning whether the drink you're about to taste was assembled by a ham-handed ignoramus who's making it up as he goes along or by someone who has spent a few years absorbing the best practices of the job from people who really know their onions.

In the early days of the American republic, when this quintessentially American art was first finding its legs, the best practices with which the wide-awake young men behind the bar had been indoctrinated were British, developed across the Atlantic and transplanted in American soil, and the laboratory in which they had been developed was the Punch bowl. We don't know precisely who invented Punch in the first place, nor are we ever likely to. But we don't know who invented the Martini, either, or the original Cocktail. Such is the history of mixed drinks. We do know that if Punch wasn't the first mixed drink powered by distilled spirits, it was certainly the first globally popular one—spirits-drinking's killer app, as it were—and that its first unambiguous appearance in writing was in a letter by an Englishman. Whoever might have invented it, it was Englishmen, or at least Britons, who fostered the formula, spread it to their neighbors, took it all around the world.

Although when I say "Englishmen," I am doing a great injustice, as much if not most of the mixing of drinks that was done in England in the eighteenth century was not done by men at all. Bartending was a woman's job. That's not to say that no men ever performed it, but the standard setup was the man as proprietor, host, bouncer and business manager, while the ones who drew the drinks and served them were female—in fact, they were often the proprietor's daughters, the prettier the better. As Thomas Brown observed in 1700, "Every Coffee-House is illuminated both without and within Doors; without by a fine Glass Lanthorn, and within by a Woman . . . light and splendid," whose job was not only to serve the customer but to chaff him and flirt with him and draw him in. I suspect that the freedom the modern bartender possesses to banter with a customer, a thing not common in the service professions, was fought for and won by those Punch-slinging young barmaids of three hundred years ago.

"The Pretty Bar Maid," Thomas Rowlandson, 1795.
BRITISH MUSEUM

Like all the best and most enduring culinary preparations, Punch was a simple formula that could grow in complexity with its executor's skill and available resources. During the two centuries of its hegemony, British Punch-makers, generously endowed with both, used them to develop a good many of what we consider today to be the hallmarks of the American school of mixing drinks. The appreciation of which liquors and wines complement each other and which don't; the ins and outs of balancing sweet and sour; the use of liqueurs and various flavored syrups for sweetening; the salutary effects of Champagne and sparkling water on drink and drinker; the affinities between certain citrus fruits and certain spirits (e.g., the orange and brandy, the lime and rum); the use of eggs, dairy products and gelatin as smoothing agents—the list is both long and technical, descending into the minutiae of proportion, technique and even garnish.

The chance to explore the British foundations of modern mixology and, even better, to delve into the rich and mostly unmined quarry of anecdote that stemmed from it is certainly motivation enough to write a book and, I hope, for people to read it. Yet there's

another, even better reason, but to explain it I'm going to have to
stoop to autobiography.

How to Win Friends and Intoxicate People

Ten years ago, I fell into a job writing about Cocktails. It began
as an amusing sideline, something to have a little fun with while
I pursued a career as professor of English literature. But it turned
out that mixing up Sazerac Cocktails and Green Swizzles, research-
ing their histories and writing anecdotal little essays about them for
Esquire magazine's website was not only more fun than grading
papers and trying to keep classes full of hormone-buzzed sopho-
mores focused on the tribulations of King Lear but also—to me,
anyway—considerably more satisfying. Perhaps I lacked academic
seriousness. In any case, before very long the sideline metastasized
into a career.

Being a professional Cocktail geek brought its own peculiar
challenges. One of them was what to do at parties. Spending all this
time in the company of delightful drinks, I wanted to share—friends
don't let friends drink Vodka Tonics, not when they could be absorbing iced dewdrops crafted from good gin or straight rye whiskey,
fresh-squeezed juices, rare bitters and liqueurs and, of course, lots
of love. But bartending is hard work, and after a couple of years'
worth of parties spent measuring, shaking, stirring, spilling, fum-
bling for ingredients, fielding requests for Vodka Tonics and, worst
of all, never getting a chance to actually talk to anyone, I was willing to relinquish the spotlight and the performative glory of mixing
drinks in front of people for a little hanging out and cocktail party
chitchat. Perhaps it was time to take a second look at Punch. After
all, the old bartender's guides I'd been steadily accumulating had
clutches of large-bore recipes tucked away at the back, and if these
were anywhere near as tasty as the Cocktails I'd been successfully
extracting from them . . .

My first attempts to fill the Punch bowl, however, were amateur at best. I treated the recipes as mere guidelines, changing things for convenience and cost and because surely I knew better than the mustachioed old gent whose work I was interpreting. Used to making Cocktails, where dilution is a no-no, I would cut back the seemingly excessive amounts of water the recipes called for. The result, of course, was chaos. I remember, dimly, one summer afternoon when I made the famous Philadelphia Fish-House Punch for the first time, leaving in the copious amounts of rum and brandy but omitting most of the water. Fortunately, it was at a house party out in the country, and nobody had to drive. Or even walk, for that matter. Even staying pantsed was somewhat of a challenge. Other times, I'd skimp on the ice, think nothing of using powdered nutmeg instead of grating it fresh, splash in Technicolor arrays of clashing liqueurs, substitute cheap bourbon for good cognac or ginger ale for Champagne and a host of other things too embarrassing to relate.

Eventually, though, I began to learn. I had help. Friends shared their expertise, their space, their liquor and, most importantly, themselves. It's not Punch if there's nobody to drink it. Ted "Dr. Cocktail" Haigh, who had put in some sterling work at the Punch bowl, was happy to share the fruits of his experience (for the record, his Bimbo Punch is a thing of beauty). Sherwin Dunner, friend to every living hot jazz musician, hosted some memorable evenings, where the Punch flowed like ditchwater and the music reached an authentic speakeasy-era level of abandon. Nick Noyes and Jessica Monaco provided guinea pigs in their dozens and in their hundreds and the booze with which to water them—and, even better, an appreciation for precisely the sort of recherché, historic formula that appealed to me. There's something stirring about gazing across a sweeping lawn full of people all mildly intoxicated on Captain Radcliffe's Punch, a recipe that hadn't seen the light of day since England was ruled by a Dutchman. I could go on, but I'll save everyone else—as many as I can remember—for the acknowledgments.

It wasn't just laziness that kept me making Punch, although Lord knows I can be plenty lazy. But if you're spending the hour and a half before party time assembling a baroque concoction that was originally created for European royalty and calls for fifteen ingredients, half of them prepared from other ingredients, sloth doesn't really enter into it. Nor was it the utter deliciousness of most of these old Punches. G&Ts are delicious, too, and they take a lot less work. But over the last seven or eight years, I've made historic Punches dozens and dozens of times, for groups as small as four and as large as 250; for friends coming over to chat, backyard barbecues, Christmas parties, book parties, weddings (a massive bowl of Punch makes a fine wedding present and produces happy wedding guests); for Victorian Societies and museums and clubs and too many lectures to count. Every time, it happens the same way.

First, while everyone else remembers those fraternal garbage cans and decides that they'll stick to the wine, thanks anyway, the veterans, those who have shared a bowl of real Punch before, step smartly up to the sideboard and ladle themselves cups. Meanwhile, a few adventurous or unusually bibulous newcomers sniff around the bowl, examining the unpromising, brownish liquid within (frat and food-magazine Punches are always as brightly and cheerfully colored as drinks marketed for toddlers) and studying the vets for signs of liver disease or just plain bad character. Then one of these will give in and ladle herself a glass, taking a tentative sip as the others look on with concern. Okay, so it's not poisonous. In fact— well, soon the knot by the bowl is making a joyful little noise, and the rest of the folks are beginning to reconsider their policy of cleaving to the Grüner Veltliner. One by one, what the heck, they drift over to see what the fuss is about, soon to be joined by whomever it was they were talking to before they excused themselves for the minute that has turned into ten or fifteen. Before you know it, everyone's chattering away with tipsy animation and it's a party. Sure, there are always a few holdouts, but sooner or later all but the most stridently resistant will get sucked in. Nobody likes to be the odd person out, particularly if all it takes to participate is to stand around sipping something truly delightful, made from a formula that Charles Dickens used to enjoy.

But that's the true beauty of Punch. The "flowing bowl," as its devotees used to call it, makes itself the catalyst for, and focus of, a temporary community of drinkers, not unlike the one you'll find on a good night at a really good neighborhood pub. Admittedly, some will drink a little more than they're used to; the limpid balance of good Punch makes that easy. One or two might be grievously over-served, but if so, it is by their own hands. The Punch bowl holds dangers as well as delights; it is freedom, and freedom is a test that some must fail. Yet for every Punch-drinker who does, there are five, six, ten, who would agree with the Edinburgh wit John Wilson that "there seems to be a divine air breathed from the surface of a circle of china . . . when a waveless well of punch sleeps within, that soothes every ruder feeling into peace, and awakens in the soul all the finer emotions of sensibility and friendship."

Punch isn't Cocktails. The Cocktail is an unforgiving drink, with a very narrow margin of safety. Two Martinis and you're fine; three and you're boarding the red-eye to Drunkistan. The little glasses of Punch—the traditional serving is about a sherry glass full, just a couple of ounces—mount up, to be sure, but it's easy to pull back before you've gone too far.[2] Whatever their octane, though, there's something particularly exhilarating to drinks based on dis-tilled spirits, and Punch will always share that. As the eighteenth-century song put it,

> *You may talk of brisk Claret, sing Praises of Sherry,*
> *Speak well of old Hock, Mum, Cider and Perry;*
> *But you must drink Punch if you mean to be Merry.*

There's the crux. Without merriment, life is scarcely worth liv-ing. I know there are people who will disagree with that statement—the ethereal, contemplative ones; the efficient, purpose-driven ones; the solitary, the angry, the superior. Punch is not for them. But for

---

2 If the Punch is cold, the ice will melt as the afternoon or evening drags on; if it's hot, the alcohol will slowly steam out. Either way, it will weaken over time, in parallel with the drinker's judgment. This is not a bad thing.

the rest of us, the ones who find solace in this grim world in the humor and good nature of our fellow humans, there's no surer way of concentrating those qualities than around a bowl of Punch.

This Book

Finally, a little bit about the present volume. Dozens of recipes for Punch survive from its heyday—hundreds if you include the transitional decades that immediately followed (by then, drink books had become a proven moneymaker, and any recipe you could use to fill a page had value, even if few were going to actually make it). Not only have they never been collected, but there's never even been a real attempt to determine which ones should be collected. In 1862, the New York firm of Dick & Fitzgerald published Jerry Thomas's *Bar-Tenders Guide*, alias *How to Mix Drinks, or the Bon Vivant's Companion*, the world's first book of its kind (you will find it referred to by each of its three names; I'll try to stick to *Bar-Tenders Guide*). Even if it hadn't been the first, it would nonetheless remain the most influential, for one reason: Thomas took the time to make the book something more than a random collection of recipes. He stood before the young and boisterous crowd of American drinks, called them to order and assigned them to classes. In the process, he recognized fine distinctions, identified defining characteristics and excluded a lot of redundant and superfluous recipes. It stands as testament to the intelligence with which he made his choices that, for the most part, his categories still stand today. Unfortunately, the one category that he let in wholesale, utterly unsorted, is Punches. Where "the Professor" feared to tread, his successors have chosen the path of wisdom and stayed their feet as well. (For more on Thomas's life and drinks, see my 2007 book, *Imbibe!*)

My first tasks, therefore, were to separate the Punches from other, similar drinks, sort them into broad categories and, perhaps most importantly, throw out as many as I possibly could. Punch was merely one of many drinks served in bowls (the preindustrial period saw much more communal drinking than was possible once people had to drive, dial telephones and operate heavy machinery). While they all have their interesting points, I had to be ruthless, lest this book require its own propulsion system to move from point A to point B. So, alas, here you will find no Wassails, Eggnogs, Possets, or other large-bore drinks that are not Punches. The eighteenth century's Negus and Bishop, Sangaree, Flip and reeking bowl of Whiskey Toddy will, alas, have to wait for another book, as will the Claret Cup and Maitrank and other nineteenth-century low-alcohol delights. They are all, or almost all, delicious drinks served in bowls, but they aren't Punch, and while I strive not to be doctrinaire in my drinking, to include them would have swelled the size of this book beyond any reasonable bounds. For the same reason, neither will you find here the individual-serving Punches that arose in great profusion once the days of sitting around the flowing bowl began to wane. For what it's worth, I address many of those in *Imbibe!*, while their Tiki-drink descendants are admirably covered by Jeff Berry in his various works.

But neither have I included every genuine Punch that wormed its way into an old book. If a recipe is here, it's because it's historically important, it helps illustrate the techniques and practices of the Punch-maker's art or it's just plain delicious. Almost always, it's some combination of the three. I've tried to get all the famous ones, at least; if it's not here, it's because I couldn't find a definitive recipe for it. For instance, as delightful as it may be, you won't find Charleston's famed St. Cecilia Society Punch here, since the earliest recipe I've been able to find is from 1939, and it bears marks of tampering. For many another, I couldn't find even that much. The most famous Punches tended to be associated with clubs, and as club life waned and the organizations shut up their houses and disbanded, the closely guarded formulae for their characteristic tipples tended to disappear into the memory hole. But who knows? With the digital revolution making rich new archives not only available but easily searchable, even from your cell phone, such deeply buried secrets might very well make their way back to the shores of light.

It's my fondest hope that anyone who reads this book will feel that it has rendered him or her fully capable of sizing up whatever the archives should disgorge and reducing it to a shopping list and a set of procedures. To that end, on top of the forty-odd Punch recipes you'll find here, I've also supplied as thorough a course in the fundamentals of Punch-making as I can provide, including notes on formulae, techniques, ingredients and equipment. Teach a man to fish, and he'll always have Fish-House Punch.

Finally, you will find a lot of very bad spelling in these pages. In stitching my text together from the hundreds of sources I've consulted, I've always tried to follow the motto of the Royal Society, *Nullius in verba*—"Take no one's word for it." Rather than rely on other, less Punch-obsessed authors' evaluations and interpretations of the historical evidence, I've done my best to draw on original, primary sources. And since English spelling was a matter of opinion and personal preference until well into the eighteenth century, many of those documents show a remarkable freedom with the forms of written English. Rather than beat them all into our narrow modern mold, I've chosen to celebrate diversity. If anything has you stumped, read it aloud and it should become clear.

BOOK I

THE HISTORY OF PUNCH

Nobody can say precisely when, where or by whom Punch was invented. That is in fact the default position for popular mixed drinks in general; few of them indeed can produce their birth certificates. But drinks don't spring out of nowhere, nor do they attain general popularity before their time—before, in other words, they supply a timely, efficient and executable answer, a best answer, to the eternal question, "What should we drink?" The Dry Martini, to consider an example at least somewhat closer to us in time, could have been invented anytime from the 1850s on, when the United States (the land of the Cocktail) began to import French vermouth and English gin in quantity. And yet it wasn't until the mid 1890s that it achieved popularity, when the increased complexity and sophistication of American city life caused fashionable tipplers to cast about for a less-alcoholic alternative to the highly intoxicating glass of barely tainted straight booze that was the original Cocktail, and the rise of the soda fountain made it imperative that that alternative not be sweet or syrupy. Similarly, to understand the origins of Punch and its rise to popularity, we'll have to try to figure out what made it necessary.

The Age of Punch as seen by itself, Thomas Rowlandson, 1810.
BRITISH MUSEUM

AQUA VITAE,
AQUA MORTIS

In 1575, Louis Le Roy, a French humanist chiefly known for his meticulous and elegant translations of Plato and Aristotle, published a Great Big Book of Everything under the title *De la vicissitude ou variété des choses en l'univers* (it was translated into English by Robert Ashley in 1594 as *Of the Interchangeable Course, or Variety of Things in the Whole World*). Most of the book is devoted to a study of the cyclical nature of change, in particular as it relates to human civilizations and the institutions that support them. Ultimately, though, Le Roy finds himself forced to concede that some aspects of his own time break the pattern. "To this age," he writes, "has been reserved the invention of many fine things that look not only to the necessities, but also to the pleasures and embellishments of life." These things are entirely new, he emphasizes, unknown to the Ancients in any form. Some of them are even powerful enough to destabilize the cycles of history. Le Roy lists only the most salient examples: the printing press, which has spread knowledge with a hitherto unthinkable breadth and rapidity, and the magnetic compass, which has enabled explorers to cross oceans and discover new continents.

There's one more great, world-changing invention he takes note of, but he hesitates to assign it to the *"belles choses,"* the "fine things," since "it seems invented rather for the ruin than the benefit of the human race."

He was referring, of course, to gunpowder, an invention that, according to Le Roy, made obsolete not only all traditional weapons but also the courage and inborn spirit that was needed to wield them (tell that to Sergeant York).

But there was another novelty of the age that he could have mentioned in almost the same words, had he deigned to lower his lofty gaze enough to bring it into view. *Aqua vitae*, it was called; "water of life."[1] All of the exhilaration and well-being contained in a quart of honest ale or a pint of good wine, ripped free from the watery and feculent elements that cushioned it and held it in check and concentrated into a glass you could drink off with a single short swallow. As with gunpowder, aqua vitae's strength could be used for good or ill, to protect or to destroy. Indeed, its dual nature was enshrined in another of its names, the paradoxical *aqua ardens*, "flaming water."

Its virtues were many. It could be made from materials not otherwise fit for consumption. It took up far less cargo space than other drinks—an important consideration in an age of travel and exploration. The high concentration of alcohol meant that it was essentially sterile and hence more or less immune to the rapid spoilage that affected beer and, to a somewhat lesser extent, wine. The alcohol could also make bad water safe to drink and was wonderfully effective at extracting and preserving the essences of the roots,

---

1 See Revelation 22:17, which reads in the Vulgate (the Latin Bible used in Europe at the time): "Qui vult accipiat aquam vitae gratis" (rendered in the King James Version as "And whosoever will, let him take the water of life freely"). This must have caused no end of hilarity among the Latin-speaking clerks of the day.

Household distilling, ca. 1500. AUTHOR'S COLLECTION

barks, herbs, spices and other botanical products that made up the bulk of the Renaissance pharmacopoeia. Even when unfortified with other drugs, taken in moderation it was invigorating in a way wine, beer or mead could never be.

On the other side of the ledger stood the fact that fortitude was useless against it. Even the mightiest potsman, a paladin who could match tankards with a whole alehouse full of swag-bellied Falstaffs and outquaff the parcel of them, would see his length measured upon the floor by less liquid than it would take to fill his hat. Traditional ways of drinking would need to be revised in order to accommodate it, lest social chaos ensue. "One should mark oneself when it comes to burnt wine,"[2] a Nuremberg physician warned in 1493, "and pay all the more attention to learning how to drink it." Not to put too fine a point on it, the Latinate wags of the day were quick to point out that a more appropriate name for it might be *aqua mortis*, "water of death," as the Lord Deputy of Ireland did in

---

2 "Geprannten weyn," another of aqua vitae's many names.

1584. If it (usually) didn't kill men outright, it certainly destroyed the health of those it ensorcelled and reduced them to penury.

Ironically, as a doctor and a German, our cautious Nuremberger was doubly culpable for the problem in the first place. Aqua vitae had begun its career as a drug, a medication, and as such, it followed the classic six stages through which euphoric drugs—that is, the kind that make you feel better whether there's anything wrong with you or not—pass on their way to acceptance: Investigation, when their powers are determined; Prescription, when theory is put into practice; Self-Medication, when their use becomes preventative; Recreation, when Commerce shows Medicine the door; Repression, when too much of a good thing proves too much; and—a step that is only granted to a precious few—Transcendence, when repression fails and society's institutions are rebuilt to accommodate the troublesome element, since people have realized that it cannot be dispensed with. This being a drink book and not a history of medicine, we're less concerned with the first three steps of the process than the last three, and as far as can be determined, it was Germany that first saw that transition from medicinal to recreational use.

I say "as far as can be determined" because unfortunately there exists no truly satisfactory history of the growth of the distilling industry in Europe. In fact, distillation in general has received far less attention than its historical importance would warrant, and I know of no up-to-date, detailed, accurate and comprehensive account of its origins and early fortunes (for a list of the most useful books that do exist, see my "Brief Note on Further Reading" on page 277). This is lamentable but not surprising. Such an enterprise would require expertise in history, chemistry, and archaeology and many years of archival research spanning four continents and documents in Latin, Greek, Arabic, the various branches of High and Low German, Dutch, Old English, Gaelic, Old and Modern French, Italian, Spanish, Portuguese, Old High Norse, Russian, Polish— even Syriac, Persian, Sanskrit and Mandarin Chinese. No doubt I'm forgetting a few. (Welsh? Persian? Lithuanian?) We are unlikely to see any such study soon.

At any rate, from what serious research has been done, we know that while distilled beverages had been used in parts of Asia for a very long time,[3] if Europeans knew before the eleventh century that one could, with fairly modest effort, isolate and concentrate the intoxicating part of wine, that knowledge was very closely held indeed. The extensive archaeological record of Greco-Roman antiquity and the early Middle Ages yields no traces of distillation at all, while all we find in the written record are mere hints and suggestions, on the order of Pliny the Elder's offhand remark that, alone of all wines, the highly prized Falernian is *"flamma accenditur"*—"ignited by a flame." (All wines will do so slightly if heated, so Pliny must have been talking about a wine that would burn at normal temperature. An alcohol-water compound won't do that unless it has been dosed with chemicals that render it undrinkable or is at least 35 percent alcohol, a concentration unattainable by fermentation alone.)

Even after Europe openly turned its attention to distillation during the so-called Twelfth-Century Renaissance, it took some two hundred years for the technology to break out of medical or scientific (that is to say, alchemical) circles and reach the Self-Medication phase. Once it did, though, it made its presence known: in 1360, for example, the city fathers of Frankfurt felt compelled to pass an ordinance regulating and taxing *der Schnapsteufel*, "the spirits-devil." By this point, grain-distilling was coming into play, a much cheaper way for northern Europe to produce spirits than by boiling down wines imported from its southern neighbors. Even with that advantage, though, it would take another century for recreational spirits-drinking to become widespread, and still there were holdouts. We can track its progress by the trail of taxes and regulations

---

3 The Chinese had a commercial distilling industry as early as the 600s, as Joseph Needham has shown in the book-length subsection of his magisterial *Science and Civilization in China* devoted to "Spagyrical Discovery and Invention: Apparatus, Theories and Gifts" (which would be volume V, part 4); however, based on postwar excavations in Pakistan, F. Raymond Allchin has been able to mount a persuasive argument that parts of India had such an industry a good thousand years before that.

any new intoxicant leaves behind itself once it is too popular, or too profitable, to ignore. Frankfurt got into the game exceptionally early, but by the end of the next century, the signposts start proliferating. Just a few examples: in 1472, the city of Augsburg began regulating the brandy trade. At more or less the same time, Ivan the Great of Russia was declaring a monopoly on "bread wine"—that is, vodka—sales. In 1496, it was Nuremberg's turn to crack down, the city fathers declaring that since *"vil Menschen in dieser Statt mit Nieszung Geprannds Weyns ein Merklicher Miszbrauch getrieben"*— "many men in this town have been markedly abusive in their enjoyment of burnt wine"—it could no longer be sold on Sundays and holidays. In 1514, France passed a licensing act; in 1556, England finally did the same—but only in its Irish colony, where it declared aqua vitae "a drink nothing profitable to be daily drunken and used."

Yet it wasn't until the seventeenth century, a full five hundred years after the alchemists' first experiments, that someone discovered a way to make spirits-drinking not just acceptable but even delightful. To understand just what a feat that was, we have to pause for a moment to consider the nature of early spirits and how they were made. First of all, distillers had to compete for raw materials with long-established professions and guilds—vintners, vinegar-makers, bakers, brewers. As a result, actual wine and beer were rarely distilled, and if they were, it was likely to be wine made from reconstituted raisins or beer made from spoiled or otherwise unsalable grain. More commonly, the still would be charged with wine lees or brewer's draff (the term of art for the leftovers of beer-making). Even when treated with unusual care, such materials—basically, industrial waste—would yield spirits of inferior flavor, as (for instance) Konrad Gesner readily acknowledged in his influential 1556 treatise on spirits, *Euonymus*. What's worse, though, the stills of the day were directly heated over an open flame, and the lees and draff were thick with suspended particles that would settle out and scorch on the hot spots produced by putting a pot on a fire, thus communicating an "empyreumatic," or burned taste, to the spirit, which was often commented on—never favorably. Even when wholesome materials were used, they were seldom so pure as to avoid this problem entirely, particularly when they were grain based.

Then there's the matter of cuts. While early works on distillation devote a fair amount of space to the need to cut off the distilling run before it comes to the "tails," or "phlegm"—the watery, oily stuff that begins to pass through the still once the bulk of the alcohol has been drawn off—there's no similar attention paid to segregating the "heads," the very first part of the still run, whose elimination forms one of the bases of modern quality spirits-making. Indeed, as late as 1753, we find one Antoine Hornot, a French distiller, insisting that those who discard the first drops off the still do so at their own loss, as they are the "most spirituous" portions of the run. The need to eliminate the heads would not be a regular precept in distillation manuals until the nineteenth century. Of course, people do a lot of things that don't make it into books, but if early distillers were regularly doing this, one would expect some notice of the practice somewhere, and I have found none (again, the lack of a detailed history of distilling is a problem). With the heads included, the distiller's handiwork would have hit the drinker with a nasty spike of methyl alcohol, acetone and other highly volatile, and toxic, aldehydes.

Taken all together, these conditions would have made for spirits with, let's say, little to offer the discriminating palate. This isn't to say that nobody was making tolerable spirits—there are scattered notices of people distilling quality ingredients in well-designed equipment over indirect heat. But such things must have been unusual. At its all-too-common worst, aqua vitae would have been a stinking, oily potion that burned like Sherman's march going down and left you the next morning with a head as pulpy and tender as a rotten jack-o'-lantern.

Fortunately, spirits-making doesn't stop with distilling. There are ways to change raw spirit into something more drinkable. They are not infinite, as a half hour of reading labels in your local Liquor Barn will demonstrate. There are really only four. You can try to mask the offending congeners (whatever's in there that isn't water or ethyl alcohol) by compounding: that is, spending days and weeks infusing your raw spirit with aromatic and pungent substances to mask the flavors of the congeners, redistilling (usually) the result and perhaps dosing it with sugar or honey to bank some of the remaining flames (examples: Chartreuse, Jägermeister). Or you can try to remove them by filtration, most commonly by passing your distillate slowly through a thick bed of charcoal and thus stripping off pretty much all of the congeners, be they good, bad or indifferent (vodka in general, Bacardi). Or you can try to "barrel out" the problem, as they say in Kentucky. Long aging in relatively small wooden casks allows some of the more volatile congeners to evaporate, mellows others and transforms still others through slow interaction with air and oak into something pleasing (Martell Cordon Bleu, Highland Park, Woodford Reserve, anything else that gets aged). For the fourth method, though, you'll have to leave the Liquor Barn and go to the nearest bar, since it involves mixing the raw spirit with a little of this and a little of that and drinking it down.

Unfortunately for the Renaissance spirits-drinker, these techniques required a good deal of trial and error to perfect, some of their principles being not nearly as obvious as they seem to us today, and only the first of them was fully understood. From the very beginning of European distilling, alchemists and physicians had been making what were essentially herbal liqueurs, pungent alcoholic elixirs that were flavored with multiple botanicals and, usually, sweetened. Although their production was originally (and still is) an Italian specialty, before long it became more or less general throughout the continent and its outlying islands. To pluck out one example among many, the late-fourteenth-century aqua vitae recipe contained in the British Library's manuscript Royal 17 A iii—if not the earliest, then one of the earliest in the English language—calls for distilling wine lees with cinnamon, cloves, ginger, nutmeg, galangal, cubeb and thirteen other herbs and spices. Drinks made thus were pungent and cloying on the palate—not the sort of thing you'd want to build an evening around. That's probably just as well, since, being in fact no purer than their base spirit, they would have induced hangovers worse than death itself. What's more, they were enormously expensive to make, lees or no, since many of the spices used were, quite literally, worth their weight in gold. The Germans had at least that problem solved by 1505, when a Vienna physician published a formula for "cramatbeerwasser"—wine (or wine lees) redistilled with juniper berries, which were plenty pungent and undeniably cheap. Once its base was switched to the more easily available grain, this ur-gin would become the spirit of the south German countryside, whence it radiated north and west until it went to ground in the Low Countries, where it has lived happily ever since. It could not, at first, have been very pleasant to drink, and its consumption did not approach social respectability until the eighteenth century, when careful Dutch hands had learned to distill a relatively clean spirit from grain.

As for the other techniques, by the beginning of the seventeenth century, the Russians were seriously exploring the possibilities of filtration, while the brandy-distillers of southwest France were in the early stages of their love affair with long barrel-aging. Yet neither practice would be even close to perfected before the end of the eighteenth century (as late as the 1730s, even the best cognacs spent no more than two or three years in oak), and hence we can set them aside and proceed to our last option, mixology. For that, we must look to England.

II

"A HORSE THAT DRINKS OF ALL WATERS"

The English have always considered themselves reliable drinkers. Iago's words in Act II of *Othello* pretty much sum up the prevailing opinion in his day: "In England . . . indeed they are most potent in potting. . . . [Your Englishman] drinks you with facility your Dane dead drunk; he sweats not to overthrow your Almaine; he gives your Hollander a vomit, ere the next pottle can be filled."

Iago has his issues, to be sure, but at least he got the players right: in any tippling contest, the Latin countries, while hardly dry, would have finished far behind the Dutch, the Germans (Iago's "Almaine") and the Scandinavians, much as they would now; and while in any man-on-man swilling match a great number of individual Russians and other Slavs would have certainly finished in the money, factors such as serfdom, Ottoman rule and the backward state of commerce would have kept eastern Europe's per capita scores low. But as for the relative superiority of the Englishman to

Dutchman, Almaine and Dane, well, it's a charming theory. Sure, as Richard Unger argues in his *Beer in the Middle Ages and the Renaissance*, what data exist suggest "drinkers in the Low Countries to have been consistent but less avid than German beer drinkers, while English drinkers kept pace with their German counterparts." And it must also be conceded that the English aristocracy and merchant class supplemented their quarts with many a pint, bottle and bowl of imported wine. But Germans and Dutchmen drank plenty of wine, too. So far, pretty much of a draw. But throw in aqua vitae and England comes up decidedly short. In 1603, when *Othello* was written, the rest of northern Europe had been sticking it away in quantity for a century and a half and was already well into the Repression phase, while England essentially abstained.

Knowing the Englishman of today, that seems scarcely possible. To merely slide your fingernail under the tab that peels the foil off a bottle of good single-malt Scotch whiskey[1] is to find one materialized at your shoulder, looking on with fond interest (or so it seems, anyway). But it's a curious fact—one of the anomalies of bibulology—that England, the very country for whom most of the world's best spirits were developed, came very late to serious aqua vitae–drinking.

It wasn't due to a failure of knowledge. The basic technology crossed the Channel at more or less the same time it reached the rest of northern Europe. There are records of English monasteries buying stills in the mid 1300s, when aqua vitae was first breaking out of the Investigation stage. Grain-distilling followed soon after, if we may judge by the passage in the *Canterbury Tales* (written in the late 1380s) where Chaucer has his Canon's Yeoman include among the many skills and knowings of his "elvish craft" the use of "cucur-

---

1 The modern convention is to spell this word with an "e" when it refers to something made in Ireland and the United States and without one when it refers to a Scottish, Canadian or Japanese product. This is a very recent rule, however, for a matter of personal preference that recognized no national borders, and since I shall be discussing aged grain distillates from several nations, rather than skipping back and forth like a spelling flea, I'll stick to "whiskey" throughout.

bits" and "alembykes" (both pieces of distilling equipment) and a familiarity with "berm" (yeast), "wort" (basically, unfermented ale) and "fermentacioun." And, to be sure, spirits were not entirely ignored: the upper classes were not slow to use them medically—it's worth bearing in mind that along with opium, alcohol was practically the only effective pain reliever in the pharmacopoeia—and distilling herbal "waters" became another of the myriad responsibilities of the mistress of a large house.

Yet by and large, while their Germanic cousins were guzzling gin and brandy on a daily basis, the English were taking it in cautious sips when feeling queasy. True, we read of Irish distillers crossing the Irish Sea in the time of Henry VIII and setting up shop in Pembrokeshire, on the coast of Wales, and Flemish ones operating in London a few years later (I should emphasize here that Ireland and Scotland were not England, and both took to spirits-drinking considerably earlier; see Whiskey Punch, Chapter XIV). But neither group seems to have gained all that much commercial traction, and it's safe to say that spirits-drinking in England didn't progress much beyond the Self-Medication stage until the 1600s—indeed, in William Harrison's 1587 *Description of England*, we find him much exercised at the inebriety of his countrymen (e.g., regarding strong ale, "it is incredible to say how our maltbugs lug at this liquor, even as pigs should lie in a row lugging at their dame's teats, till they lie still again and be not able to wag"), yet there's nary a dram of brandy or genever or usquebaugh to be found among the many drinks he lists with which they're continually fuddling themselves.

Why did the English, a determinedly bibulous people, wait so long to embrace the efficiencies of recreational spirits-drinking? For one thing, there was really no place to do it. From roughly 1300 to 1600, every time an Englishman nipped out for a drink, he had a choice of venues. Well, not every time—in most of the land, no matter who you were, you would have had to make do with the plain old alehouse—a humble, mom-and-pop sort of place, where you drank ale and beer and nothing but ale and beer, without so much as a packet of crisps (or whatever the contemporary equivalent was) to nibble on while you drank your pint or quart. Since the average Englishman/woman/child was already drinking a gallon or so of ale or beer a day at home and on the job (nobody drank water if they could possibly help it, and tea and coffee didn't appear on the scene until the mid 1600s), the alehouse offered little in the way of novelty. If you lived in one of the principal towns, though, had money to spend and looked presentable, you could also go to an inn, which had rooms to let, or a tavern, which didn't. Both sold ale (as a matter of course), but they also offered imported wines and food and a faster, more cosmopolitan clientele. The tavern was regulated with particular strictness—wine was considered more disruptive than ale, and the kind of people who could afford to idle away the hours drinking it and gambling (not traditionally a feature of the alehouse) and whatnot seemed far more likely to cause trouble than the business travelers who frequented the inn or the workingmen who filled the alehouses. Even London, the great metropolis, licensed no more than forty or so taverns, while most towns were lucky to have even one (in 1577, England had over 14,000 licensed alehouses, as opposed to 1,600-odd inns, most clustered in the major market towns, and a paltry 329 taverns).

This two-tier system was cumbersome, perhaps, but in a country where animals were called one thing by the people who raised them and another by those who could afford to eat them, it was not incomprehensible. It's no coincidence that "alehouse," like "pig," "calf" and "bull," is a word of Anglo-Saxon origin, while "tavern," like "pork," "veal" and "beef," comes from the Norman French. The two institutions faced each other across a cultural gulf that, over the centuries since the Norman Conquest of 1066, had evolved into a class one. And distilled spirits had no class. While their natural place would be in the more cosmopolitan precincts of the tavern, spirits-drinking elsewhere in Europe was too much of a plebeian activity to recommend it (spirits' early adoption by the "uncivilized" Scots and Irish didn't help things here). For the alehouse, on the other hand, well, it was enough that spirits were foreign. Even as England shook herself out of her medieval slumber and began opening herself to the larger world, her common people remained militantly, sometimes shockingly, xenophobic, even in London. A natural corollary was the deep resistance they displayed toward any novelty perceived as foreign, no matter how useful or enticing. It did, after all, take them some two hundred years to accept hops in their malt beverage, even though that addition made it keep far longer without spoiling and improved its flavor to boot.

But there was a counterweight to this conservatism. In Thomas Dekker's 1623 tragicomedy *The Welsh Ambassador*, there's a scene where several characters drink to the King of England's health, each in the preferred tipple of his people. Eldred, the king's brother, is disguised as a stereotypical Welshman (don't ask) and therefore chooses metheglin, a spiced honey wine especially prized in Wales, while another brother, disguised as an Irishman, will pledge "in usquebagh or nothing." But the Clown is an Englishman and, as he says,

> I'll pledge it in ale, in aligant, cider, perry, metheglin,
> usquebagh, minglum-manglum, purr; in hum, mum, aqua
> quaquam, claret or sacum, for an English man is a horse
> that drinks of all waters.[2]

He wasn't exaggerating. In 1587, Harrison reckoned that some fifty-six different dry, or "small," wines and another thirty-odd of the stronger sweet wines were being imported from places as nearby as France and as far afield as Persia. For those who had no access to or interest in such foreign bellywash, there were beers and ales in profusion—from the weak "small beer" everyone drank instead of water to the eccentrically named varieties of strong ale favored by Harrison's liquor-lugging maltbugs—the "huffcap, the mad-dog, father-whoreson, angels'-food, dragons'-milk, go-by-the-wall, stride-

---

2 For the record, "aligant" is a Spanish wine, "minglum-manglum" an adulterated wine of any sort, "purr" a weak cider, "hum" a fortified ale, "mum" a strong beer, "aqua quaquam" strong water of any type and "sacum" sherry.

wide, and lift-leg, etc." There were many more.[3] Add ciders, perries and other fruit wines, and the many and various honey wines (Sir Kenelm Digby, who died in 1665, left behind a collection of over a hundred different recipes for them), and factor in the unusual variety of ways in which they were sweetened, spiced, bittered and mixed, and we have the portrait of a land that had a long-standing and unusual interest in maintaining a varied and balanced diet of alcoholic beverages—with, of course, the sole exception of aqua vitae.

Flavoring strong drink with herbs, spices and fruits might be as universal as alcohol and almost as old, but this, too, the English approached with an unusual thirst for variety. Wines were sweetened, spiced, bittered, mulled or whipped up with cream and eggs to make Possets and Syllabubs; ales were buttered (if unhopped), bittered, sweetened, spiced—in fact (not coincidentally), pretty much everything that was done to the gentleman's wine was done to the yeoman's ale or beer. One example among many: if you steeped wormwood and other herbs in strong ale for a few weeks, it made "purl," a popular eye-opener. Replace the ale with wine, and you had "purl royal." Downstairs, upstairs. There were even, it must be noted, drinks that made limited use of aqua vitae in their compounding: since the 1400s, small amounts of it had occasionally been used in preparing hippocras (a spiced wine popular throughout Europe), where its extractive power came in handy, and braggott, an overstrength, spiced ale, where its advantages would have been obvious. Yet even then, it wasn't a standard ingredient in either. When the poet and soldier of fortune (a combination no longer often seen, alas) George Gascoigne needed an example of up-to-date mixology to rail against in his *A Delicate Diet for Daintie Mouthde Droonkardes*, the temperance tract he wrote in 1576 as penance for his past transgressions, the most recherché mixture he could pro-

---

3 The English still have a way with naming drinks. As proof, I adduce the Cheeky Vimto, a fairly nauseating mixture of port wine and blue alcopop claimed by its devotees to resemble Vimto, a popular (in Britain, anyway) purple soft drink.

duce was wine with "Sugar, Limons and sundry sortes of Spices . . . drowned therein."

Perhaps Gascoigne had quit his roistering too soon: by the end of the 1500s, the barriers to aqua vitae's popular acceptance were beginning to totter. Not only was it passing rapidly through the Self-Medication phase, with distillation becoming part of the apothecary's and even the grocer's skill set, but people were even beginning to turn their minds toward how it might be used to make a pleasing mixed drink. Take, for instance, the suggestion made by Sir Hugh Platt in his 1595 *Jewel House of Art and Nature*, that

> travellers may make a speedy or present drink for themselves when they are distressed for want of beer or ale at their inn if they take a quart of fair water and put thereto five or six spoonfuls of good *aqua composita*, which is strong of annis seeds, and one ounce of sugar and a branch of rosemary, and brew them a pretty while out of one pot into another; and then is your drink prepared.

While one must admire the mixological spirit displayed here, five or six spoonfuls of anise-flavored booze in a quart of water is weak sauce indeed, particularly when compared to the heady compounds lurking over the horizon. But it's a start.

Spirits were also beginning to slink into the bar. In 1572, an establishment turns up in London property records that not only foreshadowed the eventual solution to the problem of where to drink spirits but also served as a signpost for the route by which they would infiltrate and, for a time, subdue the highest reaches of English society. In a run-down row of stone buildings in Petty Wales, just east of the Tower of London, tucked in between a pair of alehouses known as the Ram's Head and Mother Mampudding's, stood the Aqua Vitae House.[4] Its location was no accident: behind

_____

4 I don't know if this was the first of its kind in England, but it's certainly the first cited in the standard sources. I have not been able to establish when it opened or who ran it.

"The Sailor's Joys," after Robert Dighton, 1782. BRITISH MUSEUM

Petty Wales, you see, lay the quays of the Thames, where cargo ships unloaded. And sailors—well, as an anonymous French freebooter observed in 1620, the sailor's way of celebrating anything *"est du boire l'eau-de-vie"*—"is to drink aqua vitae." Under Queen Elizabeth I, England suddenly had a lot of celebrating sailors.

III

"Punch by No Allowanc"

As the sixteenth century began to shade into the seventeenth, England sailed forth into the world, the Virgin Queen's canny hand loosely on the tiller. In the process, her mariners laid the foundations of what would become the greatest maritime empire the world has ever known. Having been too embroiled in internal strife to participate in the first part of the Age of Exploration, when Spain and Portugal mapped the globe and snapped up the richest parts of it, England had a latecomer's determination to pick up what hadn't yet been nailed down and, if possible, to un-nail a few things that had already been nailed. At first, ships were sent forth to America in the West and Muscovy in the East (the Queen and Ivan the Terrible were longtime correspondents, and he even proposed marriage to her; one shudders) in the hopes of finding a northern route to the riches of Asia, one that wouldn't be infested with Spaniards and "Portingales" and Hollanders and other dangerous pests of that ilk. When such a thing could not be found, they broke out the crowbar and set to un-nailing.

In 1577, Sir Francis Drake sailed for the Spanish-held west coast of the Americas, bent on exploration and plunder. He returned via the Pacific and the Cape of Good Hope, thus leading the second mission to successfully circumnavigate the globe. Unlike Ferdinand Magellan, he survived his voyage. Better yet, he came back rich with pirated Peruvian gold. Two years after his return, some of the queen's inner circle tried to capitalize on what he had learned and launched the country's first attempt at direct trade with Asia (with perhaps a little unofficial slaving and piracy at Iberian expense along the way). Led by Captain Edward Fenton, this expedition "for China and Cathay" dissolved into squabbling and disharmony and never made it out of the Atlantic. Ten years later, after the fight against the Spanish Armada had boosted England's confidence and professionalism at sea, another mission was sent east. This one actually reached Asia but left no permanent English presence there.

That would soon change. In 1600, a group of hard-nosed London merchants obtained a royal charter to form the English East India Company. The company's first trading mission reached the spice-rich islands of Sumatra and Java in 1602, but unfortunately the Hollanders had beaten them to it.[1] Nonetheless, despite Dutch harassment and interference, they still managed to establish a small "factory" (the contemporary term for trading post) there. In 1608, one of the company's men first set foot in India, although it would be another seven years before its "factors"—traders—would be able to gain a secure commercial foothold. By 1632, anyway, the company had factories dotted up and down India's southeast and northwest coasts and was on the verge of setting up its first outpost in the rich province of Bengal, where, 125 years later, its private troops would defeat a French army at the battle of Plassey and

---

1 The Dutch had been sniffing around those waters, nominally in the Portuguese sphere of influence, since 1596. They were not happy to have their fellow Protestants and erstwhile allies join them.

seize effective control of the entire Indian subcontinent, thus usher-
ing in the age of Britannia Triumphant.

But already, in those first thirty years of England in Asia,
the opportunistic, even semipiratical cadre of sailors, soldiers and
merchant-adventurers that the company sent out had made a mark
on world culture that time cannot erase nor age destroy. We know
this from a letter sent on September 28, 1632, from Armagon, one
muggy, mosquito-ridden pinprick on the Coromandel Coast, to Pet-
tapoli, another.[2] In it Robert Addams, one of the company's men-at-
arms, thanks Thomas Colley, a "factor," for a favor and wishes him
well on the upcoming mission to Bengal, on which Colley was slated
to be second in command to Ralph Cartwright. "I am very glad you
have so good compani to be with all as Mr. Cartwright," Addams
wrote, and "I hop you will keep good house together and drincke
punch by no allowanc." Thus Punch makes its debut in the written
records of history. As far as debuts go, it's not much: a name let fall
in a passing comment without definition or explanation (in this, it is
not unlike the first mention of a drink named cock-tail, in a 1798
London newspaper, which tells us only that it is "vulgarly called
ginger"). About all that we can be sure of from this famous letter is
that Punch was already a known drink and that there were those
who feared it—and that Englishmen were often savage spellers.

As with the Cocktail, it would take a few years before someone
would bother to define the drink for those playing the home game.
Punch got there in 1638, when Johan Albert de Mandelslo, a young
German adventurer, washed up at the company's factory in Surat.
There he found the factors irrigating themselves with "a kind of
drink consisting of aqua vitae, rose-water, juice of citrons and sugar."
"*Palepuntz*," he called it in the account of his wanderings published a
few years later; ungarbled, that's "bowl o' Punch," or—as the French
traveler François de La Boullaye-Le Gouz, who visited the same factory eleven years later, called it, "*bolleponge*." The Frenchman's de-

---

2 Should you seek these places on the map, they are now known respectively as Duga-
rajupatnam and Nizampatnam.

scription of it (sugar, lemon juice, "eau de vie," mace and toasted biscuit) more or less tallies with Mandelslo's, give or take a spice (and, of course, the toast garnish, traditional in English ale-based bowl drinks but a little odd here). Add the one given by François Bernier, who encountered "*bouleponge*" in Bengal in the 1660s ("aqua vitae . . . with lemon juice, water and a little nutmeg grated on top"), and we have a pretty clear idea of what these Englishmen were drinking. Aqua vitae, watered down to a more quaffable strength, soured with citrus juice, sweetened with sugar and spiced with whatever was handy, be it nutmeg, mace, rosewater or what have you—simple enough, considering that it's the foundation stone upon which all of modern mixology rests.

If the what is plain, the who, when and where are anything but. The problem is, as far as we can tell from what has come down to us almost four hundred years later, of all those early factors, of all the men who carried them from port to port, supplied them, protected them, not one took a few minutes to scribble down the origins of this new tipple. But then again, they had more pressing things to attend to than the curiosity of distant generations about their refreshments—like, for example, attempting to get the servant of the Chinese-Javan drinking-house keeper who has just tried to tunnel into your warehouse and steal your goods to give up where his master has hidden himself, a task that Edmund Scott attempted by shoving hot irons under the servant's nails and then tearing them all off, shredding his flesh with rasps, causing "cold iron screws to be screwed into the bones of his arms, and suddenly snatched out" and a dozen other demonic things (Javanese servants are tough; the man still wouldn't talk, or even cry out). Admittedly, that was in 1604, in Java, not 1632, in India, but it gives us a pretty good idea of the sort of person we're dealing with. They were not mixographers.

They certainly did like their Punch, though. Take our friend Thomas Colley. Evidently poor Mr. Colley—a rather sporty youth from London, it appears from the scant notices we have of his life— did not choose to heed Richard Addams's advice, and he probably should have: he died on August twenty-fifth, less than four months after he set foot in Bengal. He was not alone. In the first year of the factory there, four more of his companions were laid to rest, as was one of their replacements. "The Chiefe Occasion of this disease," one of the company's captains reported to his bosses in London, "is doubtless Intemperancy . . . for 'tis a place that abounds with Racke and ffruit [*sic*], and these immoderately taken Cannot Chuse but ingender Surfeits."

Once thirst and enforced sobriety weaned them of their native beverages, the English factors took to the native ones wholeheartedly; as early as 1618, some factories were already including arrack among their standard provisions. Few abstained from drinking Punch, and many abused it. Yet one can hardly blame them. Consider, for a moment, the factor's life. Thirteen thousand miles and six months at sea from home, pent up in a claustrophobic little compound (few were allowed to live outside of the factory) perched on the rim of an alien land whose people, languages and way of life were utterly foreign to anything in your experience, with little to occupy your time for weeks on end but waiting for ships to come in and trying not to think about the disease and death that were claiming all too many of your comrades. Small wonder if, as the Reverend John Ovington reported after his 1689 tour of the English factories of western India, you lost yourself in "Luxury, Immodesty and a prostitute Dissolution of Manners"—if you gambled, drank yourself insensate on Punch and solaced your existence with native whores.

Of course, some company men were just plain bad to begin with. "In those early turbulent days," as Major H. Hobbs wrote in 1944 in his marvelously chatty *John Barleycorn Bahadur: Old Time Taverns in India*, "India swarmed with unrepentant sinners who had discarded their Bibles and their consciences at the Cape of Good Hope." But not all were so studiedly wicked. Mandelslo leaves us a rather poignant portrait of how William Methwold, president of the Surat factory, would gather with three other factors after prayers each Friday, "which day being that of their departure from England," to toast with sherry and Punch the health of their wives, half the world away in England. "Some made their advantage of this meeting to get more than they could well carry away," he adds. It would take a strong man not to.[3]

But drinking something and inventing it are two different things, and with all that tippling, there was not much reflection on the origins of the factors' social drink of choice, and no informed account of its introduction has yet come to light. In the absence of eyewitness testimony, plausible assumptions tend to harden into orthodoxy. In the case of Punch, those assumptions began early. In 1658, Edward Phillips, a pioneering English lexicographer, published his *New World of English Words*. Among those new words was "Punch," which he defined thus: "A kind of *Indian* Drink." From his point of view, this was a good call. Paging through the convivial literature popular in the day—from Thomas Dekker's and Robert Greene's low and squabblesome satires and pasquinades to the various rowdy comedies by Shakespeare and his contemporaries to the 1638 *Barnabae Itinerarium*, aka "Drunken Barnaby's Itinerary" (a wet and smutty tour of England recounted in execrable verse, both Latin and English) and on up the literary scale to the elegant drinking songs of Ben Jonson and the other Mermaid wits and the suave little essay James Howell devoted to the world's drinks in 1634—he would have found no Punch. Poking around London, he might perhaps have heard of such a concoction at the East India docks. Elsewhere, the only recreational drink he would have found made with spirits would have been the newly popular pop-in (the seventeenth-century tippler's name for a shot of booze in a mug of beer or glass of wine), and he would have had to descend to low precincts indeed to find that. See, for example, Dekker's 1609 lowlife excursion, *The Bel-Man of London*, in which the senior member of the "ragged regiment of beggars" calls his crew to order while swigging from "a double Jug of Ale (that had the spirit of Aqua vitae in it, it smelt so strong)." Of course, the fortified wines coming into England from Spain at the time were made on essentially the same

---

3 In 1665, "two senior Captains" of the company estimated that for a month in India, a man would need thirty bottles of Madeira, thirty of beer and fifteen of arrack. Indeed.

principle, but wines were for gentlemen and thus received little satirical attention.

In 1676, John Fryer, a young English physician working for the
company in India, gave weight to the Punch-as-Indian-drink theory
when he noted in one of his letters home that

> at *Nerule* [Nerul, just outside Goa] is made the best *Arach*[4] . . .
> with which the *English* on this coast make that enervating
> Liquor called *Paunch* (which is *Indostan* for Five) from Five
> Ingredients; as the Physicians name their Composition
> *Diapente*; or from four things, *Diatesseron*.

Fryer's letters were published in 1698. Ever since, his offhand remark
has had the force of holy writ. In part, it's because of the erudition
displayed. Compared to the hardheaded Edmund Scotts, whom the
company usually sent east, Fryer was a gentleman, and as such, he
knew Greek (that "*Diapente*" and "*Diatesseron*") and was quick to
use his learning to fit modern phenomena into classical molds. It
helped that his etymology was plausible—the Hindi for "five" is indeed *panch*, and Punch did generally have five ingredients, except of
course when it didn't. It also helped that the idea of the drink's Indian origin appealed to not only academic sense but common sense.
Everything in a bowl of Punch but the water either came exclusively
from the East or was much cheaper there and easier to come by—but
here I am merely repeating what Joseph Addison already observed
in No. 22 of his newspaper, *The Free-Holder*, three centuries ago.[5]

---

4 "Arach," "arak," or however else this protean word is transliterated—"arrack" was
the most common in our period—is derived from the Arabic word for "sweat" or "juice"
and is generic throughout the Middle East and South, Central and Southeast Asia for
a distilled spirit; hence, when used unmodified it is no more useful for identifying precisely what someone is drinking than our "liquor." Materials it has been distilled from
range from raisins and dates in the Middle East to fermented mare's milk in Mongolia.
5 Lemons, citrons and both sweet and sour oranges were imported in increasing quantity throughout the seventeenth century, as English trade with the Mediterranean and,
particularly, Portugal developed. During the same period, the spectacular growth of the
Caribbean sugar industry meant that it went from being a rare spice to a culinary staple.

Addison's observation was particularly true when it came to the booze. The first European travelers to the eastern and southern parts of Asia found them awash in distilled spirits of various new and interesting species, none of them involving lees or draff and none needing to be spiced to mask the flavor. Antonio Pigafetta, one of the few who sailed with Magellan to survive the voyage, encountered two of the most common types on the Philippine island of Palawan in 1521. There the natives drank both distilled palm wine and distilled rice wine, he reported, the latter being the stronger and better. "It is as clear as water, but so strong that it intoxicated many of our men. It is called *arach*." When it touched at Java in 1596, the first Dutch mission to the Spice Islands found the Chinese community there ("very subtil and industrious people," as the contemporary English translation of their report puts it) also making "much aqua vitae of rice and Cocus [i.e., coconut sap], which the Iauars [Javans] by night come to buy, and drinke it secretly, for by Mahomets law it is forbidden them." Indeed, it's likely that the distilling technology in the great Southeast Asian island groups came originally from China; certainly the stills that they used, and in some places use to this day, are Chinese style.[6] But the only thing sketchier than the history of distilling in Europe is the history of distilling in Asia; in this respect, great stretches of time and territory are sunk in stygian blackness.

Only relatively recently has the antiquity of India's distilling tradition become clear. Archaeological excavations in the 1950s and 1960s in the region around the ancient trading center of Taxila, at the headwaters of the Indus in what is today Pakistan, uncovered remains of what were unmistakably distillery-grogshop complexes, each with multiple clay-pot stills. These have been dated to the time of Christ, give or take a century or two. Combine them with the sugarcane that Alexander the Great found growing in the same region

---

6 Unlike the still used in western Europe, with its high, bulbous top and external condensing coil, the Chinese still relies on a woklike cover full of cold water to induce condensation, with a cup underneath it, inside the still, to collect what drips off the bottom of the wok. It is then drawn out by a pipe through the side of the pot.

and the long-standing domestication of the lime in India, and it's not impossible that Rum Punch could be two thousand years old. Frustratingly, the millennium and a half between then and the arrival of European explorers in the 1500s remains one of those dark stretches, and I cannot say whether that ancient tradition survived unbroken or had to be reestablished through contact with the Chinese or Arabs. In any case, those explorers found not only a tremendous amount of distilling going on but some unusual people drinking the resulting spirits.

Moghul emperors, for example. Although they strove mightily to spread the faith with sword and lance and glorified it with jaw-dropping architecture (e.g., the Taj Mahal), Babur, the conqueror who swept into India from the north at the beginning of the sixteenth century and founded the dynasty; his son Humayun; his grandson Akbar and his great-grandson Jahangir all shared one great, un-Islamic weakness. Like the Javans, they could not resist a little tipple. Unlike them, however, they made no attempt to hide it. Akbar the Great, drunk on arrack, once famously raced across the rickety pontoon bridge spanning the Yamuna in Agra at a gallop. He was riding Hawai, his favorite elephant, at the time. And Jahangir, who at one point in his life was sticking away twenty capacious cups of arrack a day, scrupled not to drink it in front of William Hawkins, the East India Company's first emissary to his court, and then banish him from court for having alcohol on his breath.[7] By the time the elegant Sir Thomas Roe, who replaced Hawkins in 1615, arrived at his court, the shah had ostensibly cut back to six cups a day, although Roe still found him often "very busy with his Cuppes" and possessed by "a drowzines . . . from the fumes of Backus." And those six cups weren't even of pure arrack: Jahangir preferred "mingled wyne, halfe of the Grape, halfe Artificiall." When he offered Roe a cup of it, the aristocratic ambassador took one sip and promptly sneezed, remark-

_____

7 Hawkins got off lightly. Jahangir had others who had imbibed without authorization scourged in front of the court with barbed whips and then beaten with iron bars. And you thought *your* hangovers were bad. . . .

ing later that "it was more strong then [*sic*] ever I tasted." I shouldn't wonder; pop-in was not exactly favored by gentlemen. Ever true to his class, Roe informed his mercantile masters in his first report home that he "drancke water this 11 Monthes, and Nothing els," adding that "Rack" he could not endure.

Jahangir, who clearly could, preferred the coconut-sap variety. Although it was produced all over southern and western India, it was a particular specialty of the Portuguese-held port of Goa. In Bengal they had another type, which Bernier defined as "*eau de vie de sucre noir*"—"aqua vitae of black [i.e., raw] sugar"—a "much stronger Spirit than that of *Goa*," according to the Reverend John Ovington, who encountered it in Surat in 1689. There were plenty of other kinds, made from things like mangoes, cashew fruits, mahua-tree blossoms and what have you. India also abounded in the other ingredients that went into Punch. Although not a great producer of spices itself, it was close enough to their source in the East Indies that they were widely available, and for far less money than in Europe. Citrus fruits were abundant, as was sugar from both cane and palm. There was of course water, too, although its purity doesn't bear thinking about; but then again the same could be said of the water in London. It's safe to say, in other words, that all the ingredients for Punch were present in India. In parts of the subcontinent, people even had a tradition of drinking sherbet, an Islam-friendly tipple made by flavoring water or snow with a syrup of sugar, citrus juice (or other acid) and spices.

But possibility is not the same thing as necessity; the fact that something could have happened does not mean that it had to happen. Even if it did, we'd have another problem, since the exact same conditions existed in Java: plenty of arrack, citrus and sugar, and there the spices were even cheaper. Who's to say that our inquisitorial Mr. Scott, had he been a little more neighborly and gone to sit for a spell at the Chinese "arrack house" (as he called it) next door, might not only have forestalled that vexatious tunneling but also have taken Richard Addams's place in the history of drink by discovering that the arrack house was in fact a "Punch house," where a novel and delightful tipple was on offer? By the middle of the century, that is in fact precisely how Europeans were identifying such places in Indonesia, where they appeared to be operating in profusion, and we don't know whether the changed terminology reflects changed drinks or simply more precise knowledge of what was on offer in such places.[8]

But the real problem for the claim that Punch is an Indian creation is the dearth of actual seventeenth-century evidence of the native peoples of the region drinking the stuff. It's not mentioned in their own writings, or at least no such mention has yet filtered through to the West. If it were in fact a native specialty, one would expect that it would have been known by the likes of Jahangir, but it appears in none of the (very detailed) observations on his drinking habits. As for the Europeans who encountered it, they share a consensus that it was, as de La Boullaye-Le Gouz put it, *"un boisson dont les Anglois usent aux Indes"*—"a drink the English use in India." Even the erudite Dr. Fryer, in the midst of his lesson in etymology, says only that it's "the *English* on this coast" who are making "that enervating Liquor called *Paunch*." If it's not the English, it's the Dutch; they, at least, are the ones Bernier found also drinking it. True, a few of these travelers spent the entirety of their time in-country in one of the English factories, but others did not. Only one of the latter even so much as mentions Punch.

That was Johann Jacob Saar, who spent much of the 1640s and 1650s in Sri Lanka as a soldier for the Dutch. Upon his return, he published a wildly popular account of his travels, written with a cowriter from memory, as he had lost his notes on the voyage back. In it, he has a little section on Sri Lankan mixed drinks. There are

---

8 Indeed, in 1622, Pietro della Valle, the scrupulous Italian traveler, found the English in Bandar Abbas, near the Straits of Hormuz, drinking an aqua vitae–based tipple called "Larkin," which they had picked up in Java. He thought it so *"gagliarda"*— "potent"—and delicious that he had them teach him how to make it, although the recipe itself didn't make it into his book. It's worth noting that the company had a man named Robert Larkin in Java at the time.

three: massack, which is warm toddy—palm wine—mixed with palm arrack, eggs and spices; the very Punch-like vinperle—water and arrack boiled together with citrons, sugar, spices and, again, eggs; and palebunze, which is the now-familiar concoction but without the spices. His verdict on that one? *"Wie dem Geschmack so angenehm nicht: Also auch der Gesundheit nicht"*—"As for the taste, it pleases not; for the health, neither." Regrettably, Saar gives us no context for these most interesting concoctions. Did the locals drink them when by themselves? Were these drinks simply what they had learned to serve to Europeans in Punch houses, like the Bahama Mamas that rum-and-coconut-water-drinking Caribbean bartenders make for tourists? Most importantly, were they local inventions or merely adaptations of drinks that had been floating around the ports of the Bay of Bengal and the eastern shores of the Arabian Sea for the last generation or so?

Without this context, we can't rest half the argument for a native Indian origin of Punch on his observations—the other half resting, of course, on Fryer's etymology. That, too, is pretty shaky, seeing as the English were such inveterate manglers of foreign words— "Robidavia," a Spanish wine, became in their mouths "Rob Davy"— that it would be most remarkable if the Hindustani word for "five" emerged nearly unscathed. Furthermore, "punch" was a perfectly good English word with a number of uses, including, according to Samuel Pepys, as "a word of common use for all that is thick and short"—items that would include the "round and Belly'd" bowl Punch was usually served in (as the journalist John Dunton noted in 1728).[9] Nor can we ignore that there was a perfectly good, perfectly

---

9 Some have also thought to derive the name from "puncheon," a type of barrel, on the theory that spirits were shipped in them. Unfortunately, records do not bear that out, aqua vitae being carried in "runlets," small kegs of thirteen (U.S.) gallons, while puncheons held from sixty to ninety gallons. Such a container used as a mixing bowl, another theory, would mean that every man in the typical ten-to-twenty-man factory would have had to drink several gallons of Punch; even shared out among a typical Elizabethan ship's company that would yield between five and eight pints a man. Either quantity would be a paralyzing dose, if not a fatal one.

English model for this new drink, one that's attested to in print before the first English traveler set foot in India or viewed the palm-fringed coast of Java. That is, of course, George Gascoigne's wine mixed with "Sugar, Limons and sundry sortes of Spices." To make that into Punch, one would have to simply replace the real wine with an "artificiall" one (as Roe would describe it) made up of aqua vitae and water. Easy.

Ultimately, we have to judge this question as one does all historical ones: by the preponderance of the evidence. And that suggests that Punch was invented by an Englishman. But what sort of Englishman? I used to be content with the idea that, as one nineteenth-century commentator wrote, "punch . . . was invented by the convivial factors at Surat," and if not there, then at one of the East India Company's many outposts. After all, it first appears in their records, and they certainly drank a lot of it. But the more I delved into the records of England's early commercial enterprises out east, the more uneasy that conclusion made me. It turns out that I'm not the first to have my doubts. There are only two phyla of ink-stained wretch who can read through the eye-popping accounts of the early English experience in Asia and remain focused on that single word, "punch": mixographers and lexicographers. The Reverend Charles Bridges Mount belonged to the latter, being one of the subeditors of the *Oxford English Dictionary*. In a brief but cogent 1907 article in the indispensable *Notes & Queries*, after challenging Fryer's etymology (the published *OED* went with it anyway), Mount posited that the first man to make Punch was most likely neither a factor nor a soldier, but a sailor. The main basis of his argument rests on the popularity of the drink among English tars and the rapidity with which those of other nationalities adopted both the formula and its name. "Sailors of different nationalities," he observes, "when not fighting each other, are apt to be good comrades. . . . Moreover, they are very ready . . . to pick up from each other words which subsequently become current in the language of those who have taken the words." Reasonable enough.

But there's another, stronger basis for assigning a nautical origin to Punch. And it's not just that sailors like to drink; as we shall see, the land-bound employees of the company yielded to no man in their mastery of the bottle. Rather, it has to do with supplies, with victuals.

Traditionally, English ships had been victualed with beer for all and supplemental wine for the "gentlemen," the officers and important passengers. On the longer voyages that they were beginning to undertake in the Elizabethan years, this proved to be less than perfectly satisfactory. For one thing, beer and wine took up a great deal of space, what with each seaman's official daily ration of two to four forty-ounce quarts of beer and the so-called gentlemen good for easily half that in wine. Even on short rations, the unfortunate Captain Fenton's flagship, with a crew of one-hundred-odd seamen, managed to go through 2,300 gallons of beer and 300 of cider in under two months, with the gentlemen sticking away an average of three bottles' worth of wine a day each on top of that. When the East India Company's first trading mission set sail in 1601, its four ships and 480 men were provided with thirty thousand gallons of beer, a like amount of cider and fifteen thousand gallons of wine— some 420 tons' worth in total. Considering that the capacity of the ships totaled 1,160 tons, the burden this copious supply of fermented beverages laid on Elizabethan navigators is all too clear.

But bulk wasn't the only problem, or even the worst one. In 1588, as England braced herself for the imminent onslaught of the Spanish Armada, a fatal epidemic swept through the fleet. Charles Howard, Lord Admiral of England, attributed it to the beer, which had gone sour; quoth Howard, "I know not which way to deal with the mariners to make them rest contented with sour beer, for nothing doth displease them more."

One can hardly blame them, what with beer being the main source of their daily caloric intake. Beer going off was no unusual occurrence. Before pasteurization, it was hard enough keeping it from souring when it was stored in a cool, dry cellar. Slosh it around for a while in the fetid bilge of a ship, and every day it kept whole-some was borrowed time, even in temperate home waters.[10] In the tropics, well, as one Dutch sailor recorded in 1595, "the ex-treame heat of the ayre spoyled all our victuailes: Our flesh and fishe stunke, our Bisket molded, our Beere sowred, our water stunke, and our Butter became as thinne as Oyle, whereby diverse of our men fell sicke, and many of them dyed."

Nor did wines necessarily fare much better; evaluating some captured aboard a couple of stragglers from the armada, the En-glish reported that those from one ship were "wines but indiffer-ent, and many of them eager [i.e., sour]" and those from another good "only to make aquavitae of." But that, of course, was the answer right there. Shakespeare knew it: in *The Comedy of Errors*, written sometime in the early 1590s, he lists the special supplies purchased for a sea voyage as "oil . . . balsamum, and aqua-vitae" (act IV, scene 1). As is often the case with Shakespeare, the technical knowledge is state of the art, if anachronistic: the play is set in antiquity, but balsam of Tolu, or Peruvian balsam—a remedy for seasickness—was first described in 1574, and the usefulness of aqua vitae as a ship's store reflected experience even more recent than that. In fact, Shakespeare was one of the first to mention the prac-tice; judging from victualing records and inventories of captured ships, neither the Spanish ships that made up the armada nor the English ones that defeated it were supplied with spirits.[11]

The choleric and bibulous Captain Fenton, though, had shipped a fair amount with him, on top of all that beer and wine, ostensibly

---

10 Indeed, worse things could happen to beer than going sour, as Admiral of the Fleet Edward Russell recorded in 1689 after ten weeks at sea keeping station off the coast of Ireland: "in severall of the buts of beare, great heapes of stuff was found at the bottom of the buts not unlike to mens' guts, which has alaramed the sea men to a strange degre."

11 Oddly enough, the gin-drinking Dutch seem to have stuck to victualing their ships with beer and wine as well, although they may have changed things after the 1595 voy-age noted above, when they "learned what meat and drinke we should carrie with us that would keepe good." They were shipping aqua vitae by 1609, anyway, since Henry Hudson's men used it to intoxicate the poor Lenapes they found inhabiting Manhattan Island.

for medicinal use.[12] While his lading list doesn't survive, his journal does. Halfway through the trip, he started keeping a monthly tally of his provisions. His jottings show an interesting pattern: in the first month for which he left figures, Fenton's men go through three rundlets of aqua vitae. That could indicate something like a daily fortifying dram for each man. But then nothing for five months, during which the remaining four rundlets are kept untapped. Once they run out of beer (some of which had gone bad before they even cleared the Canary Islands) and wine, though, then there goes the aqua vitae, too. That suggests that Fenton decided to hold on to it as a sort of iron ration, a reserve that could be relied on not to spoil until the more perishable drinks were gone (leave beer, wine and water in barrels for six months at sea and they spoil; leave spirits, and they only get better). If this was a decision made on the spot, then whatever his faults, and they were many, Edward Fenton can be said to be the father of the naval rum ration.

In any case, by 1600, long-haul English voyagers were carrying a lot of spirits; the East India Company's first fleet stocked the equivalent of seven bottles per man, on top of the usual beer, wine and cider. Nor did the company's men have any trouble adapting to the indigenous spirits of Asia; indeed, they would run considerable risk to get them, as did the boatswain of Thomas Best's ship, who, when it anchored at Surat in 1612, swam ashore on the Sabbath with a couple of his comrades and spent the day "drinkinge drunk with houres [i.e., whores]," an episode for which he was ducked from the yardarm and demoted back to common seaman. By 1613, as John Jourdain (the company's chief factor in Indonesia) recorded, its ships were gladly provisioning themselves with Jakarta arrack.

But how did they drink their spirits? One point of evidence: according to the coded secret journal kept by Richard Maddox, Fenton's minister (it was that kind of voyage), the puritanical ship's surgeon pretended to pray and fast but kept a secret stash of cheese

---

12 He also had a distiller in each of his two main ships, ostensibly to provide fresh water—although who's to say they couldn't also whip up some sea-biscuit whiskey?

and bacon and drank "plenty of coole bear & aquavitte." Shots and chasers? Pop-in? One would like a little more detail. However he was taking it, the aqua vitae seems more recreational than medicinal. That was definitely the case with Robert Pike, a sailor on Sir Francis Drake's 1572 raid on Panama, who gave away an ambush after "having drunk too much aqua vitae." The problem wasn't so much that he drank the spirits, as Drake specifies in his account of the incident, but that he drank them "without water." So. If watered spirits were a common drink on English ships, that's 40 percent of the way to a bowl of Punch. We still need the sugar, spice and citrus, though.

One of history's sad ironies concerns scurvy, a fatal wasting disease caused by a lack of vitamin C, which every other animal save our fellow primates and the guinea pig synthesizes on its own. In the age of sail, it was a great killer: months and months afloat without fresh provisions meant that ships would often lose half their crews to it or more, and through the centuries, its toll must have been into the hundreds of thousands. It wasn't until the nineteenth century that the Royal Navy finally put an end to the problem with increased attention to fresh provisions and lime-juice rations. Yet the Elizabethans had known that citrus fruit was a sure cure. As Maddox recorded in his journal, after they made landfall in Guinea and took on a supply of "lymmons" (in this case, probably limes; "lemon" was used for both until the eighteenth century),

> above 50 men that wer before geven over to death ar now
> become lusty and strong, for the lymmons have scowred their
> mowths, fastened their teath [bleeding gums and loose teeth
> are among the earliest symptoms of scurvy] and purifyd the
> blood.

Some captains went to great lengths to ensure the citrus supply—the excellent James Lancaster, leader of the East India Company's first fleet, not only provisioning his ship with bottled lemon juice and stopping often for more "limons and oranges," as one of his sailors recounted, "which were precious for our diseased men, to rid their bodies of the scurvy," but even going so far as to retrace part of his route when he had run out.

We don't know whether this citrus juice was drunk straight or mixed with anything to make it more palatable. In 1617, though, John Woodall, the East India Company's surgeon general and a man of great intelligence and experience, prescribed against the scurvy "the use of the juice of lemons . . . to be taken each morning, two or three spoonfuls . . . and if you add one spoonful of aqua vitae thereto, to a cold stomach it is the better." It's also possible that, in practice, the juice was sweetened; according to victualing records, early East India men carried plenty of sugar and made sure to procure more when they could. And though I've been able to find no direct mention of the practice, it's telling that William Hawkins, who sailed east in 1593, prescribed that sailors be given, in the absence of citrus juice, two drops of oil of vitriol—that is, sulfuric acid; a little frightening, to be sure—"mingled in a draught of water, with a little sugar." Even the spices can be accounted for: Lancaster, for one, shipped fifty pounds of assorted cloves, cinnamon and nutmegs for use during the voyage.

Again, possibility is not actuality. But in the absence of direct eyewitness testimony, it's all we have: the nautical origin of Punch is a case that has to be argued on circumstantial evidence. As we've seen, there's enough of that to establish means (all the ingredients at hand), motive (failure of traditional sources of strong drink) and opportunity (months on board ship). So much for the basics. There are also circumstances that work to exclude the other most likely suspects, the company's factors. For one, they didn't have to resort to mixology to get something palatable: Shiraz wine, from Persia, was widely available in the East, as was palm wine. Then there's the "biscuit roty" garnish de La Boullaye-Le Gouz recorded; landlubbers were unlikely to float toasted sea biscuit in their drink unless they had learned to make it from someone for whom that would be a natural building block. (Sailors, it should be noted, were famous for finding novel and unlikely ways to combine the limited ingredients available to them, their odd concoctions serving to fight the salt-pork-and-sea-biscuit monotony of the nautical diet.) Making it even less likely that Punch jumped from land to shore is the sailor's well-documented antipathy to anyone aboard ship who didn't pull his weight, a category that would have most definitely included the company men for whom they heaved and hauled and sweated and froze and, shockingly often, died to carry in leisure from England to the East.[13] Finally, there were a lot more sailors out east than there were factors: even as late as 1650, it's doubtful that the company had more than a hundred men in all of India—fewer than the crew of one decent-sized ship.

It would be unsporting of me to go this far into Punch's origins without hazarding a guess of my own. Therefore, for the who, I nominate a ship's junior officer—senior officers generally having enough money to bring their own extensive stocks of wine, and ordinary seamen being more likely to adopt an officer's drink than the reverse—and an Englishman, probably, although a Dutchman is by no means out of the question (Punch would not be the first Dutch innovation that the English took over wholesale). The when is trickier. It could be as early as Fenton's voyage of 1582 and as late as 1620 or so (here I am assuming Della Valle's "Larkin" is Punch by another name), but I'll go with 1610, give or take a few years; the earlier we place it, the stranger it becomes that we don't hear of it until 1632. Where—well, at sea, of course, anyplace east of the Cape of Good Hope, where English ships called to stock up on water and citrus fruits at a time in their voyages when all beer was likely to be gone.

In any case, for the next two centuries, Punch would be the sailor's joy, as much a part of the stereotypical image of the English seaman as rough talk, stubborn courage and a proclivity to cavorting with whores. Indeed, Admiral Vernon, in the famous 1740 order

---

13 As one of his men reported, Drake was forced to land early in his circumnavigation to address and attempt to quell "controversy" and "stomaching" between "the sailors and the gentlemen [i.e., the passengers]," which nearly derailed the voyage.

directing that his sailors' daily rum ration—by 1731 the Royal Navy had, sensibly, abandoned beer for foreign postings, substituting a perhaps not so sensible half-pint of rum, brandy or arrack—be "daily mixed with a quart of water" (thus creating "grog"), came close to making it official by also adding that "they that are good husbandmen may . . . purchase sugar and limes" to make the result "more palatable to them." After a 1794 experiment, the navy took husbandmanship out of the equation and had lemon juice and sugar added to the grog before it was served out, thus preventing scurvy and, finally, making official the expedient that those intrepid, quarrelsome East India men of the early days came up with so that they would not have to drink water.

IV

THE AGE OF PUNCH

In a way, despite their isolation, those early India factors were lucky. What with civil war, regicide, religious dictatorship, two naval wars with the Dutch and a plague that killed one hundred thousand Londoners and was only extinguished by a fire that consumed most of the city, the folks back home in England didn't get a lot of enjoyment out of the middle parts of the seventeenth century. Fortunately, this being a drink book, we can skip over most of the fear, pain, and drama and concentrate on the carousing with which an often intolerable existence was solaced. On January 30, 1649, King Charles I laid his head on a Whitehall chopping block. Then came democracy, of a sort, and then Puritan dictatorship, during which conviviality was, officially, next to rascality. But on May 29, 1660, with the monarchy restored, King Charles II entered London in triumph. As he wound his way through the city's ancient streets, the fountains literally flowed with wine. Conviviality was restored.

The very next day, however, Charles issued a proclamation against the "vicious, debauch'd, and profane Persons . . . who spend their Time in Taverns, Tippling-Houses, and Debauches, giving no other Evidence of their Affection to us but in drinking our health, and inveighing against all others who are not of their own dissolute Temper." True, many of the king's supporters had in fact been using the toasting of his health as a rather shabby on-the-fly loyalty test: drink up, and you were a good Royalist; decline, and you were some sort of Puritan Roundhead and not to be trusted. But there was no dearth of people who would toast him even without coercion: life under Oliver Cromwell and the Puritans had been dreary, what with alehouses and taverns being viewed with official suspicion, sports and games of any and all sorts suppressed, and theaters shut down; and if public morals had slipped a bit in the two years since Cromwell's death, things were still rather glum. With a Charles back in charge, they would take a decided turn for the merrier, grumpy royal proclamations or no.

Then again, it's hard to believe that even Charles took that proclamation seriously. If one had to pick a theme for his reign, one could do no better than that conviviality (at least until the very end, when it devolved into a tedious web of cabals, plots, counterplots and executions). The theaters were open, the games were afoot, and the alehouses, inns and taverns were full. A moderate drinker himself, for the most part (we all get ahead of ourselves every now and then), Charles presided over a court that—well, one would have had to scour the kingdom most thoroughly to find a group to whom "vicious, debauch'd, and profane" better applied. They were rakes, roisterers and alcoholics—and, for that matter, duelists, bride-abductors, exhibitionists, atheists and poets (indeed, John Wilmot, Earl of Rochester, combined all of those things and more). What they were not, however, were Punch-drinkers, at least not at first. Being gentlemen, they drank wine. Being English, they also drank beer and ale. The latter was no doubt of a stronger and better grade than what their fellow countrymen who made up the London mob were drinking, but if those at the lower reaches of society were deprived of alcohol, it wasn't for long. Before the decade was out, they would discover spirits.

After the Second Anglo-Dutch War ended in 1667, as Daniel Defoe, a schoolboy at the time, would recall in 1727: "Suddenly . . . we began to abound in Strong Water-Shops. These were a sort of petty Distillers, who made up . . . Compound Waters from such mixt and confus'd Trash, as they could get to work from." The trash was familiar: sour or salt-water-damaged wines, "Lees and Bottoms," cider dregs, "damag'd sugars," and so forth. The resulting aqua vitae was then flavored, cheaply, with aniseed or juniper and hawked from "bulks" (shop windows) and market stalls or "by street vendors crying 'A dram of the bottle.'"[1]

Whatever their quality, spirits sales in England soared: by 1684, they were topping half a million gallons a year. The causes for this increase could have been as complex as postrevolutionary disorientation and the rootlessness brought on by out-of-control urbanization[2] or as simple as the high excise taxes that Cromwell's Parliament had imposed on beer and ale and Charles's had retained and extended. But whatever they were, they didn't just affect the urban rabble, the alehouse classes. Before long, the drinking life of the taverngoer would change as well.

By the time Charles took the throne, Punch had spread far beyond its South Asian cradle. Its earliest appearance elsewhere comes in the often-cited account of the new English colony of Barbados written by Richard Ligon, who was there from 1647 to 1650. Whatever his good qualities, and I'm sure they are many, when it came to Punch, either he got his notes a little mixed up or those early Bajans had picked up the name but not the drink that came with it.[3] In any

1 The vendors used an ancestor of the modern bartender's two-sided jigger to measure out their product: a gill—a quarter pint—on one side, half that on the other.
2 Despite plague and fire, London drew in enough migrants from the countryside to end the century a far larger and busier place than it had been at its beginning. From a city of two hundred thousand at the death of Elizabeth, in 1603, it grew to half a million by the time William III died ninety-nine years later.
3 Or—another argument for an English origin of the name—"punch" was a common English word for strong drink of whatever sort that was applied independently to both.

case, he described it as simply fermented sugar water—"very strong, and fit for labourers." Between Ligon's years in Barbados and the Restoration, the fortunes of Punch in the West are obscure. In early 1668, however, William Willoughby, the aristocratic governor of Barbados and the Leeward Islands, reporting to London on the typically unruly state of affairs in the English Caribbean, described his intention to place affairs in St. Kitts in the hands of one Colonel Lambert. With half the island being a French colony, they took some management. Fortunately, quoth Willoughby, Lambert "is a man of good reason, and at a bowl of punch I dare turn him loose to any Monsieur in the Indies." If English colonels and French monsieurs could drink Punch together, one may assume that by then the drink was both well established and, to some degree, socially acceptable in the Caribbean colonies. By then, Punch-drinking had spread to the North American colonies as well, and not only among the servants.

We know this from, among other things, the lengthy tab John Parker ran up between May 1670 and February 1671 at John Richardson's Talbot County, Maryland, "ordinary."[4] Scattered among all the charges for beer and mum and rum and brandy are entries for a total of thirteen and a half "Bowles of Punch," at sixty or eighty pounds of tobacco—the local currency—each, depending on what it was made from. Clearly, Parker was no servant—any man who could afford to spend more than eight hundred pounds of tobacco on Punch was not, in that time and place, socially negligible. Things in Maryland would only get worse: by 1708, Ebenezer Cook could write in his satirical but not inaccurate epic *The Sot-Weed Factor* about how, arriving in that same part of the colony, "A Herd of Planters on the ground / O'er-whelmed with Punch, dead drunk we found."

It's unclear exactly who brought Punch-drinking to the West

---

4 The ordinary, a seventeenth-century response to a society in which increasing numbers of people were working away from home, was essentially an alehouse that served one or two set communal meals a day.

Indies and North America, but since English sailors were customarily dismissed from their ships between voyages and had to find new ones, many of those who manned the vessels that serviced the new western colonies would have had East India Company experience. In any case, the Spanish had conveniently planted the islands of the Caribbean with sugarcane and citrus trees, so there was no dearth of raw materials with which to work, and plenty of motivation in the form of lousy beer (for various reasons, it took some time to establish a viable brewing industry in America) and expensive wine. In any case, Punch-drinking spread rapidly, and by the turn of the eighteenth century, it was near universal in the colonies.

By that time, though, Punch had conquered the mother country as well. There, at least, we know how the campaign began. The earliest reference to drinking Punch on English soil I've been able to discover comes from the diarist and author John Evelyn, who was well connected and deeply involved in naval affairs. On the sixteenth of January 1662, he accompanied the Duke of York to "an East India vessel that lay at Black Wall." Evidently the ship's officers laid out something of a spread, company style. "We had entertainment of several curiosities," Evelyn recorded. "Amongst other spirituous drinks, as punch, &c., they gave us Canarie that had been carried to and brought from the Indies." True to his class, he found the Punch curious, but it was the Canary wine that "was indeed incomparably good." Significantly, the new drink makes no appearance in the diary that Evelyn's friend Samuel Pepys, almost as well connected and even more deeply involved in naval affairs, so famously kept from 1660 to 1669. Pepys was a curious and wide-ranging tippler and a conscientious observer; if the London gentry had adopted Punch, he would have recorded it—just as he had done for so many other drinks. It's difficult to think of someone who would have enjoyed it more. Indeed, he might have had the chance to become one of its early adopters, if only Christopher Batters hadn't liked it quite so much.

A navy gunner "born and bred to the sea," as Pepys remembered him, who managed to work his way up to captaining his own ship, Batters considered Pepys his patron (Pepys, alas, considered him a "foole" and "a poor painful wretch . . . as can be"). On December 17, 1666, he put in to London to dispose of the cargo of a Dutch "fish dogger" (i.e., cod boat) he had taken. After seeing his patron, he went back aboard his ship, the *Joseph*, in the company of "one Allen, a fishmonger," to whom he sold his cargo for ten pounds. There was Punch, to seal the deal. We know that because he was overheard telling Allen that "if he drank any more Punch he should tell two shillings for one." The next morning, he was found floating in the Thames, still with his gold signet ring but with his pocket cut open and minus the sash in which he was reputed to keep fifty pounds in gold. By the time they held an inquest (most likely at Pepys's prompting), the fishmonger was nowhere to be found. "A sad fortune," quoth Pepys.[5] Who knows—had he taken on board a little less Punch that night, Batters might have survived to introduce Pepys to the joys of the flowing bowl. Pepys got there eventually, as a September 1683 entry from one of his fragmentary later diaries proves, but by that stage in life he was rather more sedate an individual and seems to have been little amused by the new beverage.

But in the 1660s, some landlubbers, anyway, must have known about Punch because it turns up in a list of drinks in *Poor Robin's Jests*, a 1666 joke book, and again the next year in *The Spightful Sister*, a rather confused tragicomedy written by the teenaged Abraham Bailey in time he should probably have devoted to his legal studies (he couldn't get it staged, and he never wrote another). In 1670, the pioneering cookbook writer Hannah Wooley even gives us an actual recipe, complete with proportions and all, in her book *The Queen-Like Closet, or Rich Cabinet*. Over the next decade, Punch would become firmly established ashore, ending up as what the sporty young gentleman would drink when he joined his friends on a spree.

---

5 But, as a look through the next century or so of London court records shows, hardly a unique one. Many a man, nautical or otherwise, would be plied with Punch until insensate, robbed and—if lucky—left in the gutter.

Yet as happens so often with mixography, just when we would like the most light we're granted the least. During those crucial ten years (if I may use a word as serious as "crucial" in connection with something so fundamentally frivolous as the art of mixing drinks), the only times Punch makes it into the written record it's still sporting its sailor suit. If it's not physicians praising it for its antiscorbutic powers, it's drinks writers acknowledging it as something "very usual amongst those that frequent the sea"—an observation amply borne out by the diary of Henry Teonge, a Warwickshire parson who joined the HMS *Assistance* as ship's chaplain in 1675 and found it flowing "like ditchwater," the officers going through several bowls of it a day. But that's pretty much it. Then, in 1680, Alexander Radcliffe, a young man-about-town who clearly espoused the then-popular principle that "*nulla manere diu neque vivere carmina possunt quae scribuntur aquae potoribus,*" which is to say "no poems written by water-drinkers are likely to last," published a broadsheet titled *Bacchanalia Coelestia: A Poem in Praise of Punch.* In it, he has the Roman gods gather in heaven to assemble a bowl of the new

Charging the Punch, from Hogarth's "An Election Entertainment," 1755 (detail). AUTHOR'S COLLECTION

drink, since, as Jupiter says, "We're inform'd they drink Punch upon Earth, / By which mortal Wights outdo us in mirth." It's not much as far as poetry goes, although plenty worse has been published. But its very existence tells us that something major has happened in the perception of Punch, for though Radcliffe was a captain, it was in the army, not the navy, and his connections were with the royal court and the dissolute wits associated with it, not the diligent moneymakers of the East India Company. If Radcliffe, a poetical protégé of the Earl of Rochester, knew Punch, Rochester knew it; if Rochester knew it, every whore and rake and freethinking young gent in town knew it.

Ironically, Punch, the Great Intoxicator, seems to have ridden into town on the back of the ensobering coffee bean. I won't delve into the history of coffee and tea in England, as fascinating as they might be in their quiet way. But the first coffeehouses began opening in the 1650s, in Oxford; by the 1660s, whether due to interest in the novelty of a stimulating drink that did not intoxicate or a conviction that if something is in Oxford then it certainly must be in London, they were all over the metropolis, too. From the beginning, coffeehouses took on a character of their own. For one thing, they charged admission: to enter, you had to pay a penny, then not a negligible sum. That penny let you read the various newspapers, pamphlets, broadsheets and ballads that were the coffeehouse's other great attraction (the tangled, bitter politics of the day threw off a lot of print). Or you could just join the general conversation that flowed freely and often heatedly among the various tables. It wouldn't be entirely wrong to compare them to modern online discussion groups such as MetaFilter or Free Republic, except with the possibility of actual fisticuffs should the snark get out of hand. In any case, they were something entirely new in the way that they brought together the more progressive young aristocrats and the more cosmopolitan members of the commercial classes, in a setting where if not the only then at least the chief currency was wit.

There were those who frequented coffeehouses for that wit but who didn't much care for the "soot-coloured ninny-broth" (as the

Grub Street satirist Ned Ward called it) that went with it. Even hipsters like to get their drink on. Yet ale wasn't quite the thing—not aspirational enough—although at first many coffeehouses served it anyway, *faute de mieux*, since the tavern licenses that would allow wine were scarce and expensive. But anyone with a coffeehouse license could sell spirits—then just at the beginning of their Recreational phase in England and hence largely unregulated—if he could persuade his patrons to drink them. John Dryden, the pugnacious poet laureate, signaled the eventual solution to that problem in a set of verses he wrote in 1691 on the legendary Will's Coffee-House, where he had been the head-wit-in-charge (so to speak) since it opened in 1660. In them, he portrays William Urwin, the house's proprietor, with "nutmeg, spoon and garter" [i.e., grater], all necessary accessories for Punch-making. And indeed by then Punch had become the standard coffeehouse antidote to all that caffeine. In fact, many a coffeehouse—such as the Little Devil in Goodman's Fields, lauded by Ward for its Punch in his 1700 masterwork of literary lowlife, *The London Spy*—was one in name only.

Yet it's unclear precisely how or when coffeehouses learned the utility of Punch; if history recorded which of them was the first to give the flowing bowl safe harbor and when that happened, I haven't been able to find where. It seems to have taken a little while: the satirical 1673 pamphlet *A Character of a Coffee House* lists, for the "Hodge Podge of Drinks" typically served, the "hot Hell-Broth" coffee, tea and chocolate (all three recent imports), plus "Betony and Rosade [a sort of herbal tea] for the addle-headed Customer," cider, mum and ale. If Punch had been in common use, the opportunity to hit at trumped-up would-be wits for fuddling themselves with a low sailor's tipple would have been too tempting to pass up.

Or maybe not: one of the factors that must have hastened Punch's adoption in England was the high standing in which the navy stood, and not just because the king's brother was Lord High Admiral. Unlike the army, which was deeply implicated in the dark deeds of the Civil War, the navy was seen as England's defender, pure and simple, and sailors themselves as stout, if rough, primitives with hearts of oak. (And besides, they were making England rich.) Well into the nineteenth century, a popular upper-class expression of patriotism was to gather a party to visit a navy ship at dock and drink Punch with the sailors. In 1732, even Alexander Pope, the great poet of the age, participated in the ritual, answering Lord Peterborough's invitation with the stirring words, "I decline no Danger where the Glory of Great Britain is concern'd and will contribute to empty the largest Bowl of Punch that shall be rigg'd out on such an Occasion." It's a wonder it didn't kill him, sickly as he was with the chronic tuberculosis that had so stunted and twisted his bones that he was barely four and a half feet tall. Such things had been known to happen: the Calendar of State Papers for November 8, 1692, records that "One Mr. Hele, a gentleman of Devonshire, went on board the Rupert at Plymouth, and drinking too freely of punch he fell asleep and never waked."

The spread of Punch-drinking couldn't have been hurt by Parliament's 1678 ban on the importation of French wines. This regulation was as much an attempt to buck up the fledgling wine trade with Portugal as it was a hit at France and its troublesome monarch, Louis XIV, but since the Portuguese, the most temperate of people, barely drank wine themselves and when they did cared little about its quality (it would take generations to create the magnificence that is port), it resulted mostly in more smuggling and spirits-drinking in England. As in turn did the various measures passed under William III—the genever-drinking Dutchman who was given the English throne in 1688 after Charles's brother James, who succeeded him in 1685, unacceptably produced a Catholic heir—to restrict the very large wine and brandy trade with France, now an open enemy, and bulk up English grain-distilling.

The moment of transition was captured perfectly by the spectacularly alluring figure of Mrs. Aphra Behn—author, spy, courtesan, wit and mixologist (we'll get to that last part in Book III)—in her play *The Widow Ranter*, published posthumously in 1690. Set in Virginia, it features in the very first scene a country justice of the peace "sick" from having been drunk the night before on "high

Burgundy Claret." Hearing this, his tippling companion wonders aloud "how the gentlemen do drink" that "Paulter Liquor, your *English French* wine." "Ay so do I," replies our over-hung J.P.:

'tis for want of a little *Virginia* Breeding: how much more like a Gentleman 'tis, to drink as we do, brave Edifying Punch and Brandy,—but they say the young Noble-men now and Sparks in *England* begin to reform, and take it for their mornings.

Although Mrs. Behn was barred by her sex from participating in the strictly stag coffeehouse culture, she nonetheless maintained a wide acquaintance among the wits (the prologue to *The Widow Ranter* was supplied by no less than Dryden himself). If drinking Punch was still low enough to satirize, it must have at least been common enough for the jab to tell.[6]

By 1690, Punch-drinking had also followed the roads out of London and taken root deep in the countryside. In 1675, when Henry Teonge joined his ship fresh from rural Warwickshire, he had pronounced the Punch of which he shared three bowls on his first night afloat "a Liquor very strange to me." Ten years later, they had even heard of it in farthest Yorkshire, judging by the fact that George Meriton included it in the locally printed booklet of verses he wrote in praise of Yorkshire ale. Not that rural Punch-tippling didn't have its problems, as Thomas Brown, one of Dryden's verbal sparring partners, who found himself marooned in Hertfordshire, complained in a characteristically amusing 1692 letter on the inconveniences of country life:

The Wine, in those few Places where we find it, is so intolerably bad, that tho' 'tis good for nothing else, 'tis a better Argument for Sobriety, than what all the Volumes of

---

6 Mrs. Behn's play, though quite Punch-sodden, wasn't the wettest of its day: in 1693, Henry Higden's *Wary Widow, or Sir Noisy Parrot* didn't make it past the third act of its one and only performance, "the author having contrived so much drinking of punch in the play, that the actors all got drunk, and were unable to finish it."

Morality can afford. . . . Where this sorry Stuff is not to be had, we are forc'd, in our own Defence, to take up with Punch, but the Ingredients are as long a summoning, as a Colonel would be recruiting his Regiment. . . . We must send to a Market-Town five miles off for Sugar and Nutmeg, and five miles beyond that for rotten Lemons. Water it self is not to be had without travelling a League for it, and an unsanctify'd Kettle supplies the Place of a Bowl. Then when we have mix'd all these noble Ingredients, which, generally speaking, are as bad as those the Witches in *Mackbeth* jumble together to make a Charm, we fall to contentedly, and sport off an Afternoon. 'Tis true, our Heads suffer for it next Morning, but what is that to an old Soldier? We air our selves next Morning on the Common, and the Sin and the Pain are forgotten together.

Reluctantly or not, the tavern class had learned to drink Punch, and it would take it another century and a half to relinquish the sport and the sin and the pain of it.

Thus arrived the Age of Punch. In 1700, Ned Ward could opine in prose that Punch "if composed of good ingredients, and prepared with true judgment, exceeds all the simple [i.e., straight, unmixed], potable products in the universe" and in verse that "Had our forefathers but thy virtues known, / Their foggy ale to lubbers they'd have thrown." As long as there were lubbers—that is, bumpkins—to keep ale alive, its triumph was not complete, but Punch did cast many of the other traditional compound drinks of Olde Englande, those turbid, egg-rich brews based on ale and wine, into the outer darkness, where is wailing and gnashing of teeth.

Over time, the informal associations that the coffeehouses encouraged hardened into formal clubs made up of like-minded men who agreed to meet at a fixed time and venue and follow certain loose rules. Not all clubs drank Punch, but most did, and since the majority of them favored the Whigs—the (semi) progressive element in English politics and the one that supported William III against his Tory and Jacobite (i.e., loyal to the deposed James II) opponents—Punch became something of a Whig drink. In 1695, when William III visited Warwick Castle, "a cistern containing a hundred and twenty gallons of punch was emptied to his Majesty's health," as one contemporary history recorded. Clearly, in a time when Whiggishness was triumphant that association did nothing to impair Punch's popularity. If the Tories, not at all progressive, stuck for a time to the traditional French wines of the English gentry, paying exorbitantly for smuggled goods when necessary, eventually they, too, would yield to the attraction of the "flowing bowl" (a phrase that was already proverbial when Matthew Prior used it in one of his poems in 1718).

Ultimately, people will drink what they will drink, politics be damned. Ned Ward, for one, was a Tory, and when he tired of Grub Street, he opened a Punch house of his own. But even if you agreed with Bishop Hoadley's then-notorious polemic on the theme "Christ's Kingdom is not of this world" and eschewed the vulgar money-getting and party politics of the day in favor of laying up capital for the next world, you could still partake. Henry Fielding's prison chaplain in *The Adventures of Jonathan Wild* supplies the justification: "If we must drink, let us have a Bowl of Punch—a Liquor I rather prefer, as it is nowhere spoken against in Scripture."

Many Punch-drinkers absorbed their portions without incident. But as Fielding also observed, this time in *Tom Jones*, "There are indeed certain Liquors, which, being applied to our Passions, or to Fire, produce Effects the very Reverse of those produced by Water, as they serve to kindle and inflame, rather than to extinguish. Among these, the generous Liquor called Punch is one." Just because clubmen were literate and of at least a middling social rank didn't mean that they wouldn't sluice themselves a little too liberally from the bowl and end the evening in a crashing, heaving general brawl. With Punch on the table, even someone as civilized as Samuel Taylor Coleridge can end up smashing glassware, windows and furnishings, as he and Theodore Hook and their fellow topers did on one late evening at "a gay young bachelor's villa near Highgate" (Coleridge brewed the Punch, so Lord knows what was in it).

But that only fit in with the times. In the early eighteenth century, London was nothing like the trim, orderly place it (mostly) is today, with its neat ranks of just-so town houses, its quiet, leafy parks and its general air of peaceful bustle. The streets in the older parts of town were dark and narrow and choked with (as Jonathan Swift put it) "filths of all hues and odour," while not even the most fashionable new neighborhoods were exempt from having herds of swine driven through them to market. Londoners were different, too. The lords and marquesses and other fine gentlemen didn't carry umbrellas but carried swords, and not just for show, while the common people weren't so much plucky and quaint as frankly terrifying—a xenophobic, violent lot who made a sport of pelting anyone who ventured into the street in fancy court-dress with some of those "filths" and could turn from curious crowd to murderous mob at the drop of a handkerchief.

They did not drink Punch. They drank gin, and far too much of it. As much as their putative betters deplored the gin habit, though, they weren't all that much better when it came to resisting the power of aqua vitae. When, in the 1730s, Parliament began to consider various prohibition measures, there were always members who could be counted on to mount passionate arguments for the exemption of Punch and its component spirits (i.e., anything but gin) from the law. In 1737, when Parliament passed the infamous Gin Act, with no exceptions, one of the first acts of protest came from the Cherry Tree Tavern in Clerkenwell (by then, taverns had followed the coffeehouses' lead in serving Punch), where "a Company of 100 Persons resolving to drink Punch . . . had a Bowl (or rather Trough) of that liquor . . . containing 80 Gallons, which was drunk out before the Company parted."[7] Reading through the Old Bailey's records of the rapes, robberies, assaults and outright murders committed under the influence of Punch, one may conclude that at times the main difference between the filth-pelter and the peltee was the price

---

7 That works out to five or six pints a head. As the *Grub Street Journal* commented, "This Bowl is called with very great propriety a trough."

of their tipple (those sword-carrying gentlemen, for example, had a distressing habit of getting quarrelsome over Punch and sticking each other, all too often fatally).

Punch was not cheap. Once it became a status drink, the literate classes made it an object of connoisseurship, in particular the spirits that fueled it. By the late seventeenth century, the days of generic aqua vitae were over. Now drinkers had preferences. If it wasn't arrack, imported at great expense from the East,[8] it was French brandy, by now (at its best, anyway) an exceedingly well-distilled, barrel-mellowed commodity, or fragrant rum from the Caribbean. For a bowl of Punch made with one of these, one might expect to pay six or eight shillings a three-quart bowl. Eight shillings doesn't sound like much, but in an age when, as a friend of Samuel Johnson observed to him, "thirty pounds a year was enough to enable a man to live [in London] and not be contemptible," it amounted to half a week's living wage—say, some two hundred dollars today. The lemons alone cost the equivalent of eight dollars each. Sure, you would split this bowl between three or four people, but it still required a rather hefty capital investment. By the 1730s, the gin-drinkers had learned to make Punch with it, which could be sold for a shilling—say, twenty-five dollars a bowl. Entirely more like it. With the creation of Gin Punch, this simple sailor's expedient completed its conquest: all levels of English—or rather British, as it had to be called since the 1707 union of England and Scotland—society were more or less comfortable with the idea that spirits could be drunk recreationally.

More or less. There would always be some who eyed Punch with suspicion. In 1727, Daniel Defoe could still sniff about "The Punch Drinkers of Quality (if any such there be)." But he was an old-timer, born just before the Restoration, and didn't quite get what

---

8 Both palm and Batavia arracks were imported, even if it meant paying the hated Dutch for the latter—Charles II had settled the Second Anglo-Dutch War, in part, by giving up almost all English claims and factories in Indonesia and the Spice Islands, receiving in return the rather drab colony of New Amsterdam as a sort of consolation prize.

was going on. People of "Quality" most assuredly drank Punch; they just didn't really respect it. Not even in the colonies: in 1739, Charles Francis wrote a friend in England from Jamaica that "The common Drink here is Madeira wine, or Rum Punch; the first, mixed with Water, is used by the better Sort; the latter, by Servants and the inferior kind of People." Now, it's safe to say that either he wasn't being strictly truthful or his Jamaican acquaintances were on their best behavior while the man from the home office was sniffing around. Jamaica was as punchy as a place could be. But it's true that even in its heyday, Punch could never quite rid itself of the whiff of the lower decks it carried with it. A gentleman or a lady could always drink French claret—even the brandy-jolted, adulterated stuff that passed under the name[9]—without giving even the severest critic grounds to so much as raise an eyebrow. But Punch, even at its most carefully compounded and wholesome, remained something of a spree drink, fuel for a devil-take-the-hindmost journey to the end of the night.

In the colonies, that didn't matter so much, since by definition no colonial was truly of the best sort. As a result, Punch, and particularly Rum Punch, was consumed by almost every rung on the social ladder. When a group of African slaves plotted with a white alehouse-keeper to burn New York and slaughter its inhabitants—the abortive uprising that would be known as the New York Conspiracy of 1741—it was over Rum Punch that they conspired. Three years later, when Dr. Alexander Hamilton of Maryland took a trip to Maine and back for his health, he found his fellow colonials sluicing themselves with the stuff pretty liberally, in just about every town he visited. And if from time to time he joined them in a bowl, what of it? It was simply the sociable thing to do, as George Washington had to learn the hard way. In 1757, when the twenty-five-year-old major stood for election to the Virginia House of Burgesses, he was

---

9 British vintners had a deplorable habit of fortifying and otherwise adulterating every last drop of wine or winelike substance that passed through their hands. Even claret—good French Bordeaux—received the stiffening shot of brandy and didn't shake it off until well into the nineteenth century.

known as an unsociable fellow who had frequently wrangled with the local "Tippling-house keepers" over their selling drinks to his soldiers. To prove his uncongeniality, he stood on principle and declined to provide the customary free drinks at his campaign rallies. He lost. The next year, he spent thirty-six pounds and change on liquors, almost half of it on Punch. He won.

After independence for a time, free men continued to club together to while away their idle hours around a bowl of Punch, just as they had when they were subjects of the king. In November 1783, when the Continental Army reoccupied New York, there was a general carouse of several days' duration. As part of it, George Clinton, the governor of New York State, held a banquet for the French ambassador at which the 120 guests emptied 30 bowls of (presumably Rum) Punch—and 135 bottles of Madeira, 36 bottles of port and 60 bottles of English beer. Or then there's the celebration held for the ordination of a New England minister in 1785, at which the eighty people present put paid to "30 Boles of Punch before the People went to meeting" and "44 boles of Punch while at dinner," not to mention 28 bottles of wine, 8 bowls of brandy and an unspecified quantity of "cherry rum." As the new republic found its legs, though, the old institution began to seem a little quaint.

By then, though, Punch was beginning to fade even in the land that first fostered it. We can see the beginning of the end in India in a letter the *India Gazette* published in 1781 from "An Old Country Captain." "I am an old stager in this Country," he writes,

> having arrived in Calcutta in the year 1736. . . . Those were the days, when Gentlemen studied *Ease* instead of *Fashion*; even when the Hon. Members of the Council met in Banyan Shirts, Long Drawers and Conjee Caps; with a case bottle of good old Arrack, and a Gouglet of Water placed on the Table, which the Secretary (a Skilful Hand) frequently converted into Punch. . . .

Note the nostalgic mode (and that wonderful word "gouglet"). The very fact that he had to write in to mention all this indicates that business was no longer conducted on these lines. By 1810, Thomas Williamson could write about Punch, in his *East India Guide and Vade-Mecum*, that "that beverage is now completely obsolete, unless among sea-faring persons, who rarely fail to experience its deleterious effects." How low the mighty have fallen! Things were no better in America, long a bastion of Punch-drinking. By 1810, Americans were no longer colonists, and they were rapidly pursuing their own mixological path, without so much as a glance over their shoulder at their traditional drinkways.

Even in England, life was changing. The ritual of the Punch bowl had been a secular communion, welding a group of good fellows together into a temporary sodality whose values superseded all others—or, in plain English, a group of men gathered around a bowl of Punch could be pretty much counted on to see it to the end, come what may. All in good fun, and something the modern world could perhaps use a little more of, but it required its participants to have a large block of uncommitted time on their hands. As the nineteenth century wore on, this was less and less likely to be the case. Industrialization and improved communications and the rise of the bourgeoisie all made claims on the individual that militated against partaking of the Lethean bowl. Not that the Victorians were exactly sober, by our standards, but neither could they be as wet as their forefathers. As Robert Chambers put it in 1864, "Advanced ideas on the question of temperance have, doubtless, . . . had their influence in rendering obsolete, in a great measure, this beverage."

This isn't the only reason Punch fell by the wayside, of course. Improvements in distilling and, above all, aging of liquors meant that they required less intervention to make them palatable. The rise of a global economy made for greater choice of potables and a more fragmented culture of drink. Central heating to some degree dimmed the charms of hot Punch. Ideas of democracy and individualism extended to men's behavior in the barroom, where they were less likely to all settle for the same thing or let someone else choose what they were to drink. Like all social institutions, the bowl of Punch was subject to a plethora of subtle and incremental strains. Eventually, by midcentury, they toppled it, with most of the pull coming from America. Punch was out and the Cocktail, the down-the-hatch, out-the-door-and-back-to-work drink par excellence, was in. The flowing bowl would serve out the rest of its days in the twilight land of the special-occasion, holiday-gathering drink.

BOOK II

A Concise but Comprehensive Course in the Art of Making Punch

Unless you're a total mixology geek, I strongly suggest you skip this entire section of the book and proceed to Book III, "The Punches." If you actually start making any of those, you can always come back here for tips, pointers and reasons why. Until then, off you go.

V

THE REASON WHY

There's something about Punch that demands generalities and grand schemes. I suppose it has to do with the not-inconsiderable investment each bowl requires in time and, some would argue more importantly, money. By contrast, a Cocktail can be lashed together from whatever's at hand. Tequila, kumquat juice and clover honey? Give it a spin. Tawny port, Cherry Heering, Holland gin and half-and-half? Why the hell not? If it proves unsatisfactory (as I suspect that last one might), down the drain it goes and no regrets. You're only out a couple of ounces of booze and the thirty seconds or so it takes to shake them up. But when it's a question of twenty minutes of squeezing lemons, a quart and a half—eighty dollars' worth, give or take, at New York prices—of pretty good cognac, and the hopes and dreams of the thirty people who shall soon be ringing your door-bell, that's an entirely different story. Punch matters. Punch has heft. As one nineteenth-century master put it, "a man can never make good punch unless he is satisfied, nay positive, that no man breathing can make better." That satisfaction comes from experience, to be sure. But it also comes from knowing why you're doing what you're doing; from, in short, a theory.

The theorizing began early—in fact, with the rather eccentric hat-merchant-cum-vegetarian-activist-cum-temperance-crusader Thomas Tryon, who noted back in 1684 that Punch was made from "four or five ingredients, all of as different Natures as Light is from Darkness, and all great Extreams in their kind, except only the *Water*" and that in the mixture the fiery spirits and corrosively acidic limes "are some-what allay'd or moderated by the friendly Ingredients, viz. *Water* and *Sugar*, which do not only render it plea-surable to the Pallate, but also more tollerable to the Stomach"— although not to the point that the "Extreams" are made "altogether *Homogeneal*," or completely annul each other (indeed, Tryon denied that this was even possible). This, the earliest statement of the fun-damental principle of making Punch, differs only in lexical and grammatical detail from the assertion Jerry Thomas made in his pioneering *Bar-Tenders Guide*, published in 1862 at the very end of the Punch era, that a large part of the "grand secret" to making Punch is making it "sweet and strong" while "thoroughly amalgam-ating all the compounds, so that the taste of neither the bitter, the sweet, the spirit, nor the element [i.e., H_2O], shall be perceptible one over the other."[1]

Indeed, this idea of Punch as the embodiment of balance was so common during its heyday that it became proverbial. One ex-ample among many: if it were permissible to compare great things to vulgar ones, Bernard Mandeville disingenuously informs us in *The Fable of the Bees, or Private Vices, Public Benefits*, his 1714 philo-sophical *success de scandale*, "I would compare the Body Politick (I confess the Simile is very low) to a Bowl of Punch." Avarice is the

---

1 Of course, these principles could be applied equally well to mixology in general: strong must be set against weak, sour against sweet, yet with the whole in a state of dynamic tension wherein the contrasting ingredients are not completely neutralized to the point of being "homogeneal."

sour, spendthrift prodigality the sweet, the water is like "the Ignorance, Folly and Credulity of the floating insipid Multitude" and the "sublime Qualities of Men . . . separated by Art from the Dregs of Nature" are "an equivalent to Brandy." Individually, the ingredients are not promising. "I don't doubt but a *Westphalian*, *Laplander*, or any other dull Stranger that is unacquainted with the wholesome Composition," Mandeville adds,

> if he was to taste the several Ingredients apart, would
> think it impossible they should make any tolerable Liquor.
> The Lemons would be too sower, the Sugar too luscious, the
> Brandy he'll say is too strong ever to be drank in any
> quantity, and the Water he'll call a tasteless Liquor only
> fit for Cows and Horses.

Mix them all "judiciously," though, and you have "an excellent Liquor, lik'd of and admir'd by Men of exquisite Palates." (It should be noted that Mandeville, not a foolish man, was describing here an ideal body politic, not the British body politic of 1714, which I would liken more to a bowl of Olde English 800 spiked with Hennessy Paradis.)

Unfortunately, this idea of Punch as the balance of opposites, while useful enough as far as it goes, appears to be pretty much the only bit of abstract or higher analysis Punch-makers or Punch-drinkers ever advanced on its behalf, and it's really not enough. Balance, you see—well, a properly constructed Dry Martini is balanced, but so is a properly constructed Piña Colada, and those are about as different as two drinks can be. Balance covers relationships but not intensities, relative ranges but not absolute values. Nor does the higher-union-of-opposites idea really explain the role of the spice, something Mandeville tacitly acknowledged by simply omitting it from his simile.

To really get inside the Punch bowl, we've got to consider what the original Punch-makers were trying to achieve. That means projecting ourselves into their world, at least a little bit. First of all, for most of the Punch Age, there was no such thing as a Cocktail. The ship's officers, India factors, Maryland planters, coffeehouse wits and other men and women who clustered around the flowing bowl at taverns, country houses, picnics and wherever else it radiated its woozy glow were wine-drinkers, beer-drinkers, sometimes even dram-drinkers. What they weren't were drinkers of pungent, concentrated, icy blasts of spirits and spice, or spirits, citrus and spice—dram-strength stimulants meant to be consumed quickly but sparingly. In fact, Britons were conversant with the basic formula for what would become the Cocktail—spirits, bitters, sugar, perhaps a little water—a full hundred years before it caught on in America, and they did little with it but make occasional use of it as a hangover cure.

That tells us we have to approach Punch differently—well, okay, we don't absolutely *have* to; there's nothing in the world to stop anyone from making a bowl-sized Cocktail and certainly nothing to stop anyone else from drinking it. But to get the most out of Punch, to enjoy it as something not only different in scale from the now-ubiquitous Cocktail but also different in kind, then yes. Differently. We have to, for a brief moment, dethrone the Cocktail, expel it from our thinking. In a drinking culture that could have embraced it but chose not to, its quick impact, concentration and intensity of flavor—for us its greatest attributes—were instead drawbacks. For someone who decries the "empyreumatick or burnt taste . . . easily distinguished by every palate in fresh distilled rum, brandy, simple and compound waters," as a writer in the *London Magazine* did in 1768, a forward presence of spirits would hardly be a recommendation.

For the first generations of Punch-drinkers, it was (as we have seen) a means of making the dram of spirits, a "Vesuvian" drink fit only for the "Bawd" and the "Country Bitch," for "swearing Porters . . . drunken Carr-men / And the lewd drivers of the Hackney Coaches" (as a 1683 satire on brandy-drinking represented its public), into something that one could drink without losing social status—something fit for, as the satire put it, "Sots of Quality." To accomplish that, it had to assimilate spirits as closely as possible to the dominant tipple of the upper class. Here, then, is the secret of Punch's success: true Punch is wine by other means. Using the gentlemanly qualities of judgment and taste, the Punch-mixer takes simple, even base materials (the spice excepted) and forges them into an artificial wine, in the process restoring some of the nobility that the industrial process of distillation has brutally stripped away.

So. An "extemporary kind of wine" (as a British medical writer defined it in 1779). What does that mean in practice? In part, nothing new: anyone who has learned to make a proper Sidecar, Margarita or Aviation Cocktail will already have mastered the art of balancing sweet and sour so that the drink is neither tooth-settingly tart nor in any way syrupy. For Punch, you'll have to do that. But you'll also have to learn to balance the spirituous and aqueous elements, so that the drink is soft and pleasant but not insipid; so that the taste and aroma of the base liquor are present enough to remind you that you're drinking spirits, but with none of its heat or bite. James Ashley, London's leading purveyor of Punch in the eighteenth century (and a man whom we shall meet again in Book III), found that balance point at one part spirits to two parts water, citrus and sugar. Assuming said spirits were roughly half alcohol, that yields a Punch that's about 16 percent alcohol (by volume)—the strength of a (very) strong California Cab or a light sherry.

But Punch has to be balanced in three dimensions, not two—after sweetness and strength have been reconciled with their opposites, there remains the question of pungency. In the nineteenth century, it was a common gambler's trick to bet someone that he couldn't eat a quail a day for thirty days. Just one tiny, tasty little quail every day? Easy money. And yet so few were able to complete the challenge that when they did it went into the pages of the sporting almanacs. For the first week, the task is a pleasure. For the second, entirely tolerable. But then the gaminess of the little birds starts to pall, then creates an aversion, and then quickly becomes nauseating. It's the same with Punch: a bowl made "interesting" with too much spice—be that the traditional sort (nutmeg, allspice, mace and the like), an unusual sort of herbal tea, copious dashes of bitters, Chartreuse and its ilk or even something as seemingly innocuous as tropical fruit—can be unusually compelling for the first glass or three, but by the time the bowl is half empty, it will cloy. Above all things, Punch must be moreish.[2] It's a long-distance drink, not a sprinter like the Cocktail. If you've made five gallons of the stuff, you want to make sure that five gallons is what people will drink, not two.

But that's more than enough theory for a book that's supposed to be about mixing drinks. Before we lift up the hood and get our hands all greasy, though, we'd better make sure we've got our tools laid out. Three-quarters of the work in making Punch is logistical: assembling your ingredients, choosing your tools, preparing your ice (should you choose to use it). We'll take these more or less in order.

---

2 Drinks writing has few terms of art entirely its own; this is one of them, and it is indispensable. It simply means "it makes you want to drink more of it."

VI

INGREDIENTS

You can make Punch out of most anything, really. It doesn't have to be the traditional arracks, brandies, rums, whiskeys and gins. Mountain men in the old Southwest frequently made theirs with mescal, about which one later recalled, "It made punches nearly equal to Scotch whisky, and solaced many a winter's evening." Or consider the Tequila Punch, "pink and of flavor indescribable," that Stanton Davis Kirkham came across a-hundred-odd years ago in a town near Veracruz. Or, for that matter, the concoction encountered in 1873 by J. A. MacGahan, correspondent of the *New York Herald*, in a Russian army camp outside the walls of the ancient Uzbek city of Khiva: "Dinner concluded," he wrote,

with a famous bowl of Russian punch. This punch is made of a mixture of vodka, Champagne, nalivka [vodka-based berry liqueur], and any other kind of wine that may be at hand. Apricots, melons, and cucumbers are put in to flavour and sugar to sweeten it, and the whole is then ignited, and allowed to burn until it boils. Though palatable and insinuating, it is the most diabolical compound I have ever tasted.

I shouldn't wonder.

As curious as such concoctions may be, though, I'll confine my general observations on ingredients to those most used during Punch's heyday, leaving oddballs and misfits to the commentary on individual Punches in Book III.

SPIRITS

Punch was born before the column still. This last device, introduced in the early nineteenth century, enabled distillers to make spirits of remarkable purity and cleanliness—think vodka (at least as we know it now), Bacardi, London dry gin; the white spirits. One thing that most of these products share is a featherweight body or texture on the tongue. Excellent in a Martini or a Daiquiri; in a bowl of Punch from the golden age, not so much. For that, you'll want the richer textures and bigger flavors characteristic of the products of the pot still. In some cases, as detailed below, that will be a problem.

Equally problematic is the question of proof. Until the 1720s, there was no even approximately effective way of measuring the alcohol content of a distilled spirit, or of anything else for that matter. Before that, distillers, merchants and the men who taxed them relied on rule-of-thumb tests involving the size of bubbles a bottle of the distillate in question produces when it's shaken,[1] or whether

---

1 This method, it must be acknowledged, can be surprisingly accurate; there are, for example, village distillers in Oaxaca who even today produce spirits of a consistent proof without using any measuring tools whatsoever.

or not a portion of gunpowder wet with it will catch fire. In 1725, though, one John Clarke came up with a hydrometer, which accurately measured how much alcohol was in a given spirit; its use would be made official in 1787 (in 1818, it was replaced by Bartholomew Sikes's improved version, which remained in official service until 1907 and unofficial service up to the 1980s). This simple device enabled the government to set a standard "proof," against which all spirits would be measured. That proof was 50 percent alcohol. But due to the way the hydrometer worked, that 50 percent was by weight, not by volume, which is how we measure it today. Alcohol being significantly lighter than water, that meant that a spirit that was 100 percent of proof (i.e., 50 percent alcohol by weight) contained between 57 and 58 percent alcohol by volume, making it 114 to 116 proof by our system. Simple, right?

I bring all this up because it has very real consequences when adapting certain old recipes. Not the seventeenth- or early-eighteenth-century ones, perhaps. For them, the proper proof of the spirits used will have to be a guess, as they could have been anywhere between 45 and 60 percent alcohol by volume, which means you'll have to balance your Punch the old-fashioned way, by tasting. But for a late-eighteenth- or nineteenth-century recipe, if all you have is an 80-proof (40 percent by volume) spirit and you're in the grip of an obsession with accuracy, you'll have to make adjustments, multiplying the amount of spirit you put in by 1.4 and subtracting as much water from the amount the recipe calls for as you've added of extra booze. Say, for example, you're making a British Milk Punch recipe from 1832 that calls for "1 quart French brandy" and all you have is an 80-proof cognac. Bearing in mind that the imperial quart of 40 ounces is what's called for here (see "A Note on Measurements," on page 98), you'll have to use 56 ounces of cognac and subtract 16 ounces from the amount of water added.

However. Even back in the day, not every spirit was sold at proof. (To contemplate the ways that old vintners' and publicans' handbooks suggest to fool the hydrometer is to despair for poor, mendacious mankind.) And, Punch being a compound beverage, the amount of water with which that spirit will be diluted in the final mixture is entirely in the hands of the person compounding it. Therefore, with few exceptions, I have not built this proof adjustment into my suggested recipes. Anyone making Punch properly will withhold some of the water anyway, adding it slowly to taste. If your Punch is on the verge of lacking, well, punch, just stop adding the water. But on to the individual spirits. Since this is not a handbook on liquor or its history, I'll keep my notes brief.

ARRACK

"Arrack," as we saw in Book I, is a generic term like "liquor," and its kinds are legion. Only two of them, however, are important for Punch-making—or three, if you find "must avoid" status to be important. That third one is the Middle Eastern type, which is flavored with anise and, generally, sweetened. Wonderful with water and ice but horrible in Punch. Unfortunately, it's also the easiest to find in the United States.

Until recently, the other two types, Batavia arrack and palm arrack, were entirely unavailable in the United States and had been since Prohibition, if not before. When, eight years ago, I first contracted my obsession with Punch, I had to have my Batavia arrack air-freighted from Germany, a case at a time, that being the minimum economical order. The day the big box came was always a red-letter one, marked with much sounding of the festive trump and slaughter of the fatted lime. Now, thanks to Eric Seed of specialty liquor importer Haus Alpenz, it is again available, if less than universally. Batavia Arrack van Oosten is the brand to seek out.

It's worth tracking down. Batavia arrack has a raw, flat tang that has a way of floating itself over the surface of the drink and right into that tiny, atavistic part of your brain that controls motor function and inhibition. It's got the funk. That should come as no surprise, though, considering how it's made. In 1820, John Crawfurd, "late British Resident at the court of the Sultan of Java," detailed the process. Rice was boiled and molded into cakes. These cakes were put in baskets over a vat, and as they fermented, a liquid dripped into the vat. That was collected, mixed with almost double its volume of molasses (diluted, we must assume) and a splash—less than a tenth of its volume—of palm wine, presumably to aid fermentation. The resulting liquid was then left to ferment for weeks, not the usual days (a long fermentation makes for a robustly flavored spirit), and was then distilled in Chinese-style pot stills. As far as I can determine, the manufacture hasn't changed all that much. These days, when the spirit comes off the still, the stuff bound for export is matured for a couple of months in large teak vats and then shipped off to Holland, where the almost three-hundred-year-old firm of E. A. Scheer stores it, blends it and wholesales it.

As for palm arrack, otherwise known as palm wine, coconut-palm or Goa arrack, this class of spirits, widely popular in South and Southeast Asia, is made not from the nut but from the watery sap of the tree itself, collected by slicing the flower bud and putting a pot under it. The resulting liquid quickly ferments into "toddy," or palm wine. The traditional method of distillation was in clay pot stills with bamboo tubing (shades of ancient Taxila), the resulting spirits coming in three grades, depending on strength. "Feni" or "fenny" was the strongest, plain old arrack the intermediate and "sura" the weakest—although according to the Portuguese it went "fenim," "fechado" and "urraca." At any rate, judging by the frequent British complaints about the strength of Goa arrack, they weren't getting the fenny.

True Goa arrack is still made, but it hasn't been seen on the world market in quite some time, and indeed the center of the modern industry has moved to Sri Lanka. Fortunately, the Sri Lankan firm of Mendis exports its palm arracks fairly broadly, and they can be found in North America if you look hard enough. They come in several grades, depending on how much time they've spent in the indigenous halmilla-wood vats and casks in which they're aged. For Punch use, there's no need to go beyond the VSOA ("Very Special Old Arrack") grade. This sourish, lightly funky spirit is definitely worth tracking down, as it makes a Punch that's uniquely delicate and integrated in flavor.

Also worth keeping an eye out for in your travels is lambanog, the Philippine version of palm arrack. At its best, it's delicate, lightly floral and utterly bewitching. At its worst, it's bubble-gum-flavored. Really. Oh, and blue. The new Asia, God love it.

BRANDY

The eighteenth-century British Punch-drinker insisted on French brandy when he wanted Brandy Punch, and preferably genuine cognac at that.[2] Sometimes he got it. Other times he got rectified molasses- or malt-spirit, colored with God knows what and flavored with extracts and essences—and often dangerous ones at that. When he could get the real stuff, it was at "strong bubble-proof," as the physician and pioneering popularizer of chemistry Peter Shaw wrote in 1731, a point upon which the French stood "to a *Punctilio.*" That, to Shaw, was unusual. Also worth noting was how "Old French Brandy, by having long lain in an oaken Cask . . . becomes a dilute *Tincture of Oak.*" And how long was long? "Sometimes twelve or eighteen months, and often two or three years." For Shaw, that (to us) brief period in wood "wonderfully takes off . . . that hot, acrid, and foul taste, peculiar to all Spirits or Brandies newly distill'd; and gives them a coolness and a softness not easily to be introduced by art."

For eighteenth-century Punch-making, in other words, a plain old VS cognac works just fine. I'm particularly fond of the Martell, although a VS from just about any of the major houses will work. Avoid anything suspiciously cheap (i.e., under twenty dollars a bottle). There are even one or two cognacs imported at cask strength, if you can find them. Otherwise, you're going to have to work with the standard 40-percent-alcohol-by-volume stuff.

I have also had tolerable results with Raynal brandy, which is

---

2 In the early Punch years in particular, if he couldn't get cognac, he'd be happy to settle for "Nantz," from the then-booming distilling region around Nantes.

French but isn't cognac and is quite cheap, and even with Paul Masson Grand Amber, which is California brandy mixed with a little cognac, and even cheaper. When using either of those, I generally make sure to supplement them with rum.

By the nineteenth century, older cognacs were available and still cheap enough to mix into Punch. There was, however, a good deal of "sophistication" in the trade, by which I mean counterfeiting, forging and adulterating. If you were lucky, all that would mean was that your cognac had been darkened or, at worst, sweetened with a little caramel. If you weren't—well, how does German potato-spirit flavored with "oil of cognac" strike you? No, I didn't think so. In any case, for the elegant clubman's Punch of the Regency period, you might want to spring for a VSOP, if possible. Your friends will thank you, if not your financial planner. As for brands, I've made many a succulent bowl of Punch with the Hennessy Privilege VSOP, and many another with the Pierre Ferrand Ambre.

GENEVER, OR GIN

The flavored vodka we know as London dry gin didn't achieve widespread popularity until some fifty-odd years after the Punch Age ended, and it couldn't have been made at all until the introduction of the column still in the 1830s. By then, Punch was already in line for the hearty handshake and the gold watch. For Gin Punch, in other words, you'll want something a good deal older in its conception. If it's an eighteenth-century style, you'll need Holland gin— genever, as its makers call it. Pot-stilled, thick and malty, it's one of the world's great distillates, as even the British realized: they greatly preferred imported "Hollands" to the home product, at least until the blockades of the Napoleonic wars forced them to improve the quality of the latter. (Be sure to use the kind known as "corenwijn" or at least oude genever; the clear, light-bodied jonge genever that leads the Dutch market is a twentieth-century style; the Bols Genever marketed in America looks like a jonge but is oude indeed and quite effective in Punch.)

If you're making a British Gin Punch from Punch's twilight

years, though, you'll need Old Tom gin, a transitional style with a heavier body and more forward botanicals than London dry—or so I understand it, anyway; for more on the vexed question of Old Tom, you'll have to consult Gaz (fka Gary) Regan's indispensable *Bartender's Gin Compendium*. Recommended brands of Old Tom are Ransom (for which, I must disclose, I played an advisory role) and Hayman's. By the time this book is in the stores, there will doubtless be more available.

Or you can just say the hell with it and use Tanqueray or Plymouth. Your Punch will still taste good, anyway—as long as it's not a hot one. Hot Punch and London dry gin are not a combination I have found to be a happy one.

RUM

If by rum you mean something as white and pleasantly inoffensive as vodka, or as sweet, mellow and woody as bourbon, then you're not talking Punch rum. Pot-stilled, high-proof Pirate Juice (see the following list), full of hogo, that's what you want. What's this "hogo," you ask? The Victorian free-love advocate Grant Allen defined it perfectly in one of his novels, when he has a West Indian planter explain: "it's our common West Indian corruption . . . of *haut goût—haut goût*, you understand me . . . or *hogo*, being the strong and somewhat offensive molasses-like flavour of new rum, before it has been mellowed . . . by being kept for years in the wood and in bottle." "Hogo" was a term of art in the rum trade since at least the beginning of the eighteenth century, when John Oldmixon used it in his history of the Americas. Derived from the term for the "high taste" of rotting meat, it could certainly be used pejoratively. But just as one cultivated the *haut goût* in pheasants and other game birds by hanging them for days before cooking them, so the hogo in rum came to be appreciated and even, to a degree, encouraged.

Rarely, though, by modern rum-makers. There are exceptions: Brazilian cachaça and the rhum agricoles of Martinique display its characteristic sulfurous "twang" in spades (as does, for that matter, Batavia arrack). But most rum-makers from Britain's former Caribbean colonies have learned to suppress it. That's a shame, since their rums grew up with Punch and were formerly precisely the kind Punch demands. Something that can heave itself up to its feet; shake off all those layers of citrus, spice, and the "element"; and say in a strong, firm voice, "Damn right, I am somebody!" *Rum.* These days, most of the rum exported by the islands of Jamaica and Barbados—two of the three main strongholds of British rum-making during the Punch Age—is sold in blends of carefully aged pot-still and column-still spirits, light in body, mellow and pleasant in flavor and absolutely nothing like the styles those islands were making fifty years ago, let alone in the eighteenth century.

In Jamaica itself, at least, the number-one-selling spirit is the hogo-rich Wray & Nephew White Overproof, which if not pure Pirate Juice (it's too light-bodied for that) will nonetheless do until one comes along (I have made many a fine bowl of Rum Punch by marrying it to a hogoless but full-bodied rum such as Gosling's). But fortunately for us, one has: Eric Seed, the man who brought us Batavia Arrack van Oosten, has also recently introduced Smith & Cross rum, a London dock–style Jamaican rum blended from aged Plummer and Wedderburn–style long-fermentation, high-ester, pure pot-still rums and bottled at 100 percent of proof (Sikes). More than that, one cannot ask. Equally good for Punch is the pure pot-still, 100 percent–proof Inner Circle Green Dot rum, from Australia. If you can't get those and can get to the duty-free shop at Heathrow, Wood's Old Navy Rum is a more than acceptable substitute (they sell it elsewhere in Britain, too). It's at proof and hails from the one part of the British Caribbean that keeps the faith on hogo in everything it makes, the Demerara River region of Guyana. El Dorado rums, also from there, are quite good, although they tend to be bottled at 40 percent alcohol by volume and lack the London dock–aging (there's something about sitting around in barrels in the soft English climate that really works for rum). Finally, Bundaberg in

Australia makes a high-proof, hogo-rich rum that, while definitely on the crude side for sipping, makes a fair dinkum Punch.[3]

By the nineteenth century, rums began to appear that moderated the hogo with a good deal of age and blending, but here we are on more familiar territory, so I won't go into detail about them. Instead, let me give a brief recap or précis of the styles best adapted for Punch use, with brands. There are three, which I have named after my own fancy; the brands I have listed are by way of example and by no means intended to be an exclusive list:

PIRATE JUICE. The full-hogo, high-proof stuff; formerly known as "Jamaica rum." Recommended brands: Inner Circle Green Dot, Smith & Cross, Wood's, Wray & Nephew White Overproof, Lemon Hart (mix equal parts 80-proof and 151-proof), Sea Wynde, Bundaberg.

PLANTER'S BEST. Older, mellower, smoother, lower in proof. Recommended brands: Angostura 1919, El Dorado (five- or twelve-year), Chairman's Reserve, J.M VSOP, Plantation Barbados five-year Grande Reserve, English Harbour five-year, Scarlet Ibis.

STIGGINS'S DELIGHT. (Christened after Dickens's rum-swilling reverend). Even older, richer, darker and more expensive. Recommended brands: Mount Gay Extra Old, Angostura 1824, El Dorado (fifteen- or twenty-one-year), most of the Plantation vintage rums.

WHISKEY, OR WHISKY

The only Irish whiskeys on the market today made the way Irish whiskey was during the Punch Age are the single-malt ones, and even those, although plenty tasty, are almost always too old and too low-proof to be the real McCoy, historically speaking. (If you can get the Connemara cask-strength, that's young and strong, if too peaty to represent the mainstream of Irish whiskey-making during our

---

3 I should note that there is such a thing as too much hogo. I can recall a couple of cases in my experience—a clairin from Haiti and a pot-stilled sugarcane-juice rum from Grenada of great authenticity—where I not only threw in the towel but burned it to get rid of the smell.

period.) But malts are a minority style now, and they were then—at least, ones made out of pure barley. The mainstream Irish whiskeys of the eighteenth and early nineteenth centuries were made from mixed grains, with healthy proportions of oats (perhaps 15 to 20 percent of the total grain) and rye (20 to 30 percent). Up until 1785, when a new malt tax was imposed, all the grain was malted. After that, only a little malted barley was used, but the same grains were used in unmalted form. The resulting rich, oily, pot-stilled whiskey remained the dominant style until the 1950s. Today, the oats and rye have gone for good from the pot-still whiskeys, only one of which even uses the malted-unmalted barley mix. That one is Redbreast, and it's delicious in Punch hot or cold.

For cold Irish Whiskey Punch, if your budget can't stretch to Redbreast or malt whiskey (the utterly sublime Bushmills ten-year-old comes at cognac prices), then John Powers is your man.

Scotch malt whiskey, on the other hand, is essentially what it was back in the day, only older (whiskey was rarely aged much, if at all) and far more expensive. A young, peaty, cask-strength single malt is what you want. Fortunately, in Scotland ten years can be considered young, and there are several fine malts that fit the bill. Laphroaig cask-strength is widely distributed and works just fine. Any cheap malt whiskey, even if challenging to sip, will make a tolerable Punch.

Finally, American whiskey. Young, strong, rye. Solution: Old Potrero. Done. (Or you can just use pretty much any bonded bourbon or rye.)

OTHER INGREDIENTS

Punch isn't just booze, of course. Some brief notes on the sweet, sour, spicy and aqueous ingredients are thus in order, with the caveat that the unusual will be discussed, should it arise, in Book III.

Punch Fruits, as seen in 1871. GREG BOEHM

CITRUS

The scurvy-killing "lymmons" of the early East India Company ships were almost certainly limes. Not until late in the seventeenth century, once Punch had taken hold and people had to really focus on their citrus, was a consistent distinction drawn. And a distinction it was: limes were, as Dr. John Covel put it in the 1670s, "a sort of hedge or crab Lemmons." That "hedge" was telling, as it was usually compounded with words such as "whore," "alehouse" or "writer" and had connotations not unlike our "Walmart." Some cloaked their distaste for the foreign lime in science: Tryon, for example, dubbed it "an immature Fruit, wherein the *Martial* and *Saturnine* Poysons are so powerful that the Sun and Elements have not had power to awake the *Balsamic Vertues.*" (Lemons are actually on average more acidic—and hence full of "Martial and Saturnine Poysons"—than limes.)

In any case, whether they were perceived as too acidic, too foreign or too colonial (Britain's Caribbean possessions were awash with lime juice), until well into the nineteenth century limes were viewed with considerable suspicion by those drinking Punch in England, who preferred the "nobler" lemon or orange. Both sweet and sour versions of the latter were available, with an edge to the sour ones (particularly in the earlier years), and it is rarely specified which kind was being used. However, the sweet kind, used alone, make for an insipid, watery Punch.

If you can find Seville or sour oranges, by all means pounce on them. Their juice, what there is of it, is nothing special—indeed, it tastes almost exactly like lemon juice, which can thus be used to supplement it. Their peel, however, makes for a memorable "oleo-saccharum," or "sugar-oil," which you will find discussed below. When preparing that compound from lemons, as is more common, the large, knobby, thick-skinned varieties tend to yield more oil than the small, thin-skinned ones, although those are easier to juice. In either case, pick the ones with the brightest, glossiest skins.

Whichever sort of citrus you use, it should be brought to room temperature and rolled hard on a firm surface before squeezing; you'll get a lot more juice that way.

Citrus fruit was not the only souring agent used in the flowing bowl. In calling for "a little Vinegar or Verjuice or Limon Juice or Lime Juice, which of them you can get," a 1695 recipe identified the true impetus for experimentation: supply. When lemons and such were scarce, people improvised. That improvising began early, if we are to judge by the records of the provincial secretary of New York, which include an entry from 1678 for money lent to one John Shakerley for "3 pints rum, 2 lb sugar and a qtt [quart] vineger . . . to make punch with Mr. Oldfeild [*sic*]." Aaron Burr, at least, liked his Vinegar Punch hot, or at least so tolerated it (it turns up thus in the journal he kept when he was in Paris in 1811), but I'm not convinced. Other, I suspect better, "sowerings" that one comes across include that 1695 verjuice, more pleasing than vinegar but not as sour, as well as tamarinds (a pretty fair substitute) and gooseberry juice, which I have not tried.

SPICE

I have no intention of giving a mini-encyclopedia of spices. Those that turn up in one Punch recipe or another are varied and legion, although few are as delightful as the one that rules them all, nutmeg. I will treat of the others in Book III, in the individual recipes they appear in, and confine my remarks on nutmeg to the observation that anyone who would spice his or her Punch with ground nutmeg out of a jar would make fettucine Alfredo with the "parmesan" that comes in a can. (I know that because I have, to my present chagrin, done both.) Whole nutmegs used to be of such value that wars were fought over them. Now they are cheap. There's no excuse.

The other spice that must be discussed is tea. Among the general instructions with which Jerry Thomas begins the section of his book devoted to Punch is the command to "us[e] tea instead of water." Hot or cold, this addition, attested to as early as 1727, makes for a much more complex Punch. There are a couple of caveats attached, however. Tea is quite astringent, and a Tea Punch will require more sugar than one without it, particularly if you're using black tea (green tea has less bite and is therefore favored by many of the authorities; it certainly preceded black tea in Punch use by several decades). Tea also has caffeine, which means that a bowl of Tea Punch can make for some very energetic drunks who will have a hard time sleeping it off. One of the worst nights I've ever had came after an afternoon of, admittedly, overindulging in an Arrack Punch made with gunpowder tea. I still shudder to recall the racing pulse, the ravaging thirst, the damp, twisted sheets. Vodka and Red

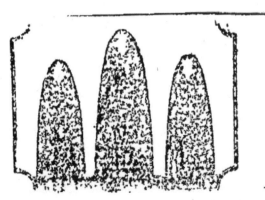

Sugar Loaves, ca. 1790. AUTHOR'S COLLECTION

Bull is Similac in comparison. These days, I only include it when the Punch will be served in the afternoon and in strictly finite quantities. In my experience, herbal teas are too highly flavored to make an acceptable substitute, as they tend to hijack the Punch and cloy.

SUGAR

Sugar that is both cheap and dazzlingly white is a thing of the modern world. True, Mandeville could speak, in the early eighteenth century, of the "glistning brightness of the finest Loaf Sugar," but that represented the flower, so to speak, of the sugar crop, and it was not for the masses. Most people had to do with a dingier, less refined product. But they would have had the last laugh, as an unrefined sugar such as demerara adds not only sweetness to Punch but also flavor, and is in fact preferable from an epicurean standpoint.

Unfortunately for the Punch reenactor, though, our sugar no longer comes in the dense loaves it used to. That does make it easier to measure out and dissolve, but it means you can't use it to rub off the oil-bearing peel of the lemon, as was the common practice. The kinds of sugar that do come in loaves—the Latin American piloncillo, or panela, and jaggery, or palm sugar, from India and Southeast Asia (highly recommended in Arrack Punch), are too soft for the task, while zuckerhut, the pointy little loaf used in Germany for making Feuerzangenbowle, is admirably white and sharp grained, but too crumbly.

If you are using piloncillo, it will have to be turned into a syrup first. Simply put the loaf in a pan with an equal quantity of water and work it over low heat, breaking it up into smaller and smaller pieces as it softens. Remember to take the water into account when you're figuring out the final dilution of your Punch. In general, equal volumes of sugar and water or citrus juice mixed will create a syrup whose volume is a little more than one and a half times that of either ingredient, a cup each of sugar and water thus making about thirteen ounces of syrup.

Jaggery, also known as gur or, in Indonesia, gula jawa (this is usually mixed with cane sugar), is softer than cane sugar and can sometimes be dissolved in citrus juice or cold water if it is broken up first. In any case, it yields an oddly fruity, cloudy syrup that does wonders for the exoticism of your Punch.

As for granulated sugars, for everyday Punch use, I generally prefer a raw sugar such as a demerara, a turbinado or an evaporated cane juice. There are a plethora of brands of both of these styles on the market; you can find them at stores that make any pretense at carrying natural foods. That includes Whole Foods and Trader Joe's. The finer the grain, the easier it is to dissolve. That holds true with white sugars as well. Those I will use only in the lightest Gin Punches or when speed of assembly is of the essence, in which case superfine sugar will be found most useful.

WATER AND ICE

Finally, the "element," as it was known. H_2O. Variations and sophistications such as the use of Champagne or soda water will be discussed in the appropriate places in Book III. Ice, however, needs a little attention. Punch, lacking the alcoholic concentration of the Cocktail, does not need to be as numbingly cold—indeed, it is best if it isn't: if it's chilled to Cocktail temperatures (i.e., below 32 degrees Fahrenheit), its fragrance is muted and its delicate harmony lost. It does, nonetheless, like to be cool, and in the summer, very cool. Ever since the end of the eighteenth century, iced Punch was considered a luxury indeed. Back then, the ice that provided the cooling had to be cut in the winter from frozen ponds and streams in large blocks and stored in insulated icehouses. That meant that Punch-makers could cut their ice to fit the bowl. The larger the block, the slower it would melt and dilute the Punch. Many preferred to avoid the dilution issue entirely by premixing the Punch, bottling it and keeping the bottles on ice, serving the Punch in small, frequently refilled bowls. Others refrigerated the bowl, either by sinking it in a very large block of ice or by putting it in a much bigger bowl and filling the space in between with cracked ice and salt. In either case, the bowl that held the Punch had to be of silver or some other, baser metal. The final option was to make the Punch extra strong and pour it over a bowl full of cracked ice. That was the American way of the nineteenth century, but then again we had already learned to tolerate ice in our drinks.

When I'm making Punch, if it's going to be ladled out over the course of an afternoon or evening, I'll use a large block of ice. This method has the advantage of ensuring that the Punch is weaker as the session progresses—not a bad thing. If it's all going to be ladled out at once, I'll go American and fill the bowl with ice cubes. It'll cool much faster and the punch will be gone before too much of the ice has melted.

To make a block of ice, you'll need a container half the capacity of your Punch bowl. Fill it with water and freeze it (for the larger quantities, this might take as long as forty-eight hours). Some people obsess about getting the block of ice to look just right, even going so far as to fill it with flowers, slices of fruit, and so on. I do not.

VII

TOOLS

I n my last book, *Imbibe!*, the section on tools took up a good
twelve pages. American-style Cocktail-making being a craft that
its first appreciators thought was best left to professionals, it required a professional tool kit. Punch-making, though, while often
practiced by professionals, was an essentially amateur art, and its
traditional tools are accordingly few and simple. *Notes & Queries*
covered most of them in 1885:

> There were certain articles which usually accompanied the
> bowl when the drink was made in the room, viz., a small gill
> measure to adjust the proportions of the ingredients; a
> peculiar strainer for the lemon juice in the form of a cup or
> small bowl, with two long flat handles or ears to rest on the
> side of the jug or vessel in which the mixture was made
> before it was poured into the bowl; and also the ladle with
> which the glasses were filled from the bowl.

This last usually took the form of a slender and graceful turned ebony or whalebone handle attached to the side of a smallish oval bowl, always of silver and usually with a silver shilling set into the bottom. Add a knife and a little silver nutmeg box, with a grater for a lid, and you were done, although there were those who would have thrown in a mechanical juicer rather than squeeze the fruit by hand. Napoleon's empress Josephine (a native of Martinique, deep in the Punch-belt) had a monogrammed one in silver. Nice.

I suppose the bowl could use a little elucidation, and we might as well take a quick look at the glasses while we're at it. England had a long tradition of mixing ale or wine with this and that and passing it around in bowls, so the line between a Posset bowl and a Punch bowl is rather a hazy one. But we know that "punchbowl" is first attested to in 1658 and that the drink was reputable enough by 1680 for those bowls to start appearing in silver.[1] Less exalted topers drank from earthenware and even wood. The large silver Punch bowl became a prime piece of institutional hardware, and every regiment, city corporation, guild, club and whatever else that very associative age could offer in the way of social organization had one: a capacious, footed silver hemisphere, with elaborate, cast handles on the sides and as much engraving as it could hold. By the middle of the eighteenth century, Britain's growing East Asia trade also supplied the booming market in Punch bowls with all the genuine china it could use. There were domestic versions, as well, often painted with political, patriotic or satirical themes (amusingly enough, Hogarth's squalid *Midnight Modern Conversation*, the print that you will find on the cover of this volume, was a popular motif).

Punch bowls came in all sizes, from the covered "sneaker" or "tiff" that held no more than a cup to the mammoth five-gallon

---

1 In 1694, the Ironmonger's Company Records contain notice of a Punch bowl made with a removable, scalloped rim so that it could also be used as a "monteith," a then-popular style of bowl used for carrying wineglasses to the table, washing them and cooling them (the stems of the glasses fit in the indentations, with the business ends resting in the cool water within and the bases hanging high and dry outside). This double-duty style of bowl became widely popular.

Hogarth's Punch Bowl. AUTHOR'S COLLECTION

Alderman's special. The default size, however, seems to have held a quart, with double and "thribble" bowls holding the requisite amounts (one must bear in mind that Punch was rarely served with ice in it, so a quart bowl of it, even if it was only one-third liquor, would still have room for a good twelve ounces of high-proof rum (the equivalent of more than a pint of 80-proof stuff). More than enough to get two people quite squiffy.

In the early nineteenth century, serious Punch-makers began turning to large earthenware jugs for day-to-day use. They didn't look like much, but they held enough for a small gathering, were easy to pour from, and did a better job of keeping hot punch hot and iced punch cold.

As for glasses, since the smaller bowls of Punch were generally passed around to be sipped from, they were not always necessary. Once the bowl reached a certain size, of course, that was no longer practical. I used to heap scorn upon the little "knuckletrap" cups that come with Punch sets. That was because they're ugly and tiny. I still do, but only because of the ugly. The Georgian silver Punch ladle in my possession, you see, holds but two ounces, just enough to fill one of the slender, stemmed V-shaped glasses from which the eighteenth century tended to drink its Punch and its wine. Not everyone agreed—there were half-pint "rummers" aplenty, and "bumpers," which technically meant any glass filled up to surface tension (hence the "bump") but in practice carried a certain notion of size, so that one might be embarrassed to identify anything less than a gill-sized glass—four ounces—as such. But in general, the glasses were not large.

That's as it should be, as I've learned. Half the fun of a bowl of Punch is in the ritual of it; in the ladling and interacting at the bowl, in the number of glasses drained, in the toasting, and so on. More small servings trump fewer large ones on all counts. One of my prized possessions is the box of thirty-six V-shaped two-ounce Libbey sherry glasses given to me by John Gertsen, of Drink in Boston. Every time it comes out, it's a party.

I've used those glasses with several different bowls. Unfortunately, not a one is a silver heirloom chased with the family crest and so large that it doubled as a baptismal font for ten generations of Wondriches. You don't have one of those, either? Pity. But here's the thing: I've made Punch successfully in silver bowls, ones of fine china and of expensive cut glass. I've also made it successfully in pasta pots, Le Creuset Dutch ovens, plastic bowls, melamine bowls, tin buckets, spackle buckets, salad spinners, highway-crew coolers (you know, the big round orange thing with the cup dispenser on the side and the spigot at the bottom), milk jugs (just cut a hole between the handle and the spout to fit the ice in), five-gallon water-cooler jugs, candy dishes, candy jars, Lexans of all sizes, nameless orange plastic things from Home Depot, large earthenware flower-pots, galvanized washtubs and a host of other miscellaneous vessels I'm not recalling. I have not made it in a washing machine, but I know someone who has. I have not made it in a building—yes, a *building*—but I know someone who has. A nice bowl is a luxury, not an essential.

These days, for small gatherings I use a ten-inch (diameter) Chinese soup bowl that holds three quarts—so technically a threbble, although I'm using ice so less liquid is involved. It cost less than ten dollars in a Chinese-restaurant supply house (a set of matching three-ounce teacups cost a dollar each). For medium parties (say, fifteen to twenty people), I find a six-quart china mixing/serving bowl works well; if you can locate one, the "Great Bowl" in the china-maker Pfaltzgraff's Aura line is just right. For large parties, I'll either use a fourteen-quart glass bowl, bought new, or, for less formal occasions, deploy the highway-crew cooler (it's insulated and holds five gallons; most efficient).

For hot Punch, a large earthenware pitcher or jug is traditional, although a fondue kit or—best of all—a Crock-Pot provides an effective modern update. About the largest size of jug available easily these days is three quarts, which is still enough for a pretty-good-sized hot Punch party. Le Creuset makes one; look for the "Sangria Jug."

The rest of a good modern Punch kit is simple. The one expensive item is a serious juicer. Punch can be a great annoyance to make in quantity if you skimp in this department. There's no finer or faster juicer made than the large, cast-aluminum Ra Chand J210, which you can get for a little over a hundred dollars. A lever-action, all-manual device, it's light and fast, and with it you can make a quart of juice in less than ten minutes—as quick as any electric juicer, and it doesn't chew up the pith (just don't put it in the dishwasher, or it will corrode). Make Punch four times and it has paid for itself in saved labor. Most of the rest of the gear is self-explanatory: measuring cups, storage containers, a good swivel-bladed vegetable peeler and a large muddler for handling the citrus peels, a chinois for straining the juice, knives and cutting boards. If you're making Punch to bottle and keep, you'll also need a fine sieve or strainer. The cloth kind made for straining cooking oil so that it can be used for biodiesel works well and is easily available for cheap on the Internet, but you can also use a clean pillowcase or T-shirt. Oh, and don't forget the nutmeg grater.

VIII

HOW TO MAKE PUNCH, OR THE FOUR PILLARS OF PUNCH

If Punch-makers were short on theoretical analysis, they were long indeed on practical tips—particularly toward the end of the Punch Age, when one begins to see magazine articles with titles like "The Poetry of Punch" and whole chapters of books devoted to the topic, such as the extensive one Charles Tovey included in his 1878 *Wit, Wisdom, and Morals Distilled from Bacchus*. By then, of course, the drink had become elaborate enough for the occasional practitioner to require such aids, and most practitioners had become occasional. Many of these tips involved specific modifications of the basic five-ingredient formula; if useful, they will be dealt with in the appropriate chapters of Book III. But there were some definite refinements to the basic technique that kept coming up again and again, albeit not always with perfect agreement. These cover four main areas of Punch-making: the handling of the citrus oil, the handling of the citrus juice, the order of assembly and the proportions of the ingredients.

You will note that none of them has anything to do with garnishing. In 1817, the opinionated Dr. Kitchiner observed in his *Apicius Redivivus* that "a few parings of the orange or lemon rind are generally considered as having an agreeable appearance floating in the bowl" (and indeed a curl of peel is visible peeking over the edge of the whopping bowl on the cover of this volume). Beyond that (and even that was controversial), classic Punches were essentially unadorned, the frippery and fanciness with which Punch is so often presented being a development of its years of obsolescence, when it was forced to rely on cosmetics and flashy clothing to seduce wary drinkers, rather than the healthy, native charms of youth. If you require such a presentation, your imagination can no doubt be your guide.

PILLAR I: THE OLEO-SACCHARUM. As Jerry Thomas wrote, "to make punch of any sort in perfection, the ambrosial essence of the lemon must be extracted." By "ambrosial essence," he meant not the juice but the oil contained in the fruit's skin. In this, he was entirely correct: the lemon oil adds a fragrance and depth that marks the difference between a good Punch and a great one (the same applies to Punch made with oranges, in particular Seville ones; if you're making Lime Punch, however, you're off the hook—lime peel is unacceptably bitter and its oil never used in classic recipes). By far the best and easiest way to incorporate this oil in Punch is to extract it with sugar, it having long been recognized that, as the *Dispensatory of the United States of America* put it in 1858, "Sugar renders . . . fixed and volatile oils to a certain extent miscible with water and forms with the latter [a] . . . combination called in pharmacy *oleo-saccharum*." I don't know when this oleo-saccharum (dog Latin for "oil-sugar") first began to be incorporated in Punch recipes, but it seems to have been on the table, so to speak, by 1670, when it appears in a very Punch-like recipe by Hannah Wooley. It was most certainly in play by 1707, when our old friend Ned Ward writes of a "Ladies *Punch-Club*, near St. *James*'s," and the member of it who shares secret nips of Punch with her chambermaid, thus rendering Mrs. Betty "fragrant of *Lemmon-Zest*, and *Nutmeg*"—a thing I must confess to finding strangely erotic.

The old-school way of preparing the oleo-saccharum, which Thomas endorses, is "by rubbing lumps of sugar on the rind, which breaks the delicate little vessels that contain the essence, and at the same time absorbs it." But as the anonymous and astute author of the 1869 *Steward & Barkeeper's Manual* observes, "this process is laborious, and seldom followed by the best punch mixers, save when a goodly number are to be supplied." Whether or not to use it is moot, however, as modern sugar is too weak. I don't mean in sweetness but rather in cohesion and abrasiveness. Nineteenth-century commentators talk of this process stripping lemons of their yellow outer skin entirely, but I've tried it with every kind of modern sugarloaf, cube and crystal I could procure and only ended up with a mass of crumbled, faintly scented sugar and a lemon undimmed in its yellowness. In this, our ancestors had the advantage on us.

If the traditional way doesn't work, then what? By far the most effective method I've found is to peel the fruit with a sharp, swivel-bladed vegetable peeler, trying to get as little of the white pith as possible. With a little practice, you should be able to turn out broad spirals of impressive length (which will make it easier when it comes time to remove them). These are then muddled firmly in a sturdy bowl along with two ounces of sugar per peel and then left to sit in a warm place for at least half an hour, and preferably twice that. During that period, if the peels are at all fresh, the sugar will draw forth an impressive amount of additional oil. After the peels are muddled again to incorporate the oil, they are ready for use.

This process is admittedly time-consuming and to some degree a laborious one. In the nineteenth century, there were those, such as the adventurous Dr. Strauss (there was seemingly not a revolution in the middle of the century that Gustave Louis Maurice Strauss didn't have a hand in, until age and impecuniousness forced him into Bohemia, writing and then, worst of all, culinary writing), who suggested substituting commercial essence of lemon for the peel, on the dubious grounds that it is "more uniform." Do not even attempt this. Others suggested that the best way to incorporate the oleo-saccharum is to put the peels in the spirits and let them infuse for a couple of hours. While this isn't ineffective, I find it produces a less vibrant lemoniness than the above method, and it takes even longer, although it is admittedly easier.

PILLAR II: THE SHRUB. The term of art for the mixture of sugar and citrus juice upon which Punch is constructed is variously given as "sherbet" or "shrub." In either case, it indicates the stage where the oleo-saccharum and the juice have been incorporated, sometimes with a little water as well, if that's needed to dissolve the sugar. "Shrub" is also used to refer to the same thing, but with some or all of the spirits added. Both nonalcoholic and alcoholic shrubs can be bottled and will keep, although their flavor will change with aging. The nonalcoholic kind is, however, more perishable and must be kept refrigerated. The boozy shrub can be kept in a cool, dark place. Either will have to be filtered after a couple of days to remove precipitates.

As an ancillary measure to employing the oleo-saccharum, there are those who suggest an additional means of adding lemon flavor to Punch. This time it's the pulp and pips we're dealing with. The more finicky of the authorities of yore, recognizing that even such Punch draff has a contribution that it could make, emphasize that it should not be discarded without having its flavor extracted. For some, this is accomplished simply by waiting to strain the juice until after it has been mixed with the oleo-saccharum. The real adepts, however, favor running a little boiling water over the strained solids, in order to leach out the flavor from the unbroken juice cells and dissolve and incorporate the jellylike coating of the pips, which is reputed to be rich in lemoniness. I have not found this to be essential, but neither have I found it to be in any way detrimental to the final flavor of the Punch.

PILLAR III: THE ORDER. Then there's the whole vexed and dog-matized question of when to put in what, which is tied in with the issue of temperature. William Maginn, one of the reigning literary wits of the Regency years, stated the general principles most con-cisely in one of his popular "Maxims of ODoherty [*sic*]," many of which are devoted to Punch and its manufacture: "In making hot toddy, or hot punch, you must put in the spirits before the water: in cold punch, grog, &c., the other way." The rationale behind this distinction, which Maginn declines to provide, appears to be two-fold. One, sugar dissolves poorly in spirits unless they're hot. For cold Punch, therefore, it's best to dissolve the sugar in the water before adding the booze. Two, hot Punch should be as hot as possi-ble. If you add the water first, it will cool as you stir it to dissolve the sugar. Therefore, since dissolution is much less of a problem in hot liquids, it can go in last. This sounds fairly logical, and yet there were those who disagreed, and bitterly. Dr. Strauss, at least, was civil about it when he suggested that the best procedure with the water was a two-part one: put some in (hot or cold, depending on how the Punch will be served) with the sugar and lemon juice, to dissolve it. Then add the spirits. Then add the remaining water. Revolutionary or not, he was a sensible man.

PILLAR IV: THE PROPORTIONS. Finally, the proportions. Are they "Two of sour, and one of sweet, / One of strong, and two of weak"? Thus, at least, a reviewer in the *Monthly Review* claimed "our grandmothers used to say." That was in 1756 (and it only makes sense if the size of a single part differs from line to line). Or is it the Caribbean "One of sour, two of sweet, / Three of strong, four of weak" (as the author of the 1844 novel *Edith Leslie* insisted)? Or was that "Four of strong and eight of weak" (as that formula was quickly amended)? Or "Two of strong and one of weak, / One of sour and one of sweet" (1851)? "One of sour and three of sweet / Four of strong and four of weak" (1908)? Or—or, as Thomas wrote with an uncharacteristic note of uncertainty, "the precise portions of spirit and water, or even of the acidity and sweetness, can have no general rule, as scarcely two persons make punch alike."[1] Beyond that, lemons and limes vary in acidity, sugar varies in sweetness by kind and spirits vary in proof. Many classic Punch recipes decline to specify quantities at all for the citrus, sugar and water. In part, this has to do with the fact that, as one of Thomas's recipes notes, "the acidity of a lemon cannot be known till tried, and therefore [the amount of sugar] must be determined by the taste." But it's more than that. Punch-making is an art, and arts cannot be legislated.

That said, it would be poltroonish to hide behind the shield of art. This is my book about Punch, and I cannot duck so vital a question. For the record, then, my favorite proportions are these: One of sour, one of sweet, / Four of strong and six of weak. They are my own, and they are, simply and without possibility of argument, the best. You may change them, but remember the words of Dr. Walsh, who upon listening to his friends' suggestions as he was brewing the evening's Punch replied, "I'll tell you what, gentlemen. The Punch may not be quite so good as you could wish, but by God if you *mend* it at all, you'll entirely *spoil* it."

Whatever proportions you use, though, remember that you'll have to put more sugar in than you would in a Cocktail, because the sugar has to not only balance out the sourness of the citrus juice but add texture to all that water as well. And if you're using tea, you'll need a lot more: tea soaks up sugar like a ShamWow does off-brand cola.

---

1 By "wrote" here I mean "plagiarized," as the comment was swiped verbatim from Gibbons Merle's 1842 *Domestic Dictionary and Housekeeper's Manual*.

Punch Cold and Hot

Finally, here in step-by-step form are two reference recipes, one for cold Punch and one for hot. Both are scaled to a single, 750-milliliter bottle of liquor. (For the question of how many people that will serve, see the introduction to Book III.)

COLD PUNCH

1. PREPARING THE OLEO-SACCHARUM

Using a swivel-bladed vegetable peeler, peel three lemons, avoiding as much as possible cutting into the white pith. Reserve the lemons and put the peels into a large, nonreactive bowl.

Add 6 ounces of sugar. Using a muddler, mash the peels into the sugar until it is wet with the lemon oil. Let sit for at least thirty minutes, and preferably an hour.

VARIATIONS AND REFINEMENTS

If using loaf sugar, you'll need a different procedure. Peel the three lemons. Then prepare a syrup by melting 6 ounces of the loaf sugar (or roughly one-third of a 500-gram loaf) in 6 ounces of water over low heat. When the sugar has melted, remove from heat and muddle in the peels.

For Lime Punch, skip this stage entirely.

2. PREPARING THE SHRUB OR SHERBET

Squeeze the reserved lemons and enough others to get 6 ounces of juice. Pass the juice through a fine-mesh strainer (this step is optional, but it yields a clearer Punch and—no small consideration—makes everything easier to clean). Stir the juice into the oleo-saccharum and then remove the lemon peels with a slotted spoon and discard them (unless, that is, you prefer to keep them in as garnish).

If using a coarse-grained raw sugar, such as turbinado or, even better, demerara, you'll need to use a somewhat different procedure. Before adding the juice, pour 6 ounces of boiling water over the oleo-saccharum and muddle the sugar hard in the water. You may end up with a little undissolved sugar at the end, but don't worry about it.

If determined to extract flavor from pulp and seeds of the squeezed-out lemons and the strained juice, squeeze the lemons through a strainer into a separate container. Then put all the residue into a fine-mesh strainer and put that over the bowl with the oleo-saccharum. Pour 12 ounces of boiling water onto the residue, stirring as you pour. Press the solids in the strainer to extract whatever can be extracted and discard them. Stir the sugar in the hot water until it has dissolved. Then add the reserved juice.

If you are making Tea Punch, add the hot tea to the oleo-saccharum before incorporating the juice. For this recipe, you'll need 4½ cups of weak tea (made with 3 teaspoons of loose tea or three tea bags and infused for less than five minutes). If making this for bottling, however, reduce the water to only 1½ cups.

3. INCORPORATING THE SPIRITS AND WINES

Add to the sherbet one 750-milliliter bottle of spirits. Use what you like, of course, but for the purposes of illustration, let's go with the Bushmills 10—or perhaps a mixture of 9 ounces of Smith & Cross Jamaican rum and 16 ounces of Martell VS cognac. Stir. Taste.

At this stage, your Punch base is done, and it can be bottled for keeping.

4. DILUTION, COOLING AND SPICE

Before serving, add to the Punch base 4½ cups of cool water. Taste. If too strong, add more water unless you're adding ice. If you are doing so, do it now, deploying either a quart-sized block if the Punch is meant to be ladled out slowly, or enough ice cubes to fill the bowl halfway if it's meant to be served all at once.

Grate about a quarter of a nutmeg on top.

Garnish? What's that?

VARIATIONS AND REFINEMENTS

If you've been making Tea Punch, don't add water, as you've already done so, unless it's the bottled version. For that you'll need to add 3 cups when you serve it.

HOT PUNCH

Hot Punch is considerably simpler to make.

1. THE OLEO-SACCHARUM

In a mixing bowl, prepare an oleo-saccharum, as on page 95, with four lemons and 8 ounces sugar (hot Punch needs to be sweeter than cold Punch). When this is ready, scrape it into a large earthenware jug that has been prewarmed by rinsing it with boiling water (or, of course, a hot Crock-Pot). Add 12 ounces boiling water and stir.

2. SPIRITS AND WINES

In short order, add one 750-milliliter bottle of spirits—here, let's go with the Bowmore Legend single-malt Scotch.

3. WATER AND SPICE

Add another 3 cups of boiling water. Taste. If too strong, add a little more water.

Spice is not strictly necessary here, but if you wish to add it, now is the time; as above.

4. AFTERCARE

To keep your Punch hot, you'll need a fireplace complete with roaring fire to put it in front of, with a napkin stuffed into the mouth of the jug to keep in the steam, as Dickens suggests. Or, of course, the Crock-Pot.

A Note on Measurements

Arhaic English currency, I can understand. Four farthings make a penny, twelve pennies a shilling, five shillings a crown, four crowns a pound, twenty-one shillings a guinea. Archaic English measures of length, piece of cake. Archaic English measures of liquid volume, though. . . . The part that makes my head explode isn't so much the measures themselves, which are simple enough (anyone who was born in the land of inches, feet, yards and miles has also grown up with ounces, cups, pints, quarts and gallons). Four ounces are a gill or quartern, four gills or quarterns a pint, two pints a quart, two quarts a pottle and two pottles a gallon. Quantities beyond that we're unlikely to use. I can even get around the uncertainty about what to call the measure that fits between a gill and a pint. Is it a tumbler, a breakfast cup or merely a half-pint (by far the most common designation)? No matter. What does matter, though, is the fact that a gallon is not always a gallon nor a quart a quart. It depends, you see, on what you're measuring and when and where you're doing it.

If you were measuring ale in England before 1824, you used a gallon of 282 cubic inches. If, however, it was wine you were measuring, that gallon would only be 231 cubic inches. Quarts of either were proportioned accordingly. There was, believe it or not, some kind of method in this. Ale foams, wine does not, and nobody wants to pay for foam. So let's just make the ale measures bigger, to allow for that foam—let's say, add another quarter, so that four ale quarts equal five wine ones. The system worked more or less tolerably as long as it was just ale or beer you were measuring on the one side and wine on the other. But what if it was, say, aqua vitae? Which measure do you use then? The original rationale for the two-tier system having been forgotten pretty much as soon as it was instituted, there was a lot of confusion about that, and confusion plus money equals litigation. By the middle of the seventeenth century, it was a settled point of law that spirits used wine measures. Fair enough.

But then there's the problem of bottles. Wine and spirits, when not sold directly from the tap, were put in quart bottles. Only the quart wasn't a quart. "It is the custom of the trade," as *The English Mechanic and World of Science* noted in 1886, "to sell six bottles to the [imperial] gallon," while still calling them quarts. About that imperial gallon: in 1824, George IV got rid of the wine gallon and made the ale gallon the standard but kept the wine-sized ounce, which is to say a pint suddenly went up by 25 percent to be 20 ounces, making a quart 40 and a gallon 160. That meant that those wine quarts held only 26 ounces. America, having opted out of that whole empire business, kept the wine gallon as it was and ditched the ale measures; that meant that we had only five "quart" bottles to the gallon. I have grossly oversimplified this, but it's complicated enough this way.[2] All I can say is, when you see a quantity specified in an old Punch recipe, let taste be your guide. Oh, and the quantities in my "Suggested Procedures" and "Notes" accompanying the recipes in Book III are wine or American measures—unless, of course, they're metric. Speaking of which, the metric equivalents below are approximate, for ease of use.

	WINE OR AMERICAN MEASURE	IMPERIAL MEASURE
Gill; quartern	4 oz. or 120 ml	5 oz. or 150 ml
Half-pint; tumbler; cup	8 oz. or 240 ml	10 oz. or 300 ml
Pint	16 oz. or 480 ml	20 oz. or 600 ml
Quart	32 oz. or 960 ml	40 oz. or 1200 ml
Pottle	64 oz. or 1920 ml	—
Gallon	128 oz. or 3840 ml	160 oz. or 4800 ml

2 For example, a U.S. ounce is actually only .96 of an imperial ounce. Let's just ignore that, shall we?

BOOK III

THE PUNCHES

Every written recipe is by its very nature incomplete. Each one assumes shared knowledge and judgment between the writer and the reader. Even an instruction as straightforward as "stir with ice" presumes a great deal of contextual knowledge. Over time, though, that contextual knowledge falls away, so that the older the recipe, the less certain we can be of our interpretation of it. We read "stir with ice" in a Cocktail book published last year and we'll fill a mixing glass two-thirds full of ice, slide the bowl of a twisted-handled bar spoon down to the bottom of it and waltz the contents around in neat, counterclockwise circles, pushing the spoon with our fingers away from us and pulling it back toward us until we have counted to fifty. Even if we're not quite so adept as that, at least we've seen people who are do it and have a general idea of the process. In 1862, however, that may have meant twirling the liquid around once or twice with a single lump of ice the size of a pigeon's egg, thus producing a drink not nearly as cold as what we're picturing and a hell of a lot less diluted.

Reconstructing historic recipes is full of pitfalls, involving as it does culinary history, social history, linguistics and a whole lot of other "istics" and "ologies," all blended with a healthy shot of guesswork. It's far too easy to use our own assumptions to fill in the blanks. As a check against these assumptions, I've done my best to provide a verbatim transcript of my source for each recipe before giving any interpretation of my own. That way, should my interpretation prove unsatisfactory, as no doubt sometimes it will, you have a foundation upon which to build your own. For the more straightforward recipes, my interpretation is confined to a set of explanatory notes; for the others, I've provided a complete recipe. But please bear in mind that my suggestions are just that. If you've got a better way of doing it, trust yourself. The brands I've included are by way of example; if there's something you prefer, use it.

Only a handful of recipes or reconstitutable descriptions for Punch have reached us from the seventeenth century; I've included most of them here. There are many more from the eighteenth century, but most are redundant. I've tried to include the ones that aren't. In the nineteenth century, recipes for Punch multiply into an ungodly profusion. At the same time, what was direct and elemental becomes complex and ornamental. Variation shades into dissipation, and novelty replaces innovation. I've included far less of them.

In assigning the Punches to their species and kinds, I've tried to the best of my ability to do it in a way that the people who made and drank Punch in the years of its dominion would have recognized. The resulting categories, therefore, reflect a somewhat uneasy mix of history and mixology—but then again, so do the generally accepted categories of Cocktails. In any case, my categories are at least a starting place.

The terms "Pirate Juice," "Planter's Best" and "Stiggins's Delight," used to categorize rums, are explained in Book II.

Finally, I've given an approximate—very approximate—yield for each recipe, in cups. In 1862, Jerry Thomas suggested one should "allow a quart for four persons," but he also noted that "this information must be taken *cum grano salis*; for the capacities of persons for this kind of beverage are generally supposed to vary considerably." Too true, too true. A cup of Punch is four eighteenth-century-sized glasses, after which many people will stop. Others will get much deeper into the bowl. In other words, you'll have to figure out how much your friends are good for; I can't help you with that. They're *your* friends.

IX

ARRACK PUNCH, ALIAS RACK PUNCH

On February 1, 1659, Henry Aldworth, an East India Company factor in Bengal, wrote his friend Thomas Davies that he and his colleague Job Charnock—one of the great names in the company's history, who would go on to found Calcutta—greatly missed his fellowship, "which wee have often remembered in a bowle of the cleerest Punch, having noe better liquor." There is an irony here: once Punch caught on in England, there were many very fancy people indeed for whom there was "noe better liquor" than the Arrack Punch with which Messrs. Aldworth and Charnock were forced to make do.

Henry Fielding made use of that fact in his popular 1730 farce, *The Tragedy of Tragedies, or The Life and Death of Tom Thumb the Great*, in which he has King Arthur issue one of the great royal decrees in literature: "To-day it is our Pleasure to be drunk, / And this our Queen shall be as drunk as we." While his queen is nothing loath in theory, she does have her scruples:

> *If the capacious Goblet overflow*
> *With* Arrack-Punch—'*fore* George*! I'll see it out;*
> *Of* Rum, *or* Brandy, *I'll not taste a Drop.*

The king answers with the magnanimity that is the sign of true-bred royalty:

> *Tho'* Rack, *in* Punch, *Eight Shillings be a Quart,*
> *And* Rum *and* Brandy *be no more than Six,*
> *Rather than quarrel, you shall have your Will.*

True, this is fiction. But these were in fact the prevailing prices at the time, eight shillings being the very rough equivalent, in percentage of a yearly living wage, to $250. Not cheap. (That makes the day in 1736 when Robert Hobart, an underage student on an allowance of seven shillings a week, spent thirty-five shillings on Arrack Punch "sent to his lodging" from Gally's Coffee House a truly memorable spree.) In the real England, one of the participants in the temperance debates of 1736, when Parliament, seeking to quash the gin trade and thus dry out the lower classes, also considered banning the retail sale of Punch, correctly identified the class that would be most affected when he noted that "our drinkers of Arrack Punch will most of them betake themselves to the drinking of *French* clarets."

Although in point of plain quality, "rack," as it was commonly known, was probably better than any other available spirit save the most carefully sourced French cognac, it was nonetheless a taste that needed acquiring, and some preferred not to. "I don't love rack punch," Jonathan Swift wrote to his beloved Stella in 1711; "I love it better with brandy; are you of my opinion?" History is silent as to whether she was or not. Swift never did reconcile himself to it, judging by the lines he wrote years later to his Punch-swilling friend

Dr. Sheridan: "But if rack punch you still would swallow / I then forewarn'd you what would follow." Whether it excited fear of its notorious ability to cause hangovers or fastidiousness of taste or pocketbook, Rack Punch did have a way of creating strong dissenters. William Hickey, for example, who encountered it frequently during the 1760s in the better London brothels, had, as he put it in his memoirs, "an uncommon dislike" of it and would just pretend to take sips from the passed bowl, focusing his energies rather on "romping and playing all sorts of tricks with the girls." (I'd like to think that one could do both.) Nonetheless, the dissenters were a minority, and Arrack Punch retained its primacy throughout the English-speaking world and beyond.[1] In the later part of the century, one of the practices of London insurance companies was to ladle out Arrack Punch to customers both actual and potential when they stopped by the offices. Beats a plastic key chain, anyway.

Even in America, the Land That Rum Built, there was real Arrack Punch from the early days, and it was popular enough. In 1728, when Colonel William Byrd struck out deep into the American hinterland on a mission to determine the Virginia-Carolina border, he found the locals moistening the clay with such rustic concoctions as Bombo—basically, strong Rum Toddy (i.e., rum, sugar and water) without the crucial scrape of nutmeg that makes it fit for civilized ingestion—and the by turns frightening and alluring "Fricassee of Rum" ("They Fry'd half a Dozen Rashers of very fat Bacon in a Pint of Rum, both which being disht up together, serv'd the Company at once for meat and Drink"). But he also found Colonel Harvey Harrison, whose "good house was enough to spoil us for Woodsmen," as he wrote in his diary: there they "drank Rack-Punch" in the evening and "trod on Carpets" when they went to bed.

Considering that mercantilist trade policies dictated that that arrack had to be shipped from India or points east to England be-

---

1 In 1776, Sweden put it at the head of a list of prohibited foreign luxuries. That prohibition didn't take, and bottled Arrack Punch base became one of the characteristic drinks of the Swedish people, only to be eclipsed by vodka in the late twentieth century.

fore it could be transshipped to America, where it then had to be carried practically by hand into the backcountry, you can imagine what it cost. Even in the more settled parts of the country, it was expensive. In 1736, when Virginian William Randolph bought a twenty-four-hundred-acre tract of Crown land that happened to include a parcel his friend Peter Jefferson had had his eye on, he agreed to sell Jefferson two hundred acres of it for fifty pounds and another two hundred in return for, as the deed reads, "Henry Weatherbourne's biggest bowl of arrack punch to him delivered."[2]

By the opening decades of the nineteenth century, though, Arrack Punch had begun to lose its grip, both in America and in the mother country. In 1829, *The Southern Review*, published in Charleston, South Carolina, gave notice of that when it mocked Louis Eustache Ude, who had been cook to the unfortunate Louis XVI, for recommending in his 1827 magnum opus, *The French Cook*, that certain characteristic English dishes

> are to be washed down . . . with the *Ponge au The*, or the *Ponge a la Rhom*, or *a la Rac a l' Anglais* . . . it being well known that rum punch and arrack punch are in great request among all the upper classes of society in England!

A rrack Punch didn't die out entirely, to be sure, at least not right away; there were always a few epicures for whom anything else was a mere understudy—men like Henry William Herbert, the

---

2 This might be a nominal price, but it wasn't entirely nominal: the inventory of Wetherburn's tavern made upon his death in 1760 values his arrack at a hefty one pound, or twenty shillings, a gallon, wholesale. Unfortunately, history is silent as to how big that bowl was, but colonial taverns definitely stocked ones far larger than the standard single, double and treble: William Black, visiting Philadelphia in 1744, recorded in his diary a literally staggering regimen of Punch morning, noon and night, all served in bowls "big enough for a goose to swim in." Wetherburn's largest Punch bowl thus could have held as much as eight or ten gallons, with a third of that being arrack. Considering that his tavern was the best in town and no doubt marked its booze up accordingly, that bowl of Punch may have cost ten pounds—making Randolph's gesture to Thomas Jefferson's father the eighteenth-century equivalent of charging a night of bottle service at a New York nightclub today.

pioneer American sportswriter, who always made himself a glass of Arrack Punch before retiring for the night. But its fate foreshadowed that of Punch in general: from daily service, it was remanded to the reserves, only to be called up in times of great mixological crisis. The wealthy and the celebrated stopped sluicing themselves with it, those who would be either stopped affecting it and those who would be neither stopped aspiring to it. In 1838, as if to put a period on its years of imperium, its greatest proponent died.

From the last years of the old century until 1831, when he resigned his post at age eighty-six, Captain Charles Morris was the spirit presiding over the venerable and riotous London institution known as the "Sublime Society of Beef Steaks," founded in 1735. At five o'clock every Saturday from November to June, twenty-five aristocratic sports and their guests gathered together to eat nothing but grilled steak (with a few fixings) and drink nothing but port wine and Arrack Punch (the society had been limited to twenty-four until 1785, when George Augustus Frederick, the Prince of Wales, wanted in). Morris, who had an extraordinary facility for throwing together impromptu verses and songs, many of them quite frank in their diction, was sort of a song-leader and, more to the point, the man in charge of making the Punch. "It was amusing to see him at his laboratory at the sideboard," one initiate later recalled, "stocked with the various products that enter into the composition of that nectareous mixture: then smacking an elementary glass or two, and giving a significant nod, the fiat of its excellence." Alas, if Morris's exact recipe survives, I have not been able to find it; all we have are tantalizing descriptions of the "mantling beauties" of this "potent" and "fascinating draught 'That flames and dances in its crystal bound'" (the quote is from Milton's youth, before England knew Punch). In any case, these sparse descriptions of the captain's Punch-making suggest that in his rendition, it was somewhat more elaborate than the old East India Company version; after all, he was mixing for royals and aristocrats, and the Prince of Wales, for one, had very elaborate tastes indeed when it came to Punch (see Regent's Punch in Chapter XVII).

Captain Morris holds forth. AUTHOR'S COLLECTION

At least the society's arrack would've been genuine Batavia.
That was not always the case—London's Vauxhall Gardens was famous for serving an Arrack Punch in which the "arrack" was in fact nothing more than cheap rum flavored with benzoin, a kind of tree gum. As Thackeray notes in *Vanity Fair*, a work in which Vauxhall's Rack Punch plays a brief but pivotal role, "there is no headache in the world like that caused by Vauxhall punch." Thus speaketh experience. But right through the end of the nineteenth century you could still find true arrack if you looked hard enough, although it grew increasingly uncommon in the English-speaking world (Germany, the Netherlands and Scandinavia kept it much more present). Imagine the dismay those Punchy old-timers felt when they stopped in at the spirits merchant's for a bottle of his finest old Batavia only to be told "we don't get no call for it anymore, sorry." That's the

risk one runs by having archaic tastes, by standing against the general degeneration of the age. I felt the same heartsink when they stopped importing the old Bols green-bottle genever or when, one after another, the bonded bourbons were edged off the liquor-store shelf to make room for another flavored vodka. For the arrack-drinker, it must have been vermouth, crème de violette and London dry gin that did the dirty deed.

But we live in times of wonder, and the rack is back—which means that this chapter need not be a purely theoretical one. Here, then, are five ways of making Arrack Punch, two from the beginning of its career and three from what was until recently the end.

Bombay Presidency Punch

Unfortunately, the earliest descriptions of Punch, even when they are obliging enough to list its component parts, are silent when it comes to how much of each was employed in its mixing, and in mixology, proportions are everything. In 1694, however, General Sir John Gayer, governor of the East India Company's Bombay "Presidency" (as its possessions in northwest India were known), diverted a fraction of his attention from encouraging trade and repairing the damage inflicted on its capital by the Mughal emperor Aurangzeb, who five years before had laid siege to the place and effectively destroyed it, to regulating the small but important matter of Punch. Because Gayer was a bureaucrat and not an artist, he did not shrink from specifying proportions for the prime ingredients. For this alone, his formula is valuable. But beyond just specifying them, he specified good ones, with a liberal dose of lime juice (limes were cheap and plentiful in India). Indeed, I have found them so excellent that, under the regrettably imprecise name of "Bombay Government Punch," I made them my standard ones and have tested them with a plethora of arracks, rums and brandies, alone and in combination, and never found them wanting (see the epilogue). Made as it is detailed in the following instructions, though, with an attempt at re-creating the precise formula dished out in the Punch houses of the company's Indian dominions, Gayer's Punch is as simple as it is delicate, and it possesses an elusive charm that is quite unlike that of any other Punch, Cocktail or mixed drink.

Be forewarned, though: as one of the governor's predecessors wrote in 1676, "the usuall effect of that accursed Bombay Punch" involves its consumers "besotting themselves with drunkenness" and then quarreling, dueling and committing any number of other acts "to the shame, scandall, and ruine of our nation and religion." I haven't seen any dueling yet when I've trotted out this formula, but there's been an argument or two, and no end of blaspheming.

THE ORIGINAL FORMULA

If any man comes into a victualling house to drink punch, he may demand one quart good Goa arak, half a pound of sugar and half a pint of good lime water; and make his own punch. If the bowl be not marked with the clerk of the market's seal, then the bowl may be freely broken without paying anything either for bowl or punch.

SOURCE: **Order Book of the Bombay Government, August 13, 1694**

SUGGESTED PROCEDURE

Break up 8 ounces of jaggery or palm sugar and put it into a three-quart Punch bowl. Add 8 ounces lime juice and muddle together until all the sugar has dissolved. Add 1 quart Sri Lankan palm arrack (or any other palm arrack) and stir. Add 5 cups water and grate nutmeg over the top.

YIELD: **10 cups.**

NOTES

While this recipe is a good place to play around with exotic Asian palm sugars, they are not essential to its success (and it should be noted that they are not all alike: if yours is hard, you might have to dissolve it first in 1 cup boiling water, subtracting that amount from the water that goes in at the end). You'll notice that Gayer's order said nothing about dilution, presumably because if you're brewing the stuff yourself you can add however much water you like (it would be useful, however, to have a close look at one of those seal-stamped bowls). Another government regulation, this one from the mother country in 1736, suggests that Punch should have no more than two parts water to one of spirits, but the spirits then were generally higher in proof than much of what we get now, so it's best to start with equal parts and adjust upward. The order also makes no mention of spice. Nutmeg is always appropriate, though, but you can also use Mandelslo's rosewater—start with no more than a teaspoon, and adjust from there—or Bernier's mace, in which case you'll need to muddle a blade of it in with the sugar before adding the lime juice.

If you want to go straight seventeenth century, you'll need some sea biscuit to float on top, an item not nearly so common as it once was. And yet it's still a staple in Alaska, Hawaii still goes through a fair amount of it and Maine consumes its share. Look online for "hardtack" or "pilot bread." In the brief period when bread was considered a useful part of Punch, common toast was spoken of as an effective substitute for the sea biscuit, and I've had acceptable results from Carr's Table Water Crackers, although it's not something I shall repeat. If you want to add ice, authenticity be damned, go right ahead.

Meriton Latroon's Bantam Punch

India wasn't the only Punch-drenched part of the East. We must not neglect Java and Sumatra and their neighboring islands. The ports of Batavia and Bantam and, a little later, Bencoolen[3] were packed cheek to jowl with Punch houses. When the English privateer Woodes Rogers put into Batavia in 1710, he noted that some of his crew "were hugging each other, others blessing themselves that they were come to such a glorious Place for Punch, where they could have Arack for 8 Pence *per* Gallon, and Sugar for 1 Peny a Pound."

While we may share the sailors' joy, it doesn't help us much with the mixology. Nor, alas, do the accounts of other contemporary travelers. It is as if once they put into these ports, the seafarers found something there to creep in through their mouths and steal away their brains. Fortunately, there exists one source that communicates some details about what Punch meant in the eastern parts of the East Indies. In 1665, one Richard Head—perhaps early English prose fiction's most disreputable practitioner, and that's saying something— published the work for which he is remembered: *The English Rogue: Described in the Life of Meriton Latroon, a Witty Extravagant*. For "witty extravagant," read "utter scumbag." Latroon, the book's narrator, is a runaway apprentice who steals, swills, swives and swindles his way through England and Ireland until the powers that be decide that the best place for him is anywhere else and transport him abroad (and that's only the censored version; as Head's friend William Winstanley wrote, the book in its original form "being too much smutty, would not be Licensed, so that he was fain to refine it").

---

3 Modern-day Bengkulu City, on the southeast coast of Sumatra, where the British established their last toehold in the archipelago in 1685.

Head, an expert at swilling himself, renders his hero's swilling in considerable detail. Ultimately, that swilling even extends to Punch, marking its earliest appearances in English fiction. That Punch-drinking doesn't happen in the British Isles, though, but rather in Bantam, where Latroon finds himself after a chain of unfortunate and highly unlikely events. There, in the street called "China Row," he not only drinks "very immoderately of punch, rack, tea & c. which was brought up in great china jugs holding at least two quarts" but marries the Indian Punch-house keeper who supplies it to him. (Nobody said he was stupid.) It's unclear from the text whether the rack and tea were combined to make the Punch or whether they were separate drinks. But then again, one shouldn't wonder at the confusion: neither Head nor Francis Kirkman, who published a 1668 continuation of the book (probably without Head's collaboration) that picks up where the first volume left off and thus begins with Punch-drinking, had ever been to the Indies.

Whether the recipe was cribbed from an as-yet-undiscovered travel book or picked up from a sailor in a bar, the Punch detailed in *The English Rogue* is of doubtful provenance, and even though there's nothing about it that explicitly forbids us doing so, it would be rash to take it as an authentic depiction of what was being mixed and drunk in Java.[4] Yet if we disregard such qualms and do our best to re-create the recipe as if it were indeed authentic, using what would have been available at that time and place, we end up with a beverage that is as dark, rich and almost meaty as the Bombay Presidency Punch is light and delicate, and thus have the two poles of Punch-making in its original rangeland.

---

4 The fact that the author of the continuation clearly doesn't know what "rack" or "lime" mean in his recipe, conflating them as he does into the nonsensical "rack-lime," which he explains as "lime-water," suggests that Kirkman and not Head wrote the passage, since Head got that part right in the original book.

For we had not only the country drink called toddee, which is made of the juice of several trees, and punch, which is made of rack-lime, or lime-water, sugar, spices, and sometimes the addition of amber-grease, but we likewise drank great quantities of Persian wine, which is much like claret, and brought from that country in bottles.

SOURCE: Richard Head/Francis Kirkman, *The English Rogue, Continued, in the Life of Meriton Latroon and Other Extravagants. Comprehending the Most Eminent Cheats of Most Trades and Professions. The Second Part,* 1668

SUGGESTED PROCEDURE

In a mortar or small bowl, muddle a piece of ambergris the size of a grain of barley with an ounce of Indonesian gula jawa or other dark, funky sugar until it has been incorporated. Add 2 ounces Batavia arrack and muddle again until sugar has dissolved. Break up 5 ounces of gula jawa, put it in a two-quart jug with 6 ounces lime juice and muddle together until the sugar has dissolved. Add the ambergris-sugar-arrack mixture and stir. Add the remains of the 750-milliliter bottle of Batavia arrack from which you have removed the 2 ounces to mix with the ambergris, stir again, and finish with 3 to 4 cups water, according to taste. Grate nutmeg over the top.

NOTES

Ambergris is clotted whale cholesterol, secreted in large lumps that float around until they wash ashore. That doesn't sound very appetizing, but by the time it washes up, ambergris has aged into a lightly, sweetly and very persistently fragrant substance that most resembles soap. What with the present state of the whale, it is also hideously expensive, but then again, it was never cheap (see "Sources for Rare Ingredients and Tools," page 281). Since it is essentially a fat, it must be rendered mixable before it can be used, which the above process will do. If the trouble, expense (it goes for about twenty dollars a gram) or squick factor is too much for you, it may easily be omitted, although it does add a subtle, insinuating I-know-not-what to the Punch that cannot otherwise be replicated.

For muddling the ambergris, regular demerara sugar is better at absorbing the fragrance, if less authentic. If you can't get gula jawa, which is a sticky, funky mix of palm and sugarcane sugars, then muscovado, piloncillo, panela or jaggery will do. But it's worth tracking the real stuff down, as it gives the Punch its porterlike color and a good deal of its umami-driven brothiness. If you don't have a pitcher, a bowl will of course work just fine. I don't recommend ice here, although an hour in the refrigerator will do no harm.

If you wish to incorporate tea, as Head's brief note seems to suggest, add 3 cups of hot green tea, made with 3 teaspoons of loose tea or three tea bags, to the sugar–lime juice–ambergris extract mixture, stir and then add the arrack. Add, if necessary, another cup of cool water at the end.

YIELD: 8 cups.

ODoherty's Arrack Punch

The Arrack Punch drunk in Britain in the early eighteenth century was, as far as I can determine, essentially indistinguishable from the Rum Punch and the Brandy Punch, save in its motive element. As the century wore on and the use of that element grew less and less general, though, the definition of Arrack Punch seems to have changed, from "Punch made from arrack" to "Punch with some arrack in it." Captain Morris's Punch, I suspect, was of the latter variety.

Not that there's anything wrong with that: one of my favorite recipes from Jerry Thomas's book has long been the one he gave for "a very pretty three tumblers" of Arrack Punch. Indeed, when I had to pick one of his drinks to make at the Slow Food tribute to him that was held at the Plaza Hotel in 2003, it's the one I chose. Even when I learned, years later, that the recipe was lifted, pretty tumblers and all, from William Maginn's "Maxims of ODoherty," a widely popular series of crotchety observations on drink, cigars and life in general that appeared in Edinburgh's *Blackwood's Magazine* in 1824, it did not diminish my enjoyment of it, although it did do fatal injury to my cherished mental picture of the young Jerry Thomas learning to make genuine Arrack Punch at the side of one of his grizzled bunkmates on the *Annie Smith*, the ship from which he ran away to the goldfields of California as soon as it docked in San Francisco in 1849. No matter. American sailor or Scottish physician, whoever committed it to paper knew his Punch. Indeed, to drink a bumper of it is to understand Captain Morris's most famous lines:

> *'Tis by the glow my bumper gives*
> *Life's picture's mellow made;*

The fading light then brightly lives,
And softly sinks the shade;
Some happier tint still rises there
With every drop I drain—
And that I think's a reason fair
To fill my glass again.

THE ORIGINAL FORMULA

Maxim Seventy-Third

In making 'rack punch, you ought to put two glasses of rum to three of arrack. A good deal of sugar is required; but sweetening, after all, must be left to taste. Kitchener is frequently absurd, when he prescribes by weight and measure for such things. Lemons and limes are also matter of palate, but two lemons are enough for the above quantity; put then an equal quantity of water—i.e., not five but six glasses to allow for the lemon juice, and you have a very pretty three tumblers of punch. Mix in a jug.

If you are afraid of head-aches—for, as Xenophon says of another kind of Eastern tipple, 'rack punch is κεφαλαλγές [i.e., "headache-making"]—put twice as much water as spirits. I, however, never use it that way for my own private drinking.

SOURCE: Morgan ODoherty (William Maginn), "Maxims of ODoherty,"
Blackwood's Magazine, 1824

SUGGESTED PROCEDURE

In a large pitcher, dissolve 2 ounces demerara sugar in 2 ounces boiling water. Add 2 ounces lime juice and stir. Add 6 ounces Batavia arrack, 4 ounces dark, full-bodied rum and 12 ounces cold water. Refrigerate or stir with large cubes of ice and pour into glasses. Grate nutmeg on top of each.

NOTES

The one thing that Thomas adds to the recipe is to specify, correctly, that the glasses should be two-ounce wineglasses. Maginn is correct about the sugar—I suggest the above amount of sugar in full knowledge that I risk falling into the same absurdity as poor Dr. Kitchiner, who wrote the 1817 *Apicius Redivivus, or The Cook's Oracle*. If you're comfortable with white sugar here, the Punch will be quicker to assemble, as you can ditch the boiling water. Or you can use 2 ounces of 2:1 demerara sugar syrup, alias rich simple syrup (simply stir two parts demerara sugar and one part water together over low heat until all the sugar has dissolved). As for the arrack, Batavia Arrack van Oosten, available domestically, is what you'll want here, unless you can get the 116-proof Boven's from Germany. (Dr. Kitchiner, to his credit, believed that "arrack punch . . . is always made with that spirit alone.") For the rum, go for a good, pungent Pirate Juice or, even better, a half-and-half blend of funky Pirate Juice and mellow Planter's Best–style rums. I'm particularly partial to a fifty-fifty mix of Smith & Cross and Plantation Barbados five-year. Like ODoherty, Kitchiner held that lime and lemon juice were both acceptable here, although where ODoherty preferred the latter, he chose the former. I agree with Kitchiner. About his contention that "the flavour of the Seville orange interferes too much with the peculiar flavour of the arrack, which proves so grateful to most tastes, though to many very unpleasant," I can only agree with the second part; the Seville orange will only step on the rack if you make an oleo-saccharum, which for an on-the-fly Punch such as this is entirely unnecessary. But yes, there are some poor benighted souls to whom the savor of Batavia arrack is not pleasant. *Suum cuique*.

YIELD: 3 cups.

COZZENS'S ARRACK PUNCH

Outside of Indonesia, where it's mostly drunk straight or mixed with soda pop, the most common use for Batavia arrack these days is in something called Swedish Punch, an achingly sweet, slightly citrusy, low-proof, arrack-based liqueur that seems to have been originally designed as a sort of Arrack Punch concentrate: just add hot water and Sven's your uncle. Ironically, in the two decades just before Prohibition, this Scandinavian specialty was making great strides as a Cocktail ingredient, ensuring that the distinctive flavor of arrack, having been shuffled out mixology's front door, was slipping in through the back. These days, unfortunately, Swedish Punch is imperiled even in Sweden, where this former drink of the people—traditionally consumed on a Thursday, before a bowl of pea soup; I'm not making that up—has largely been replaced by the same rootless, internationalized Highballs and club drinks for which the rest of western Europe has traded its drinkways.

The formula was an old one, anyway, and not just Scandinavian: follow the instructions in this recipe, and you're left with two quarts of something essentially indistinguishable from Swedish Punch. It can also be drunk as is, either cold or hot. If you choose the latter, it's worth heeding the words appended to it by F. S. Cozzens, the discursive New York wine merchant from whose newsletter this recipe hails: "those whose impatience will not permit them to wait until it is cold, should use it with caution." Even cold, "it should only be drunk from small glasses." Fair warning.

THE ORIGINAL FORMULA

To one bottle of old Batavia arrack, add six lemons, in thin slices, and let them steep for six hours. Take them out very carefully, without squeezing. To one quart of boiling water add one pound of loaf sugar. When the sugar is dissolved, add the hot solution to the arrack. Be sure to remove the lemons first.

SOURCE: F. S. Cozzens, *Wine Press*, June 1854

NOTES
This recipe is meant for bottling. If you're going to lay it down for keeping, it will need filtering after a few days. If arrack is lacking, it may be replaced here with cognac, in which case you will have Bimbo Punch, a Jerry Thomas drink and a very fine one at that. Either way, this formula is simply too sweet to be drunk as Punch without dilution. A little boiling water, though (say, equal parts), and it's a most festive holiday drink—and what's better, one that can be prepared days, weeks or even months in advance.

YIELD: 8 cups.

UNITED SERVICE PUNCH

London's United Service Club was founded in 1816, after the two-headed specter of Napoleon and revolution was safely laid to rest, in order to bring senior officers in the army and the navy together. Once they were so brought, they all seemed to have agreed that the best strategy for coexistence was to sink into their deep leather armchairs and not move until it was unclear whether they even could. The most exciting thing recorded in the club's history was when the Duke of Wellington, a member, disputed a bill and got three shillings taken off.

The club's general outlook on life is mirrored in the extreme conservativeness of its Punch. Then again, few Punches are as fundamentally sound. I'm not saying that there's a correlation.

Dissolve, in two pints of hot tea, three-quarters of a pound of loaf-sugar, having previously rubbed off, with a portion of the sugar, the peel of four lemons; then add the juice of eight lemons, and a pint of arrack.

SOURCE: Jerry Thomas, *Bar-Tenders Guide*, 1862

SUGGESTED PROCEDURE

Begin with an oleo-saccharum of four lemons and 12 ounces Florida Crystals or other restrained raw sugar. For the tea, nothing fancy: plain old black tea works fine. The pint here is of course the imperial one, so you'll need 5 cups of tea (made with five tea bags or 5 teaspoons loose tea) and 2½ cups of Batavia arrack. My instinct is to deploy the nutmeg grater here, but whenever I move to do so I see those red, jowly faces glowering at me and beat a hasty retreat. This is good either hot or cold.

YIELD: 9 cups.

X

Brandy Punch,
Rum Punch, and
Brandy and Rum Punch

Once Punch made it out of Asia and into Britain and her Caribbean possessions, it didn't take very long for it to go native. As we've seen, by 1670 people had learned to replace the exotic, expensive and often hard-to-get arrack with brandy in England and rum in the Americas—the former because it was the best thing they could get, the latter because it was the only. Brandy Punch properly made being a most delightful drink indeed, there were many who were of Swift's opinion and considered the substitute superior to the original. Most of the rest were at least willing to see it mentioned in the same breath, so that the Scottish agriculturalist William Mackintosh could lament that his countrymen had learned to scorn the humble ale of his youth for imported wine or, if that was unavailable, "a Snaker [*sic*] of Rack or Brandy Punch." That was in 1729. By the middle of the century, brandy had become the safe, almost middle-class choice for spirit to go in your Punch. Even a relative nonentity, such as the small-town Sussex shopkeeper Thomas Turner, who kept a meticulous diary in the 1760s, could occasionally indulge in "an agreeable bowl of punch" made with smuggled French brandy (it helped that he was friends with the local officer of excise, who would contribute confiscated bottles to the cause). Over the next decades, Brandy Punch would move up and down the social ladder by a few rungs, depending on the state of Britain's relations with France. When cannon and bayonet did the talking, brandy climbed out of reach of the aspirational classes (unless you count "British brandy," which was doctored malt spirit—essentially, bad whiskey). At other times, you would have scenes like Bob Sawyer's little bachelor's party in *The Pickwick Papers*, complete with mismatched glassware, jugs of warm Brandy Punch and a long-unpaid landlady who cuts off the hot water supply just when it's most needed.

But what of Rum Punch? At first look, it certainly had a different core clientele from its vinous cousin. Men like the members of

Captain Low holds forth. AUTHOR'S COLLECTION

the Bermuda General Assembly, whom their ostensible lieutenant governor described in 1724 as preferring to spend their days "wandering from one uninhabited Island to another (in their sloops), fishing for wrecks, and trading with Pyrat's, and living not like animals that are imbued with reason." On the rare occasion these vagabonds could be called together, he continues, "It is fitter to be imagin'd, than for me to tell . . . the effects which Rum Punch produces in an Assembly of 36 men, such as I have describ'd." Rum Punch wasn't served at every sitting of every colonial assembly, but—as a look at some of the surviving tavern bills quickly displays—it was far from an unknown beverage. But it isn't so much assemblymen whom we associate with Rum Punch as the fellows with whom those Bermudians were trading: pirates.

There's an oft-cited passage in the *General History of the Robberies & Murders of the Most Notorious Pyrates*, published by the pseudonymous "Captain Charles Johnson" in 1724, that the author claims was copied from the journal of Edward Teach, or Blackbeard himself:

(Such a day)[1] rum all out; our company somewhat sober; a damned confusion amongst us; rogues a-plotting; great talk of separation; so I looked sharp for a prize; (such a day) took one with a great deal of liquor on board, so kept the company hot, damned hot, then all things went well again.

This vivid scrap of prose—among the most vivid in the English language—has helped spawn countless scenes of pirates swilling rum from the bottle and cask, stinking drunk, vile and filthy.

Those last three things might certainly be accurate; most pirates were not overcareful of their linen and liked a drink of rum from time to time. But when it comes to the way they drank that

---

1 The interjections of "such a day" here are generally and wrongly interpreted as exclamations; they are, in fact, the editor's way of saying "day x" and "day y," rather than reproducing actual dates from the ship's log—if, indeed, he didn't make the whole thing up in the first place.

rum, modern writers have underestimated the freebooters' palates. The notorious Captain Avery, for example, "was one of those who are mightily addicted to Punch." John Rackham was taken when his ship was surprised while hove too near another vessel so that he and his men could share a bowl with the other crew. The psychopathic Ned Low kept a two-gallon silver Punch bowl of which he made frequent use (such luxuries are easier to maintain if you don't have to pay for them). When one of his more genteel captives declined to split a smaller bowl with him, Low picked it up in one hand and a cocked pistol in the other and offered him a stark choice: drink with a murderer or die. We may assume that he took the bowl.

Good Americans, the pirates liked a little lubrication when they had official business to conduct. The mutineer Howell Davis was elected captain at a council of war "called over a large Bowl of Punch," and Bartholomew Roberts, who succeeded to his office after Davis was ambushed by the Portuguese, was elected in the same manner. When he had a disciplinary problem, Roberts would call a hearing and, over the customary pipes and "large Bowl of Rum Punch," he and his officers would hear the evidence, consult the law and generally keep up "the Form of Justice"—which, as Johnson wrote, "is as much as can be said of several other Courts that have more lawful Commissions for what they do." (Roberts's crew once tried to recruit a clergyman by "promising he should do nothing for his Money but make Punch, and say Prayers"—note the order. For whatever reason, he declined.)

Rum Punch wasn't restricted to pirates, of course; it belonged to sailors in general, as discussed in Book I. Between the colonial connotations and the nautical ones, you might expect that it would get high-hatted in the mother country, that to drink it would brand one as a hick and a rube and a ruffian. And yet that did not happen, due in large part to two forces that trump even class anxiety: patriotism and greed. Unlike arrack or brandy, which were made by foreigners in foreign lands and had to be bought with good British gold that then stayed in foreign pockets, rum was made by Britons in lands that were nominally British, and thus any gold spent on it ended up in British pockets—and some very high and deep pockets at that. The dynamic is aptly summed up in a 1772 letter to *Town and Country Magazine* giving the character of one "Mr. Prywell," who "considers it as high treason to drink brandy punch, being a complete Antigallician [i.e., French-hater], and having the rum trade, and the good of the West-India islands strongly at heart."

It wasn't just the powerful interests on rum's side that made it popular in Punch (although they might have had something to do with the way medical writers kept proclaiming it the most wholesome and least harmful of all spirits). It was also delicious, at least when well made and properly aged—"in order to make Rum palatable to any Person of nice Taste," one expert opined during the 1737 Gin Act debates, "it must be carefully kept in a good Cellar for several Years"—with much of the twang of Batavia arrack but a richer, smoother body. If not well made or aged, Ned Ward's description of it as "that damn'd Devil's Piss" might have been closer to the truth, but by the middle of the eighteenth century, there was plenty of good rum to be had. And if you formed an *entente cordiale avant la lettre* and teamed it up with real French brandy, so much the better: the brandy smoothed out the rum, and the rum added savor to the brandy.

Not everyone was so adventurous, at least not right away: looking through Punch recipes from the early eighteenth century, it seems like there was a general sentiment of "when I drinks brandy I drinks brandy, when I drinks rum I drinks rum." Not until the second half of the century does a mixed Punch begin popping up. In 1763, the *St. James Magazine* could mention "hot rum and brandy-punch" without pausing to explain. And if the unhinged, dissipated and violent Stephen Fovargue (among other things, he horsewhipped a Cambridge servant to death) could claim in his eccentric 1767 book of opinions on matters sporting and musical, *The New Catalogue of Vulgar Errors*, that a "charming Bowl of Rum and

Brandy Punch mixed" could "inspire . . . with generous sentiments," his counterexample didn't wreck its career. By the early nineteenth century, it was utterly unobjectionable, and many of the best authorities insisted on it.

But on to the Punches. Here are five recipes for Brandy Punch, Rum Punch, and Brandy and Rum Punch that are all about the generous sentiments, and no horsewhipping.

DR. SALMON'S PUNCH

This simple, early and quite tasty recipe for Brandy Punch appears in *The Husbandman's Jewel*, a 1695 collection of remedies, recipes, and household and agricultural hints issued under the name of Gervase Markham, the pioneering agricultural writer who had died in 1637 and therefore had nothing whatsoever to do with the book. The "Salmon" to whom the recipe is attributed must be Dr.—or rather, "Dr."— William Salmon, a self-taught Grub Street polymath who was, by the standards of the day, a quack (by our standards, of course, so were all his educated contemporaries). Unfortunately, I can't say which particular work of his it comes from, as they are too prolific to search in detail—or at least for an impatient mixographer to do so (I gave up at the British Library after the fourth or fifth fat, small-print volume failed to yield the recipe; there were many more to go). In any case, the use of lime juice instead of lemon marks it as an early recipe and one that is not fully assimilated to European conditions.

THE ORIGINAL FORMULA

To Make Punch

Take two Quarts of Water, one Pint of Lime Juice, three quarters of a Pound of fine Sugar, mix and dissolve the

Sugar, then put three Pints of choice Brandy; stir them well together, and grate in a Nutmeg. This Liquor cheers the Heart, and revives the Spirits beyond any other Liquor, Moderately drunk helps Digestion, restores lost Appetite, and makes the Body profoundly Healthful, and able to resist the Assaults of all Diseases. Salmon.

SOURCE: Quoted in "Gervase Markham," *The Husbandman's Jewel*, 1695

NOTES

This recipe is as close to self-explanatory as any from the seventeenth century I've seen. The only real issue here is the balance of sweet and sour. If you don't have a heroic tolerance for tartness, you'll find that this will need a little more sugar or a little less lime juice (say, a pound of the former, or 12 ounces of the latter). If only the last part of the recipe were true. What a wonderful world it would be.

YIELD: 16 cups.

Major Bird's Brandy Punch

As has been noted, arrack was expensive in Britain, whereas French brandy was cheap, or at least cheaper, particularly when it was smuggled in to avoid the excise. Major Thomas Bird, anyway, was no smuggler, nor was his brandy, advertised in 1707 at eight and a half shillings a gallon, all that cheap. But he had been established in the business since 1689, if not before, and was a pillar of the community—that "Major" came from his position as second in command of one of the six regiments of the London Militia—and we can be pretty sure the "Old Coigniac [*sic*] Brandy" he stocked at his Pudding Lane warehouse was at least genuine, a qualification that was far from universal. Perhaps I'm only willing to give him the benefit of the doubt because the recipe for Brandy Punch that accompanied some of his advertisements is such a sound one. One could ask for no better proof that by Bird's day, mixologists had established that just as rum has its mate for life in the lime, brandy rejoices in the lemon.

THE ORIGINAL FORMULA

Major Bird's Receipt to make Punch of his Brandy.

Take 1 Quart of his Brandy, and it will bear 2 Quarts and a Pint of Spring Water; if you drink it very strong, then 2 Quarts of Water to a Quart of the Brandy, with 6 or 8 Lisbon Lemmons, and half a Pound of fine Loaf Sugar: Then you will find it to have a curious fine scent and flavour, and Drink and Taste as clean as Burgundy Wine.

SOURCE: Quoted in John Ashton, *Social Life in the Reign of Queen Anne, Taken from Original Sources*, 1882

SUGGESTED PROCEDURE

Begin with an oleo-saccharum of four lemons and 1 cup fine-grained raw sugar, such as Florida Crystals. Add 8 ounces lemon juice and stir until sugar has dissolved. Add 1 quart VS-grade cognac and 2 quarts cool water. Grate nutmeg on top.

NOTES

I've suggested the oleo-saccharum here to reflect the increasing sophistication of Punch-making in the eighteenth century. Unless your cognac is "full Proof" like Bird's (whatever that meant in 1707), even the lesser quantity of water will not make this "very strong." If you're adding ice, in fact, you might want to use even less. If you should find yourself short a cup or so of the brandy and had just that amount of Smith & Cross Jamaican rum or other hogo-bomb loitering around with nothing to do, matters might be arranged to the benefit of all concerned.

YIELD: 13 cups.

GLASGOW PUNCH

If you happened to be in Edinburgh one Saturday night in the 1770s and wished to go where the Quality went, you would in short order find yourself diving below the sidewalk into a dimly lit, smoky cellar packed with parties of the fanciest men and women in town, all eating oysters, drinking porter (there was no wine) and, when the spirit moved them, dancing reels. Once the repast was cleared, it was time for Punch. Brandy or rum—ladies' choice. Edward Topham, who dived in 1775, noted that "the ladies, who always love what is best, fixed upon brandy punch." But then again, they were Edinburgh ladies; had they been Glasgow lasses, the answer would have been different.

Glasgow, you see, was wholly and famously dedicated to Rum Punch. It being in Scotland, one might expect something different. But to this day, if the first thing you do when you walk into a drinking establishment is make a quick inventory of the available potables, you'll very quickly notice something odd going on in many a Scottish pub, particularly if it's within caber-toss of salt water. Half of the speed-pourers will be full of not malt whiskey, or even blended whiskey, but obscure, inky stuff that travels under the names "Old Trawler" and "O.V.D." Rum. Dark, heady demerara rum, at that—the kind that's all about the "hogo" (O.V.D. = "Old Vatted Demerara"). Go figure.

It's not all that strange when you really think about it, though. As a glance at the map of Scotland reveals, there's an awful lot of coastline there, and the Scots have always been seafarers as a result. And seafarers—sailors— drink rum. Small wonder, then, that the native Punch of Glasgow, a major hub for transatlantic trade in the eighteenth century and shipbuilding in the nineteenth, was based on rum.

Uncharacteristically for Hibernian Punches, Glasgow Punch is generally made cold, at least by, as Sir John Sinclair wrote in 1807, those "who value themselves on the superior flavour of their rum and fruit." Perhaps this is because Glasgow's maritime climate is warmer than that of the rest of the country or because shipbuilding is hot work. Or perhaps it simply has to do with the observation made in another of ODoherty's Maxims that would be plagiarized by Jerry Thomas (or, to be fair, his editors) that "the beautiful mutual adaptation of cold rum and cold water . . . is beyond all praise . . . being one of nature's most exquisite achievements." I might not go that far—but then again, ply me with Glasgow Punch and I very well might.

The following recipe comes from a note appended by the busy nineteenth-century editor R. Shelton Mackenzie to his edition of the *Noctes Ambrosianae*, a widely popular series of convivial and philosophical dialogues that shared the pages of *Blackwood's* with the "Maxims of ODoherty."[2] Mackenzie purloined it in turn from another of the *Blackwood's* wits, John Gibson Lockhart (Sir Walter Scott's son-in-law and a friend of Goethe's—another Punch-drinker, by the way), who included a scene of people making it in his 1819 satirical novel, *Peter's Letters to His Kinsfolk*. Peter, it must be admitted, did not have such a wonderful experience with it. "Nature," he writes his friend the morning after, "must have given bowels of brass to the Glasgow punch-drinker. On no other principle can the enormous quantities of punch, which

---

2 In fact, Mackenzie appended a slightly altered version of the same note to his edition of "ODoherty," a note that was reprinted verbatim, down to the final injunction to "Imbibe," as the recipe for Glasgow Punch in Jerry Thomas's *Bar-Tenders Guide*.

the natives here swallow with impunity, be accounted for."
The joke here is, as Sinclair observed and Lockhart's own
description of the Punch's making bears out, that

> the punch that was the ordinary drink of the people
> of Glasgow . . . was in general made weak. . . . This
> kind of liquor might be drank in large quantities with
> safety; it passed freely off by the kidneys and skin;
> and seldom occasioned a head-ache.

Peter, in short, was a pussy. Headache or no, he was lucky to
get any Glasgow Punch at all: by the early nineteenth century,
it was on its way out as a day-to-day drink, and as Sinclair
noted, if it was drunk, "instead of one overflowing social
bowl, in the preparing of which more attention was paid to
the cookery, every guest now makes his own punch in a
separate glass or tumbler."

THE ORIGINAL FORMULA

Glasgow Punch is cold. To make a quart jug of it, melt the
sugar in a little water. Squeeze a couple of lemons through a
hair-strainer, and mix. This is Sherbet, and half the battle
consists in it being well-made. Then add old Jamaica rum, in
the portion of one to six. Finally, cut two limes in two, and
run each section rapidly round the edge of the jug, gently
squeezing in some of the more delicate acid to complete the
flavor. This mixture is very insinuating, and leaves those who
freely take it, the legacy of splitting headaches, into the day-
use of which they can enter the next morning.

SOURCE: R. Shelton Mackenzie, ed., *Noctes Ambrosianae*, 1854

SUGGESTED PROCEDURE

In a one-and-a-half-quart jug or bowl, dissolve 6 ounces fine-grained
raw sugar, such as Florida Crystals, in 6 ounces water. Add 4 ounces
strained lemon juice and 20 ounces cold water. Stir in 6 or 7 ounces

strong Jamaican-style rum ("Great care was taken to use none but the best old Jamaica rum"—Sinclair), cut two well-ripened limes in half, run the cut sides around the rim of the jug or bowl and hand-squeeze the juice in. Serve.

NOTES

Don't worry too much about the headaches, not unless you drink at least a jug of this yourself. In fact (if you don't mind getting past the "portion of one to six"), this will taste a lot better, while still remaining light and quaffable, if you use 10 ounces of rum and a pint (American) of cold water, making a portion of one to three. However much rum you use, don't forget the limes; they are, as Lockhart wrote, the *"tour de maitre"* here—the master's touch.

YIELD: 5 cups (1 imperial quart).

CHARLES DICKENS'S PUNCH

Charles Dickens needs no introduction. A dedicated Punch-maker, he was known among his friends for his ritualized performance as he worked up a bowl or jug, complete with running commentary on his ingredients, techniques and progress. His characters were, if anything, more dedicated to the flowing bowl than their creator. If, however, I were to invite Pickwick and Micawber and Sam Weller and all of Dickens's other Punch-drinkers in to sit for a spell, I would soon find myself entirely without space to write about anything else. Instead, I shall send the more mixologically minded among you to Edward Hewett and W. F. Axton's *Convivial Dickens*, if you can find it, and everyone else to *The Pickwick Papers*, one of the most pleasantly tipsy books ever written. And here, to moisten your journey through the book, is Dickens's own recipe for Punch, or at least the one he sent to his friend Henry Austin's sister, with the hope that it would make her "for ninety years . . . a beautiful Punchmaker in more senses than one." With this sophisticated brandy-rum formula (ever the sign of the epicure), she could not have failed.

THE ORIGINAL FORMULA

TO MAKE THREE PINTS OF PUNCH

Peel into a very strong common basin (which may be broken, in case of accident, without damage to the owner's peace or pocket) the rinds of three lemons, cut very thin, and with as little as possible of the white coating between the peel and the fruit, attached. Add a double-handfull [*sic*] of lump sugar (good measure), a pint of good old rum, and a large wine-glass full of brandy—if it not be a large claret-glass, say two. Set this on fire, by filling a warm silver spoon with the spirit, lighting the contents at a wax taper, and pouring them gently in. [L]et it burn for three or four minutes at least, stirring it from time to time. Then extinguish it by covering the basin with a tray, which will immediately put out the flame. Then squeeze in the juice of the three lemons, and add a quart of <u>boiling</u> water. Stir the whole well, cover it up for five minutes, and stir again.

At this crisis (having skimmed off the lemon pips with a spoon) you may taste. If not sweet enough, add sugar to your liking, but observe that it will be a <u>little</u> sweeter presently. Pour the whole into a jug, tie a leather or coarse cloth over the top, so as to exclude the air completely, and stand it in a hot oven ten minutes, or on a hot stove one quarter of an hour. Keep it until it comes to table in a warm place near the fire, but not too hot. If it be intended to stand three or four hours, take half the lemon-peel out, or it will acquire a bitter taste.

The same punch allowed to cool by degrees, and then iced, is delicious. It requires less sugar when made for this purpose. If you wish to produce it bright, strain it into bottles through silk.

These proportions and directions will, of course, apply to any quantity.

SOURCE: Letter from Charles Dickens to "Mrs. F." (Amelia Austin Filloneau), January 18, 1847

SUGGESTED PROCEDURE

Use an enameled cast-iron pot for the "common basin," or at least something heatproof. Six ounces of demerara sugar should do—particularly if you can get the sort that comes in rough cubes. Use 20 ounces of rum and 6 of Courvoisier VSOP cognac (the brand Dickens kept in his cellar) to be authentic, or 16 ounces of rum and 10 of cognac if you don't want the brandy to get completely lost in the mix; for that rum, I find a sixty-forty mix of Pirate Juice and Planter's Best styles works well here, although you can also go all out and deploy something in the Reverend Stiggins's Delight line. Indeed, Dickens's cellar also held a number of bottles of "fine old pine-apple rum" (the good reverend's favorite), which may be approximated by combining 12 ounces Smith & Cross Jamaican rum and 20 ounces Angostura 1919 rum in a sealable jug along with an eighth of a pineapple, sliced, for a week; strain, let the solids settle, siphon off the clear rum and bottle.

Whatever you do in the way of rum, the fire will melt the sugar and extract the oil from the lemon peel. Dickens's advice about lighting the spirits from a spoon is extremely sound: always bring the fire to the alcohol, not the alcohol to the fire. (And a stainless steel spoon is fine—anything but pewter or, God forbid, wood or plastic.) The rest of his advice is also sound, as befits a man who was an acknowledged master of the art. The water should probably be an imperial quart, or 40 ounces.

YIELD: 8 cups (more than "three pints," but who's counting?).

BILLY DAWSON'S PUNCH

There are those in this topsy-turvy world of ours who insist that a Margarita—essentially, nothing more than a glass of strong Tequila Punch—is greatly improved by having a portion of Budweiser or other vaguely beerish beverage incorporated into its fabric. That technique, smacking as it does of frat-house experimentation, is nothing new. And I don't just say that because Chita Rivera was already teaching the bartender at Sardi's how to make 'em like that in 1985. It's a good deal older than that: in his 1807 exegesis of Glasgow Punch, John Sinclair noted that some believed "half a pint of old strong beer, in a moderate bowl of punch, will mellow the fire of the spirit considerably." He took no position on the practice, but there were plenty of skilled nineteenth-century Punch-makers who considered it another *tour de maître*. One of them I have already quoted in Book II, on the impossibility of making good Punch unless one is convinced that "no man breathing can make better."

Henry Porter and George E. Roberts, who recorded this gentleman's opinion in their 1863 *Cups and Their Customs*, identified him as "the illustrious Billy Dawson (more properly Bully Dawson, spoken of by Charles Lamb in his 'Popular Fallacies'), whose illustricity consisted in being the only man who could brew punch." They do not strike me as unserious men: Porter was a doctor and Roberts a geologist. And yet, to identify the gentleman in question as Bully Dawson they must have been so deeply in their cups to have altogether abandoned sense and reason.

Bully Dawson, you see, was a Restoration-era thug-about-town, famous for brawling and punking and roistering and, of course, bullying his way through the lower reaches of coffeehouse society. Indeed, his reputation was sufficient to earn him a place, after he had dodged his last bailiff, in the *Letters from the Dead to the Living* by Tom Brown, whom we last encountered in Book I, riffing on the hardships of the rural life. Considered as language, Brown's impersonation of Dawson, writing to his fellow bully from the shades below to castigate him for his laziness, is one of the virtuoso pieces of the English sporting vernacular. But nowhere does it, or any of the other scanty notices of Dawson's life, have him introducing London to Punch.[3] And even if Bully Dawson had been the only Londoner to know how to make Punch, he wouldn't have made it the way it is detailed here, and he couldn't have uttered the exclamation "kangaroos": that word only entered the language with the voyage of Captain Cook, in 1770. Whoever Porter and Roberts's Billy Dawson was (all we can say is that he must have been a Londoner, as Mutton Hill was near Clerkenwell), he knew how to make Punch: his method makes for a peerlessly smooth, integrated bowl with a great depth of flavor. Kangaroos indeed.

THE ORIGINAL FORMULA

The man who sees, does, or thinks of anything [else] while he is making Punch, may as well look for the North-west Passage on Mutton Hill. . . . I can and do make good Punch, because I do nothing else; and this is my way of doing it. I retire to a solitary corner, with my ingredients ready sorted; they are as follows; and I mix them in the order they are here written. Sugar, twelve tolerable lumps; hot water, one pint; lemons, two, the juice and peel; old Jamaica rum, two gills; brandy, one gill; porter or stout, half a gill; arrack, a slight dash. I allow myself five minutes to make a bowl on the foregoing proportions, carefully stirring the mixture as I furnish the

---

3 Perhaps the authors were mixed up by the scene in Oliver Goldsmith's hugely popular farce *She Stoops to Conquer*, in which Bully Dawson is mentioned in the same breath as the insolent Mr. Marlow, who has pretensions as a Punch-maker.

ingredients until it actually foams; and then, Kangaroos! how beautiful it is!!

SOURCE: Henry Porter and George E. Roberts, *Cups and Their Customs*, 1863

SUGGESTED PROCEDURE

In a stout earthenware bowl that holds at least a quart and a half, muddle the peel of two lemons with 4 ounces demerara sugar. Add 8 ounces boiling water and stir until sugar has dissolved. Add 3 ounces lemon juice, 10 ounces Jamaican rum, 5 ounces VSOP cognac, 1 ounce Batavia arrack and 3 ounces good porter or Guinness stout, stirring all along. Finish by slowly stirring in 12 ounces boiling water. Grate nutmeg over the top and serve.

NOTES

This is another case where I like the rum to be a mixture of equal parts Pirate Juice, for funk, and Planter's Best, for mellowness. When using porter in Punch, the proportion used here—roughly one part to twelve or thirteen of everything else—shouldn't be exceeded. You don't want to taste it so much as feel it. If this is to be made in advance and let cool, put all the hot water in before the lemon and spirits and add a block of ice at the end.

YIELD: 5 cups.

XI

PUNCH ROYAL

It's a natural human impulse, I suppose. Thing a is good and thing b is good, but b is defined as being "not a." Therefore, being who we are, we must somehow find a way to have both a and b. Hence Tofurkey, Tex-Mex food and reality television. Hegel had a law about it as it applies to history, and I suppose mixology must have one, too, considering the number of $a + b$ drinks in existence. Things such as the Bronx Cocktail, which reconciled the Cocktail and the drink it replaced, Punch, in one glass. Or, God help us, the Apple Martini, in which we catch the staid old 1950s-style Martini in flagrante delicto with a barely postpubescent fruity schnapps. Or Punch Royal.

In seventeenth-century England, a mixed drink often came in two grades. There was the normal, you-an'-me-an'-Joe version, based on beer or ale. Then there was the so-called royal version.

That was the same thing, but based on wine. Thus, "purl" was beer with wormwood and other herbs steeped in it, and "purl royal" was the same, but with Canary wine. Hence, when, impressively soon after it reached English shores, some unknown tinkerer took Punch and the drink it was meant to replace, wine, and mixed them together, Punch Royal was born.

Not everybody called it that—then, as now, most of the tippling public ignored the technical language of mixology. In fact, its earliest appearance, which also happens to be the first honest-to-God recipe for Punch, omits the "royal." But this recipe, from Hannah Wooley's 1670 *Queen-Like Closet*, calls for "one Quart of Claret wine, half a Pint of Brandy, and a little Nutmeg grated, a little Sugar, and the Juice of a Limon" and is therefore Punch Royal all right. And a hell of a drink it is, what with the only nonalcoholic liquid in it being the juice of one little lemon.[1] Made thus, Punch Royal is a hot-rails-to-hell spree drink, not unlike the Prohibition-era French 75, which combined bathtub gin with a little lemon and sugar and a healthy glass of Champagne, or whatever was passing for it. In 1736, when John Richardson, ship's carpenter of the pink—a type of smallish, shallow-bottomed cargo vessel—*St. John*, after hitting his captain on the head with an ax and throwing him into the Mediterranean, saw to it that one of the ship's apprentices "went down into the Cabbin, and brought up 2 Case Bottles—a Bottle of Brandy, and a Bottle of Rack—and they propos'd to make Punch Royal, that is, with Wine in it," we can be pretty sure that time Punch Royal didn't have any water in it at all.

Over time, Punch Royal would gain some dilution and finesse. It would also gain a reputation for causing vicious hangovers; George Roberts, forced to drink it by pirates, tried in vain to beg off

---

1 Speaking of the general public and technical language, the recipe right under that one bears repeating: "Take one Quarrt of Sack, half a Pint of Brandy, half a Pint of fair Water, the Juyce of two Limons, and some of the Pill [i.e., peel], so brew them together, with Sugar, and drink it." The name of this only marginally less intoxicating drink? Not "Punch," nor "Punch Royal," but "Limonado." Huh.

by pleading, "it is in a Manner Poyson to me, because I never drank any of this Liquor . . . but it made me sick two or three Days at least after it." He was not alone. But when the wine is used not as a substitute for the water but as a supplement to it, a sort of bridge between the aqueous and the spirituous elements in the formula, it makes for some of the most insinuating Punches known to the art. Here are five of them.

CAPTAIN RADCLIFFE'S PUNCH

With this 1680 paean to Punch, Captain Radcliffe earned himself a minor reputation as a poet and, if Jonathan Swift is to be believed, a major one as a mixologist—Swift was still referring to him as the author of the "true original institution of making punch" more than fifty years after his recipe saw the light of day. Perhaps that's as it should be; the twenty-eight couplets of Anacreontic tetrameter (no simple iambs for Radcliffe) that make up the "Bacchinalia Coelestia," or, roughly, "Heavenly Cocktail Party," are court poetry at best: light, forgettable and, as the most successful examples of the genre are, irreverent without being in any way dangerous.

The same could not be said about the Punch whose recipe the poem lays out—it's as polite and pleasant to your face as any courtier, sure, but what it's doing behind your back is a different matter.

SOURCE: Alexander Radcliffe, "Bacchinalia Coelestia, or A Poem in Praise of Punch," 1680

THE ORIGINAL FORMULA

Bacchinalia Coelestia

A Poem in Praise of Punch

Compos'd by the Gods and Goddesses in Cabal.

The Gods *and the* Goddesses *lately did feast,*
Where Ambrosia *with exquisite* sawces *was drest.*
The Edibles *did with their Qualities suit,*
But what they did drink, *did occasion dispute.*
'Twas time that Old Nectar *should grow out of fashion,*
A Liquor they drank long before the Creation.
When the Sky-coloured Cloth was drawn from the Board,
For the Chrystalline Bowl *Great* Jove *gave the Word.*
This was a Bowl *of most heavenly size,*
In which Infant Gods they did use to baptize.

Quoth JOVE, *We're inform'd they drink* Punch *upon Earth,*
By which mortal Wights outdo us in mirth.
Therefore our Godheads *together let's lay,*
And endeavour to make it much stronger than they.
'Twas spoke like a God, *Fill the Bowl to the top,*
He's cashier'd *from the Sky that leaves but a Drop.*

APOLLO *dispatch'd away one of his* Lasses,
Who filled us a Pitcher *from th' Well of* Parnassus.
To Poets new born, this Water is brought,
And this they suck in for their Mornings draught.

JUNO *for Lemons sent into her Closet;*
Which when she was sick she infus'd into Posset:
For Goddesses *may be as qualmish as* Gipsies;
The Sun and the Moon we find have Eclipses;
Those Lemons *were call'd the* Hesperian *Fruit,*
When vigilant Dragon was set to look to't.
Three dozen* *of these were squeez'd into Water;*
The rest of the Ingredients in order came after.

VENUS, *the Admirer of things that are sweet;*
And without her Infusion there had been no Treat;
Commanded her† *Sugar-loaves, white as her* Doves;

Supported to th' Table by a Brace of young Loves.
So wonderful curious these Deities were,
The Sugar they strain'd through a Sieve of thin Air.

BACHHUS *gave notice by dangling a Bunch,*
That without his Assistance there could be no Punch.
What was meant by his signs was very well known,
For they threw in a Gallon‡ of trusty Langoon.

MARS, *a blunt God, though chief of the Briskers,*
Was seated at Table, still twirling his Whiskers;
Quoth he, fellow-Gods and Coelestial Gallants;
I'd not give a Fart for your Punch without Nants:
Therefore Boy Ganimede I do command ye,
To put in at least two Gallons§ of Brandy.

SATURN, *of all the Gods was the oldest,*
And we may imagine his stomach was coldest,
Did out of his Pouch three Nutmegs produce,
Which when they were grated, were put to the Juyce.

NEPTUNE *this Ocean of Liquor did crown*
With a hard Sea-Bisket well bak'd in the Sun.
This Bowl being finish'd, a Health was began;
Quoth Jove, Let it be to our Creature call'd Man,

'Tis to him alone these Pleasures we owe,
For Heaven was never true Heav'n till now.

Since the Gods and poor Mortals thus do agree,
Here's a Health unto *CHARLES* His Majesty.

* Changed in 1696 to "Six dozen"
† 1696: "two"
‡ 1696: "three gallons"
§ 1696: "To fill up the Bowl with a Rundlet"

SOURCE: Alexander Radcliffe, "Bacchinalia Coelestia, or A Poem in Praise of Punch," 1680, and *The Works of Capt. Alex. Radcliffe*, 1696

SUGGESTED PROCEDURE

Squeeze seventy-two lemons, or as many as it takes to end up with 7 pints of juice, into a seven- to ten-gallon bowl or krater (if it's the latter, and it's decorated in black figure with depictions of the saucy pastimes of the Olympian gods and their progeny, so much the better; if it's "chrystalline" and fontlike, well, you shall find me on bended knee, offering my obeisance).

Sweeten with 7 pounds of pulverized demerara sugar (we must assume the gods, possessing force beyond that with which we mortals are endowed, are capable of reducing sugar loaves into a soluble state with their bare hands), stirring until it has dissolved.

Add:

> five 750-milliliter bottles of Sauternes or other white French dessert wine
>
> eight 1-liter or ten 750-milliliter bottles of VS-grade cognac
>
> 2 gallons cool water (Apollo's pitcher would have to be a generous one)

Stir well until remaining sugar has dissolved.

Let sit in a cool place for two hours.

Stir again, grate two nutmegs over the top and float lightly toasted hardtack or pilot bread on top.

NOTES

Since Radcliffe's Muse denied him knowledge of the size of Apollo's pitcher or the volume of sugar in Venus's loaves, I've fallen back on my rules of thumb for each, which dictate using as much sugar as citrus and at least as much water as spirit. The latter can be increased by half if you prefer a less heroic beverage, in which you can extract another thirty-odd servings from the bowl.

Note that in the version of the poem published in 1696, Captain Radcliffe very sensibly doubled the size of Venus's offering; I have followed that version. At the same time, he also increased the amount of wine and, presumably, brandy (a rundlet holds eighteen gallons; while he is vague as to how much of that actually goes in the bowl, it's safe to assume it's more than the two-plus gallons previously called for). In that, I have chosen not to risk singeing my wings.

The sugar can be melted in advance with an equal amount of hot water (which should be subtracted from the water added at the end), in which case it will not have to be pulverized first.

As for that "Langoon." This, it turns out, is wine shipped from Langon, in the Graves near Sauternes and Barsac. We know that at the time it was a "yellow wine," as one traveler recorded, and in all likelihood it was sweet. Your best bet is a cheap Sauternes, if there were such a thing. If not, look for a dessert wine from the Loire area, such as a Coteaux du Layon. The wine is here chiefly as a softening agent, to tame the brandy without making the Punch watery. For the brandy, while the gods might have had access to well-aged cognac at the time (who knows what treasures lie racked in Olympian cellars?), it's highly doubtful that Captain Radcliffe did. A decent VS cognac will do just fine. Radcliffe's proportion of spirits to wine, two to one, is a common one for Punch Royal and an excellent default position.

For the biscuit, you can either use hardtack or improvise as best you can (in Radcliffe's day, landlubbers would use toast). Personally, I usually say "Neptune be hanged" and proceed without his assistance, but then again I'm not a seafaring man.

One sensible addition is a large block of ice—let's call it the gift of Pluto, god of the frigid underworld. In that case, you

should use care in adding additional water beyond the
2 gallons called for (you'll also need a larger bowl).

This recipe yields some 88 cups, or 5½ gallons. For a less
Olympian quantity, try: one 750-milliliter bottle of wine, two
750-milliliter bottles of brandy, 8 ounces of lemon juice,
8 ounces of sugar, 1½ to 2 quarts of water and about a third
of a nutmeg.

Admiral Russell's Punch

If you thought the last one was large . . .

As the year 1694 wound down, for the first time in its history
the English fleet did not sail back home to go into winter
quarters. Instead, it put into the southern Spanish port of
Cádiz, from where it could keep the bulk of the French fleet
bottled up in the Mediterranean (England and Spain were
then both at war with France). It was an effective strategy,
but as the naval historian Michael Lewis notes, Admiral
Edward Russell, the fleet's impressively ill-tempered
commander, rather balked at the idea: "I am at present under
a doubt with myself whether it is not better to die," as the
admiral wrote his bosses at the Admiralty. I don't know if it
was despite his irritation or to spite the men who caused it,
but on Christmas Day 1694, Lord Russell threw a huge party
in the garden of a house belonging to Don Francisco de
Velasco y Tovar, governor of Cádiz, which he had taken over
for the winter. If the Admiralty wanted him to stay away
from home, let it pay for his amusements.

News of his "extraordinary feast" traveled quickly; by
February, it was all over London. "150 dishes—the first course
an Ox rusted whole; . . . the Admiral had 800 men to wayt on
him," one Londoner wrote to his cousin in the country; "this
was amazing to the Spaniards." Well, okay, it wasn't just the
food and the entourage that amazed the Iberian grandees and
"all the English and Dutch merchants and officers, belonging
to the fleet" who attended (as Dr. William Oliver, who was
there, described the crowd), or the neat and shipshape way that
everything was arrayed on four long tables, each running the
length of one of the walkways, all shaded with lemon and
orange trees, that radiated from the center of the garden.

What really got people's attention was what lay at the center of the garden: the large, Delft-tiled fountain with the canopy rigged over it, filled with "12 hoggsheads of punch." And, of course, the "little boy that was in a boat swimming on the punch sea and deliver[ing] it to the Company."

If there's one item of drink-related memorabilia I could have, it wouldn't be Jerry Thomas's lost second book or his silver bar kit; it wouldn't be Charles Dickens's nutmeg grater or Captain Morris's Punch ladle or even the toddy stick used by Orsamus Willard—America's first celebrity bartender— behind the bar at the City Hotel. It would be that little boat, knocked together by ships' carpenters, crewed by a boy bred to the sea and christened in an ungodly huge batch of Punch Royal.

After Russell and the guests of quality toasted one another's health to the point of satiety, as Dr. Oliver recalled,

> they drew off, and in went the mob, with their shoes
> and stockings and all on, and like to have turned the
> boat, with the boy, over, and so he might have been
> drowned in punch; but to prevent further danger they
> sucked it up, and left the punch-bowl behind.

For Russell, the day was a success. Reporting back to London on his general progress with the Spaniards, "I may say," he wrote, "without appearing vain, I have settled . . . myself as much in the Spaniards' esteem, as I could do." Indeed.

We're unusually lucky in having not just one detailed account of what went into that fountain but two: Dr. Oliver's, first printed in an almanac for 1711, and a second, better-known one, which I have been unable to trace back further than 1772, when it appeared in the *Edinburgh Advertiser*. Although this second one begins with an obvious error, placing the feast on October 25th, it has details that Oliver's lacks and can't be dismissed out of hand. That's unfortunate when it comes to the actual Punch, since both accounts, while agreeing broadly on its basic ingredients, differ widely on the important matter of proportion (and both differ on the matter of total quantity with Richard Lapthorne, the man who wrote his cousin about it, each of them making some one thousand gallons, give or take, or one and a half times his twelve hogsheads). To paraphrase one of the principles of textual scholarship, when there are two recipes, there are none. I have therefore given both and suggested a method of proceeding that takes each into account. Since it would be silly to suggest that this be made full size, I have broken my rule and given what is, as it were, a scale model of Admiral Russell's Punch. The standard scale for ship models these days appears to be 1/700, so that's what I've used.

THE ORIGINAL FORMULA

There was in the middle of a garden of lemons and oranges . . . a fountain which was set with Dutch tiles in the bottom and sides, and was made as clean as a Japan punch-bowl. In this fountain, on Christmas-day, was poured six butts of water, half a hogshead of strong mountain Malaga wine, two hundred gallons of brandy, six hundredweight of sugar, twelve thousand lemons, and nutmegs and sugar in proportion.

SOURCE: Francis Moore, *Vox Stellarum Being an Almanack for the Year of Human Redemption*, 1711

THE OTHER ORIGINAL FORMULA

In the said fountain were the following ingredients, viz. four hogsheads of brandy, eight hogsheads of water, 25,000 lemons, 20 gallons of lime juice, 1300 weight of fine white

**Whores Drinking Punch, from Hogarth's *Rake's Progress*,
1732–33 (detail).** AUTHOR'S COLLECTION

Lisbon sugar, 5 pound of grated nutmegs, 300 toasted
biscuits, and last a pipe of dry Mountain Malaga.

SOURCE: *Edinburgh Advertiser,* **1772**

SUGGESTED PROCEDURE

In a two-gallon Punch bowl or small tiled fountain, dissolve 2½
cups demerara sugar in 1 cup boiling water. Add 18 ounces strained
lemon juice and 4 ounces strained lime juice and stir, incorporating
any remaining undissolved sugar. Add two 750-milliliter bottles of
VS cognac and 18 ounces Montilla or oloroso sherry, stir again, and
finish with 1½ quarts cold water. Grate nutmeg over the top, float
a Playmobil rowboat with ship's boy at the oars and make sure the
mob has divested itself of shoes and stockings.

NOTES

Aside from the fact that you'd need eight hundred sailors
squeezing lemons, the admiral's Punch was pretty

straightforward. The strong and/or dry Mountain Malaga is a bit of a problem, though. If you can get Montilla, a Spanish fortified wine that isn't sherry, it will work well. If not, sherry or Madeira also works very well. This recipe is fairly strong and could tolerate another 2 to 4 cups water or ice. If you wish to add ice, though, you might want to omit the rowboat, to avoid any maudlin *Titanic* moments. The Playmobil set you're looking for is number 4295.

YIELD: 18 cups. To make full scale, multiply all quantities by 700.

GRUB STREET PUNCH ROYAL

The life of the scuffling writer has always been a difficult one, distinguished by hard work for sums of money that are rarely more than nominal, perpetual frustration at the squandering of one's gifts and all-consuming envy of those who do the same thing but with more success. Sometimes all of that makes one do things that aren't very nice. Take the person who, in or around 1701, compiled the pamphlet subtitled *A New and Easie Way to Make Twenty-Three Sorts of Wine, Equal to That of France*. Fair enough. But he (or she, I suppose, although that's far less likely) tacked *The Way to Get Wealth* on the front of it as the title. Not cool. In 1697, you see, Thomas Tryon had published a book by the name of *England's Grandeur and Way to Get Wealth, or Promotion of Trade Made Easy and Lands Advanced*. Tryon, you might recall, was a staunch advocate of temperance and foe of Punch. And yet, there on page 62 of the 1701 volume is a recipe for "Punch Royal." What's worse, the pamphlet has been passed off as one of Tryon's ever since. What's even worse than that, the person who so traduced Tryon's ideals may well have been Tryon himself (the pamphlet says, right there on the cover, that it is by the author of a book that Tryon indisputably wrote, although such claims were often falsified). As I said, the pressures of Grub Street can make people do things that they're not proud of.

The recipe, at least, is—with certain key modifications—a good one, spicy and rich. Indeed, it's the most elaborate, and elaborately spiced, Punch recipe of the early years. Too bad that it was stolen, with small alterations, from John Yarworth's 1690 *New Treatise of Artificial Wines*. Grub Street.

Take one pound and a half of Loaf Sugar, and dissolve it in
two quarts of Water; and if there be any dross in the Sugar,
strain the Liquor through Cloth; then add a Pint of Rhenish
Wine, six ounces of Limon Juice, or the Juice of four large
Limons, seven or eight drops of the true Spirit of Salt,
and a Dram of Alkermes or two Grains of Musk, three of
Ambergreese, a quart of strong Brandy, and a whole Nutmeg
grated, with half an Ounce of Cinnamon, and a quarter of an
Ounce of Ginger finely scraped, or beaten; stir these till they
are very well mixed, and then head it with good Toast or Sea
Bisket; you may likewise, when it is thus prepared, in what
quantitie you please, proportionable to these directions, bottle
it up, and it will keep long, and drink exceeding brisk.

SOURCE: *The Way to Get Wealth, or A New and Easie Way to Make Twenty-Three
Sorts of Wine, Equal to That of France*, 1701(?)

NOTES

While the procedure and order of assembly here are clear and
correct, the ingredients present some problems for the modern
mixologist. For one thing, that's too much sugar and too little
lemon juice. Half that amount of demerara sugar—12 ounces,
or 1½ cups—is good; dissolve it in 1 pint boiling water and
then add the rest of the water cold (and don't worry about
straining out the dross, unless you want to go super old-school
and use piloncillo). Twelve ounces of lemon juice is more like
it, but the reason there's less here might be those drops of the
"true Spirit of Salt," which is otherwise known as hydrogen
chloride, or hydrochloric acid. It may safely be omitted. The
wine should be a German Riesling. Alkermes, a then-trendy
strong water infused with aloe, amber, musk and other such
items and colored with the shell of the kermes bug (akin to
cochineal), is, incredibly, still made, by the Italian pharmacy
of Santa Maria Novella (and several low-budget producers in
northern Italy, although I doubt they use the traditional

formula). Benedictine works well as a substitute; use a teaspoon. For the ambergris, see Meriton Latroon's Bantam Punch; use a piece the size of three grains of barley, muddled with 3 ounces of the sugar and 3 ounces of the brandy, which should be VS cognac (for true authenticity, use 45 ounces and subtract 13 ounces from the water). The cinnamon (use one stick) can be ground and sprinkled on top with the nutmeg or muddled in with the sugar. For the biscuit, see Bombay Presidency Punch.

YIELD: 16 cups.

RUBY PUNCH

I don't know exactly how old this recipe is—something very much like it, with less lemon, and rum instead of arrack, shows up in the 1827 *Oxford Night Caps* as simply Punch Royal. But I doubt if it's that recent: like the United Service Punch, which it closely resembles, it's constructed strictly along eighteenth-century lines, if not seventeenth-century. Whenever it was first concocted, it's a perfect synthesis, a plush and seductive Punch that practically drinks itself. The arrack adds fragrance and bite to the port; the port, depth and weight to the arrack. How nice when we all get along.

Ruby Punch was never a hugely popular tipple, as far as I can ascertain, but it had its devotees; when a group of New York's movers and shakers met in 1884 to organize an annual observation of Evacuation Day (the day in 1783 upon which the British army pulled out of New York and the Continental Army marched in), the assorted Jays, De Lanceys, Van Cortlandts, Pells, Gallatins, Barclays, Livingstons and other worthies, whose names are familiar from the street map of New York, toasted the new enterprise in Ruby Punch. Appropriate.

Dissolve, in three pints of hot tea, one pound of sugar; add thereto the juice of six lemons, a pint of arrack, and a pint of port wine.

SOURCE: Jerry Thomas, *Bar-Tenders Guide*, 1862

NOTES

Since this recipe appears in an American book, let us assume the measures are American, too, and that a pint is sixteen ounces. For the tea, use six tea bags; I like a rich black tea here, but it also works well with green tea. For the port, use a nice ruby (naturally). This is not the place to use that 1966 Delaforce. The arrack should be Batavia. And nutmeg, if ever there was a place for it. This is equally good hot or cold.

YIELD: 12 cups.

Punschglühbowle

There is a long and honorable tradition of Punch-making on
the European continent that I am shamelessly and
determinedly ignoring in this book. I can only plead lack of
space and competence in some of the languages necessary for
bringing it to light (my Dutch, like everyone's, is hopeless). As
we've seen, Dutch and French sailors learned to drink Punch
almost when the English ones did, and they, too, took it home
with them. Eventually, the formula spread throughout
the spirits-drinking regions of Europe. It didn't catch on
everywhere—in France, it wasn't until late in the eighteenth
century that it became common—but where it did, it sent its
roots deep. As we've seen, the Scandinavians clung to their
Arrack Punch to the very threshold of the twenty-first
century. The Germans didn't stick with it quite that long, nor
did they come to it as early as the Dutch (it was still a novelty
in parts of Germany as late as the 1760s), but as long as they
did, they yielded to nobody in their dedication to the bowl.

If, in general, the Continental versions of Punch were similar
to those current in England and her colonies, the Germans
proved their dedication by coming up with something rather
different: *Feuerzangenbowle*, or "Fire-tongs bowl." This bears
roughly the relationship to Punch Royal that the Blue Blazer
does to the Hot Scotch Whiskey Skin: pretty much the same
thing, but on fire. You lay a pair of fireplace tongs over a
heavy, fireproof pot full of wine and set a loaf of sugar on top
of them. Then you soak the sugar with high-proof booze, light
it up and let it melt into the pot. The origins of this practice
are beyond my ken, although it can be seen as a mashup
between Crambambuli, an oddly named liqueur created by
melting sugar in flaming brandy or rum that goes back at
least to the mid eighteenth century, and mulled wine, which is

infinitely older than that. In any case, by 1814 it was a part of the culture, since then we find E. T. A. Hoffmann, the German Romantic to whom we owe that whole Nutcracker business, writing rhapsodically (or however it is that Romantics write) about the "salamanders" bred in the dancing flames of the burning sugar.

The following recipe for "Punchglowbowl" comes from one of the more eccentric relics of the imperial Germany of Kaiser Wilhelm II, a little book titled *Bowls and Punches for the Use of the German Army in the Field and on Maneuvers*. Set in dense, black-letter Gothic type, it oozes heavy Teutonic conviviality. As one scans the recipes for Punches, Cups, Bowls, Crambambulis (or whatever the plural of that is) and even American Cocktails, most of them contributed by the various regiments of the kaiser's army,[2] it's impossible not to hear young male voices raised in hearty song. This particular recipe was contributed by Field Artillery Regiment 67, which would go on to fight on both eastern and western fronts in the Great War, suffering 166 men killed.

THE ORIGINAL FORMULA (TRANSLATED)

In a large earthenware pot heat ten liters light, red country-wine and five liters Arrack, stirring constantly. While it is simmering, stir in a pound of sugar and four Seville oranges or regular oranges, and also two or three lemons, in slices. Having taken special care to ensure that the slices are free of seeds, simmer them in the mixture for five minutes and then pour it into a bowl and serve it flaming. A further dilution through the addition of more light, red country-wine will not obstruct its effectiveness.

SOURCE: *Bowlen und Punsche fur den Feld- und Manover-gebrauch der Deutschen Armee*, 1900 (for the original text, see the appendix)

---

2 The Cocktails, however, were pinched from the bilingual *Bartender's Manual* published by the great American mixologist Harry Johnson.

SUGGESTED PROCEDURE

In a large enameled pot or Dutch oven, heat six bottles of light, red table wine to the simmering point. Remove from heat, rest on a trivet away from any kindling, and add one bottle of Batavia arrack and two Seville or regular oranges and one lemon, sliced and seeded. Lay a pair of fireplace tongs over the bowl (or, of course, the special gizmo they make in Germany for this purpose; do not use kitchen tongs, as they tend to have a C-beam construction with internal gutters that have a disconcerting way of wicking the flaming liquid away from the bowl and onto the table). Rest a zuckerhut, the pointy, 250-gram German sugarloaf, on the tongs (or use half a loaf of piloncillo). Soak the sugar with more Batavia arrack, letting the overflow run into the bowl (no need to be stingy here), pour some more arrack in a ladle and light it. Bring the ladle to the sugarloaf, light it and then ladle the flaming liquid from the bowl over the sugar until it has melted. Serve flaming in teacups.

NOTES

The original recipe is clearly voluminous enough to upset the aim of a whole battery of gunners. It also, as the sharp-eyed reader will notice, fails to feature the whole tongs business, in part because it's simply too large. I have taken the liberty of cutting the recipe by more than half and incorporating the tongs. I've also cut the booze down even further. We are not artillerymen in the field now, are we? A Côtes du Rhône works particularly well for the wine here, but anything not too strong, oaky or jammy will do fine. If you can't get the arrack, use a Pirate Juice–type rum, preferably one at least 55 percent alcohol by volume.

XII

MILK PUNCH

If there was one complaint Punch elicited from its habitual consumers, it was that it was rather acid on the stomach. Well, that and the "legacy of splitting headaches," as the indefatigable Shelton Mackenzie noted in 1854. Everyone knew how to avoid the latter but chose not to. The former, however, was a constant spur to experimentation. The obvious way to counter the acidity was to reduce the amount of lemon juice, but this led to an insipid Punch, while simply adding more sugar made it sticky and cloying. This dilemma lead the alchemically-minded to seek that one magic ingredient that, when added to a bowl of Punch, would suddenly make all harmonious. This probably explains the "Langoon" in Captain Radcliffe's Punch, and certainly does the porter in Billy Dawson's. The very best solution, however, was discovered very early indeed in Punch's history: milk. When added to Punch, it curdles pretty much immediately, making a disgusting mess that when strained out leaves a Punch that is not only clear but also exceptionally smooth and creamy-tasting without actually being creamy.[1]

Unlike Punch Royal or, for that matter, Punch itself, we even have someone's name to attach to this innovation. The eighteenth-century English antiquary William Oldys, who specialized in the history of the stage, recorded hearing from one old thespian that "the first person he ever knew or heard of, who made the liquor called Milk Punch" was none other than the endlessly intriguing playwright Aphra Behn. Not only would an actor be well placed to collect this sort of information, but this particular actor, John Bowman, happened to have appeared in at least three of Mrs. Behn's plays, including the Punch-sodden *The Widow Ranter*. To add mixologist to her accomplishments would be, well, delicious. Unfortunately, there's little corroborating evidence, other than numerous mentions of Punch in her works and the fact that Milk Punch's first mention, in William Sacheverell's account of the ramble he took around the Scottish island of Iona in 1688, comes during her lifetime. But even if we can't prove that Mrs. Behn gave birth to the drink, I'm of the belief that she should nonetheless be awarded custody in reward for her services to the flowing bowl, nowhere better exemplified than in the words she gave to her bawdy, brash and brassy character, the Widow Ranter: "Punch! 'Tis my Morning's Draught, my Table-drink, my Treat, my Regalio, my every thing."

Milk Punch more or less lay doggo until the middle of the eighteenth century, when it suddenly, for whatever reason, became all the rage. Once popular, it remained so for almost a hundred years, particularly in its bottled form. Pickwick was happy to take "a most energetic pull" on a bottle of it, and Queen Victoria so liked the version Nathaniel Whisson & Co. bottled that in 1838 she had them named "Purveyors of Milk Punch to Her Majesty." Its agreeableness, however, didn't stop Milk Punch from fading out in the

---

1 This technique is, in fact, a version of the modern one known as "fat washing," in which an oil or a fat is mixed with liquor and, after it has contributed its flavor, coagulated (here by refrigeration) and removed.

middle of the nineteenth century with the rest of its tribe. Being more complicated to make than most, it would be denied even the half-life accorded to a special-occasion drink. Its name alone lived on, attached to a single-serving drink made on the spot with fresh milk, a very different procedure from the laborious (but rewarding) classic one, which involved much waiting, straining, bottling and waiting again.

Scan the archives of mixology and you'll find many a good and even illustrious recipe for classic Milk Punch. If one examines all the Victoria Punches, California Milk Punches, Norfolk Milk Punches and suchlike closely, one quickly discerns that give or take some spices or a little playing around with the spirits, they're all pretty much the same: Milk Punch was no sooner invented than perfected. I shall therefore give but a single version; once the technique is mastered, it can be tinkered with or applied to any combination of spirits.

MARY ROCKETT'S MILK PUNCH

This, the oldest extant recipe for Milk Punch, has the advantages of (relative) simplicity, strength and deliciousness—and, appropriately, it was written by a woman. According to Montague Summers, who unearthed this recipe in 1914, it hails from "a tattered manuscript recipe book, the compilation of a good housewife named Mary Rockett, and dated 1711." Milk Punch is just about the most conservative corner of the kingdom of Punches; Mrs. Rockett's recipe agrees on all cardinal points with those of her successors, right through the 1860s.

Like all Milk Punches, the result of this process is something between a Punch and a liqueur. Most people, rather than constantly repeating the time-consuming procedures necessary to make it, would prepare it in quantity, bottle it and cellar it—without the milk solids that would otherwise go rancid, Milk Punch would (and will) keep almost indefinitely. To help with that preservation, it was generally made with a rather richer, sweeter texture than on-the-spot Punches. Poured straight from the bottle, if chilled it's silky and unctuous enough to close a meal. As an aperitif, though, it requires additional dilution.

THE ORIGINAL FORMULA

To make Milk Punch. Infuse the rinds of 8 Lemons in a Gallon of Brandy 48 hours then add 5 Quarts of Water and 2 pounds of Loaf Sugar then Squize the Juices of all the lemons to these Ingredients add 2 Quarts of new milk Scald hot stirring the whole till it crudles [*sic*] grate in 2 Nutmegs let the whole infuse 1 Hour then refine through a flannel Bag.

SOURCE: Quoted in Montague Summers, *Memoir of Mrs. Behn*, 1914

NOTES

As archaic as this recipe sounds, it's actually quite
straightforward and laid out in most efficient order. Twenty-
four hours are more than enough for infusing the peels (which
should be cut very thin with a vegetable peeler). Four quarts
of water should be enough with the weaker spirits of today. In
general, Milk Punch was made with brandy, although we hear
of rum as well; if using rum, use a mild, mellow one of the
Planter's Best grade. Arrack would be, well, challenging, but
Scotch and Irish whiskey had their proponents, and with
reason. I have heard tell of people these days making Mezcal
Milk Punch—well, one person, Scott Marshall, of Boston (he,
being a maniac, also cubed and fried the strained-out curds,
which though edible are somewhat unappetizing without the
application of boiling fat). The milk in 1711 would have been
unpasteurized, naturally, and with all its cream; if raw milk is
legal in your vicinity, that's the thing to use (check the
farmers' market, if you've got one). Otherwise, whole milk will
do. You'll need to strain this through a tight-woven cloth, so
that you can squeeze the curds to extract every bit of Punch;
try that in a paper towel and you'll be starting over in no time
(see Chapter VII). After "refining," bottle this and refrigerate
it until what needs to precipitate has precipitated and what
needs to settle has settled. Siphon off the clear liquid, rebottle
it and you can store it at cellar temperature.

There were those who recommended adding jelly, the other
great softening ingredient, to Milk Punch (see Oxford Punch).
As *Oxford Night Caps* observed in 1827, this is gilding the lily,
"as the milk will sufficiently temper the acrimony of the
lemon juice."

YIELD: **36 cups or twelve 750-milliliter bottles (a bottle of Milk Punch makes an
excellent Christmas present).**

XIII

ORANGE PUNCH

J ust as there were those who were partisan about the species of
liquor with which their Punch was powered, there were those
who felt strongly about the species of citrus with which it was
soured. If Brandy and Rum Punch get a chapter of their own, then
it's only fitting that Orange Punch does, too.

Orange Punch is a particularly mild and agreeable beverage of
considerable antiquity—indeed, if Punch was first made on the
East India Company's ships, it's worth bearing in mind that they as
often had oranges as they did limes. In Britain, oranges start showing up in connection with Punch as early as 1691, when they appear
in a definition of the drink in John Worlidge's *Vinetum Britannicum*.
At first they were only used to supplement lemons, but eventually
there arose a faction of tipplers who made their Punch with oranges
alone. Some of them could even be found in America, the land of
the lime, judging from a 1741 notice in the *Salem (Massachusetts)*

Gazette for "Extraordinary good and very fresh Orange Juice, which some of the very best Punch Tasters prefer to Lemmons, at one dollar per gallon." That business about the "best tasters" requires a caveat, as it depends on the kind of oranges used. Made with the common sweet orange, Orange Punch, for all its pleasantness, lacks that dynamic tension that the best Punches maintain. In the sport of Punch-making, it's like going for an easy field goal rather than trying for a touchdown.

In any case, Orange Punch was popular enough by 1732 for Jonathan Swift to have a little bit of fun with it in "An Examination of Certain Abuses, Corruptions and Enormities in the City of Dublin." The basis of said fun was an old bit of small-scale political theater. Back in the days of William III, scion of the House of Orange, those who continued to support the deposed and exiled James II made it one of their practices to drink toasts to "the squeezing of an orange." Silly enough, but doing just that was one of the bases for the charge of treason on which Robert Charnock, Edward King and Thomas Keyes were tried for their lives in 1696, found guilty and executed. "Past all doubt," Swift begins,

> this liquor [i.e., Punch] is by one important innovation, grown of ill example, and dangerous consequence to the public. It is well known, that, by the true original institution of making punch . . . the sharpness is only occasioned by the juice of lemons, and so . . . Oranges, alas! are a mere innovation, and in a manner but of yesterday. It was the politics of Jacobites to introduce them gradually . . . cunningly to shew their virulence against his sacred Majesty King William, of ever glorious and immortal memory. But of late, (to shew how fast disloyalty increaseth) they came from one or two, and then to three oranges; nay, at present we often find punch made all with oranges, and not one single lemon.

Of course, Swift knew full well that most of the people who were squeezing oranges into their Punch weren't doing it as symbolic magic against their political enemies (i.e., "as I squeeze this Orange so may the D——d Whigs be squoze"). They were doing it because they liked the way the oranges tasted. His beef here was not with the drinkers of Orange Punch but with the paranoid and conspiracy-obsessed. And besides, if he were seriously impugning the drinkers of Orange Punch, he'd be impugning anyone who drank at James Ashley's, and no man of sense would want to mess with the litigious Mr. Ashley.

JAMES ASHLEY'S PUNCH

At the beginning of 1731, Ashley, a thirty-three-year-old
"wholesale dealer in cheese," abandoned that line of work, it
"not suiting his turn" (as the *Monthly Magazine* wrote in
1796). Instead, he opened the "London Coffee-House and
Punch-House," on the north side of Ludgate Hill right
next to the old medieval gate. The cheese trade must have
been good to him, as it seems to have been a pretty large
place, not wide but very deep, with rooms ranged along a
narrow passageway that led to a court in the back from
which one could scuttle through other passageways and
end up at the Old Bailey. But Ashley was no dope. Those
who knew him described the Northampton native as "an
intelligent cheerful man" who was "intimately acquainted
with every remarkable transaction in the history of
London" and "well versed in the history and laws of his
country." Perhaps too well in the latter: according to the
Monthly Magazine, his business "would have been greatly
productive, had he not contracted a taste for litigation,
which involved him in many tedious and expensive law suits."
This statement is borne out by Ashley's sole publication, a
1753 pamphlet giving his side of one of them. It would
probably have been better for him, and for us, if he had
written about something he knew even better than law and
history—making Punch. Ashley, you see, was no ordinary
Punch-maker; he was, in fact, the world's first celebrity
mixologist, the first man to become famous for compounding
and selling a mixed drink.

Everybody knew James Ashley. Some did from drinking Punch
at his establishment: Hogarth was a patron, the young James
Boswell stopped in one night in 1763 for "three threepenny

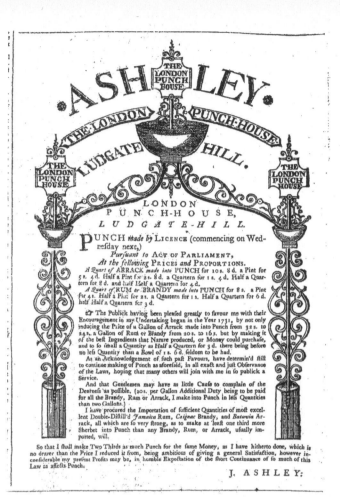

One of Ashley's early advertisements. AUTHOR'S COLLECTION

bowls" in between bouts with sixpenny whores,[1] Oliver
Goldsmith took the temperature of the town there and, for a
time, Benjamin Franklin's "Club of Honest Whigs" was one of

---

1 He was still pronouncing Ashley's "pretty agreeable" seventeen years later, when he
had given up the other sort of amusement; *vinum longum, amor brevis.*

the many it hosted. Others knew him from the newspapers—not so much from the editorial content, although he appeared in that often enough, as from the advertisements. I don't think a day went by between March 1731, when Ashley first took to print, and July 1776, when he died, that one of his ads didn't appear in a London newspaper. Not everyone drank in Punch houses or lounged around in coffeehouses reading newspapers, but even those who didn't would have known Ashley, if only because Ludgate Hill was a major shopping street and if you walked down it you couldn't miss the two iron Punch bowls on ornate openwork pedestals that flanked his door, with a third above it. If those didn't grab you, the words he had painted in massive letters on the front of his building would:

PRO BONO PUBLICO
JAMES ASHLEY IN 1731
FIRST REDUCED THE PRICE OF PUNCH
RAISED ITS REPUTATION
AND BROUGHT IT INTO
UNIVERSAL ESTEEM

They certainly made an impression; for many years whenever anyone made protestations that their profitable actions were being done "for the public good," Ashley and his "pro bono publico"—"for the public good"—was sure to be invoked.

Not that his claim was wrong, mind you. It was overstated, to be sure—Alexander Radcliffe, Ned Ward and Lord Russell might have given him an argument about the last three lines (then again, Russell would argue with anybody about anything). But Ashley's constant promotion certainly did nothing to hurt Punch. And the price part was absolutely correct: as Fielding's Tom Thumb confirms, "the settled Price throughout the Town" (as Ashley's earliest ads noted) was eight shillings for a quart of arrack made into Punch, and six for brandy or rum. Ashley's prices? Six and four shillings respectively. His innovations didn't stop there. Six shillings was still a hell of an outlay, the equivalent of almost two hundred dollars. Of course, a quart of spirits made for a large bowl; there were smaller. But if Ashley is to be believed, even those customarily only went down to one shilling sixpence, or just shy of fifty dollars, for which you would get a half-pint of liquor. Here he broke ranks: rather than a half-pint, he set as the smallest quantity of spirits he'd make into Punch the almost trivial measure of a half quartern, or two ounces. Suddenly we're in Cocktail territory: rather than a bowl of Punch, this would give the drinker one not very large glass. For that, he would pay three to four and a half pence, depending on the liquor—say, eight to twelve dollars. (A quart of porter, by contrast, also cost threepence.)

The London Punch-House's titular beverage was not only retailed by the glass (known as a "sneaker," "tiff" or "rub"), but going by the claims in Ashley's ads, it was also mixed to order— "the Sherbett is always brought by itself, and the Brandy, Rum and Arrack in the Measure"—and so quickly that "Gentlemen may have it as soon made as a Gill of Wine can be drawn." To make a system like that work, Ashley had to prepare his shrub in advance—the "acid" in it being "all Orange Juice"—and bottle it. Then it was easy: show the customer the spirit in the measure, pour it into the proper-size bowl, pour in two measures' worth of shrub (I would've used the same measure), nutmeg and done. The fact that Ashley made rather a big deal of all these practices indicates that they were not standard, as does the amount of time he spent complaining in his ads about imitators and even the amount of time some of his imitators spent frankly acknowledging his influence.[2] This was professional Punch-making on a higher level. This was bartending.

---

2 Take, for example, the 1734 ad for James Bowman's Punch house in Bristol, in which its proprietor holds Ashley up as a model and then claims his Punch is "in all Respects to be made to as great Perfection as by . . . Mr. Ashley." By 1736, there was even a Punch house on Ludgate Hill that copied Ashley's signage and offered a quart of brandy or rum made into Punch for three shillings fourpence. Ouch.

And yet it's unlikely that Ashley himself was doing any of it. Sure, someone was in the little compartment set in the wall that served as a bar in eighteenth-century Punch- and coffeehouses; someone was serving out Punch to the "egregious sots / Who pour its Poison down devouring Throats / . . . standing at the Bar / At *Ashley*'s," as Joseph Mitchell wrote in his 1735 "A Curse Upon Punch."[3] But that somebody was in all likelihood not James Ashley for the simple reason that, as we have noted, in England, "bar-keeper" was not a man's job. And indeed, along with portraits of Ashley and his wife, we find that his friend Thomas Worlidge (alias "the English Rembrandt") executed one of "a Mrs. Gaywood, their bar-keeper." So. A mixologist, perhaps, our Mr. Ashley, but not a bartender. Whatever he was, he did it well enough to stay in business for forty-five years: when he died, on July 7, 1776, the London Punch-House was still going strong.

THE ORIGINAL FORMULA

ADVERTISEMENTS.

At the Foreign Brandy, Rum and Arrack Cellars, under my House on Ludgate Hill,

Are to be sold, choice and good as ever were imported, and warranted entirely neat,

Brandy and Rum at 7 s. 6 d. per Gallon, but in no less Quantity than five Gallons; all under 8 s. per Gallon.

A parcel of superfine Batavia Arrack, at 12 s. per Gallon.

This House I opened solely for making of Punch (*and was the first that undertook to make it in small Proportions, and reduced the extravagant Price.*)

---

3 The takeaway: "Punch! That no mortal man alive wou'd drink, / Had he but Power or Willingness to think." Evidently Mitchell once drank too much of it.

Where, to the greatest Perfection, the said most excellent Brandies, Rum and Arrack made into Punch, viz.

A Quart of Arrack made into Punch for 6 s. and so in proportion to half a Quartern for 4 d. half penny.

A Quart of Rum or Brandy made into Punch for 4 s. and so in proportion to half a Quartern for 3 d.

And, that the Fairness of this undertaking may appear to every one, the Sherbett is always brought by itself, and the Brandy, Rum and Arrack in the Measure; by means whereof there can be no Imposition either in the Quality or Quantity.

As also, for the better accommodating Gentlemen at their own Houses, I do undertake (by a peculiar Management in the Acid, which is all Orange Juice) to make any Quantities of the said most excellent Brandies or Rum into Punch, as they shall order, at 4s. per Gallon, (one third whereof to be Brandy or Rum;) and I will warrant it to keep so, that there shall not be the least Variation or Alteration for 12 Months, and shall retain the same Life, Quickness and Perfection, to that Time, as no person can discover but that its [*sic*] just made.

Buy and sell for Ready Money only,

London Punch-House   J. Ashley.

SOURCE: *Grub Street Journal,* January 1736

SUGGESTED PROCEDURE

For a four-shilling bowl, prepare an oleo-saccharum with the peel of four Seville oranges and 1 cup of light raw sugar, such as Florida Crystals. Add 16 ounces of hot water and stir to dissolve sugar. Add 8 ounces of strained Seville orange juice and stir. Add enough water to bring this up to a full quart, pour it into a clean bottle, seal and refrigerate.

To serve, pour a quart of this "sherbett"; a quart of proof-strength (i.e., around 57 percent alcohol by volume) VS-grade cognac, Jamaican rum or (for a six-shilling bowl) Batavia arrack; and a quart of cold water into a bowl and grate nutmeg over the top. If you wish to add ice, add ice. This is enough for one treble, or three-quart, bowl.

NOTES

I have recommended the oleo-saccharum here to reflect a line in the 1738 poem "Brandy," by "A Youth," which has Ashley's festooned with "od'rous orange-peels, in rows thick strung, / Trophies of num'rous past exploits." Now, this suggests that the peels were tossed into the bowl and fished out later as mementos of the bowls sold (we've all been to joints that do something similar). Equally, they might have been hung up to dry so that they could be reconstituted when Seville oranges were out of season (simply simmer them in water and add sugar). At least we know that orange peel fitted in to the proceedings somehow. We know that the juice was strained because in May 1731, after only being open for a couple of months, Ashley was advertising for the return of his "Silver Orange Strainer," which some light-fingered toper had walked off with.

We're equally ignorant as to the exact procedure Mrs. Gaywood and her colleagues followed in serving their Punch— we know the spirits and the "sherbett," or shrub, were presented separately, but was the sherbet fully diluted or did water have to be added as well? I'm assuming that it was made in bulk and cellared, in which case it would keep better if less diluted. Accordingly, I've kept most of the water on the side. That also allows one to serve this Punch hot (use boiling water). More importantly, Ashley's specialty being Brandy Punch, this allows us to achieve period accuracy by compensating for the understrength brandy we usually get: for that treble bowl, simply use 44 ounces cognac and cut the added cold water back to 20 ounces. (Truth be told, I would

have found the eighteenth century challenging, as I find this
Punch plenty strong with a mere quart of 80-proof brandy.)

YIELD: 12 cups.

AMERICAN ORANGE PUNCH

On March 4, 1829, Andrew Jackson, just sworn in as the
seventh president of the United States, hosted a grand
inaugural reception at the White House. As an expression of
his small-"d" democratic principles, he broke precedent and
threw it open to the people who had elected him. The public
(okay, mostly office-seekers) turned out in droves and—well,
let's let a contemporary newspaper tell the rest.

> All the lower rooms of the President's house were
> filled. Among a great deal of well behaved company, it
> was painful to see a large number who seemed to forget
> the dignified occasion and the respectable place where
> they were assembled. . . . A profusion of refreshments
> had been provided. Orange punch by barrels full was
> made, but as the waiters opened the doors to bring it
> out, a rush would be made, the glasses broken, the
> pails of liquor upset, and the most painful confusion
> prevailed. To such a degree was this carried, that wine
> and ice-cream could not be brought out to the ladies,
> and tubs of punch were taken from the lower story
> into the garden to lead off the crowd from the rooms.

He never did *that* again.

This recipe hails from Jerry Thomas, who adapted it from the
1858 *Bordeaux Wine and Liquor Dealers' Guide: A Treatise on
the Manufacture and Adulteration of Liquors*. This intriguing

little volume, which has nothing to do with Bordeaux, is accurately subtitled at least, with a heavy emphasis on the adulteration part. The following formula is pretty much the most wholesome thing in it. At least it doesn't call for "spirits of nitre" or "acetic ether." If made with Seville oranges, this will be sweet and complex; otherwise, sweet and mild.

THE ORIGINAL FORMULA

From a recipe in the *Bordeaux Wine & Liquor Guide*

The juice of 3 or 4 oranges.

The peel of 1 or 2 oranges.

¾ lb lump sugar.

3½ pints of boiling water.

Infuse half an hour, strain, add ½ pint of porter; ¾ to 1 pint each, rum and brandy (or either alone 1½ to 2 pints) and add more warm water and sugar, if desired weaker or sweeter. A liqueur glass of Curacoa, noyau, or maraschino improves it. A good lemon punch may be made by substituting lemons instead of oranges.

SOURCE: Jerry Thomas, *Bar-Tenders Guide*, 1862

NOTES
Prepare an oleo-saccharum with the peels and the sugar (use a light, raw one), then add the boiling water and proceed with the porter and liquors. For rum, deploy the usual Pirate Juice style, or at least a blend of that and a Planter's Best one, and best to go for the full pint of both it and the cognac. The question of liqueurs will be addressed later, under Regent's Punch. Ice is highly recommended here.

YIELD: 16 cups.

XIV

WHISKEY PUNCH

A rrack Punch is all well and good if you don't mind sending your hard-earned £, *s*. and *d*. to foreigners living at the approximate ends of the earth. The same objection applies to "Coniack" and "Nantz," save that the foreigners are nearer, better armed and much more French. As for "kill-devil," or rum, it was a domestic product by some standards, but the excise tax on it went to Parliament and the profit to the pockets of those with the wherewithal to finance sugarcane plantations three thousand miles across the ocean and man them with slaves. Nothing in any of 'em for the yeomen of Britain, for the farmers.

One man, at least, tried to help them. William of Orange, being a canny Dutchman and thus free from some of the prejudices of the English when it came to potables, pushed a series of acts through Parliament for the encouragement of grain-distilling in England and the discouragement of the importation of foreign wines and spirits. These were effective, up to a point: between 1684 and 1694, English grain-distilling almost doubled, to well over a million gallons a year. And yet the only people who drank this domestic malt spirit were those who could get no better. (We'll talk about them in the next chapter.) The English opinion of grain spirits remained decidedly low. In 1696, French brandy went for a hundred pounds a barrel, while English malt spirits—essentially, whiskey—fetched less than a quarter of that. As late as 1744, the philosopher George Berkeley, a member of the Anglo-Irish aristocracy, could sniff that "Whiskey is a spirit distilled from malt, the making of which poison, cheap and plenty, as being of our growth, is esteemed, by some unlucky patriots, as a benefit to their country." Far better to drink "tar-water," as he recommended. In Ireland, where Berkeley was born and intermittently lived, his was distinctly a minority opinion.

By 1700, the Irish and their fellow Celts the Scots had been drinking aqua vitae made from grain—usquebaugh, uisce beatha, whiskey[1]—recreationally for well over two centuries. The Irish in particular gained an early reputation for heroic consumption, but that may be only because the English, having seized the greater part of their country, could observe its population more closely. In any case, by Shakespeare's day, their spirits-tippling was proverbial: "I will rather trust a Fleming with my butter," says the jealous Master Ford in *The Merry Wives of Windsor*, "Parson Hugh the Welshman with my cheese, an Irishman with my aqua-vitae bottle, or a thief to walk my ambling gelding, than my wife with herself." Well, okay. But Shakespeare might have had a point about the Irish part, anyway, if we're to believe James Howell's description of how they drank the stuff. First off, they weren't really mixing it with anything. Uisce beatha was a raw grain distillate infused with raisins and spices in the medieval manner. In England, where there were a few, anyway, who appreciated it, it was drunk in "aqua-vitae measures"—basically, shot glasses. In its native land, however, as

---

1 The Gaelic terms are literal translations of the Latin.

Howell wrote in 1645, "it goes down . . . by beer glassfuls, being more natural to the nation."

In Scotland, the consumption seems to have been fully as large but not as well recorded. The fifth of the Statutes of Icolmkill, a set of stipulations negotiated in 1609 between the principal chieftains of the Western Islands, cited as one of the major causes of the continuing barbarity and poverty of their lands "thair extraordinair drinking of strong wynis and acquavitie" brought in among them by merchants. Their solution—to ban the importation of wines and spirits, but allow all men the liberty of brewing "aquavitie and uthir drink to serve thair awne housis"—would only have encouraged whiskey-drinking. As in Ireland, the Scots seem to have drunk their whiskey in infused form, with honey and spices. We must bear in mind that even in undoctored form, what Scotland and Ireland were making was a far cry from what we consider today to be whiskey—the unaged liquor was raw and oily and redolent of peat smoke, and also very strong. Few outsiders could even bring themselves to try it.

A rare exception was Captain Edmund Burt, an English engineer who spent most of the 1730s in the Scottish Highlands. Normally, he avoided the native tipples by traveling with a bottle of his own brandy and the necessary lemons and sugar for Punch. But even the stoutest oak must yield to a gale, and one evening found him in a hut with nothing to drink but river water or the whiskey a parcel of smugglers were transporting down from the glens. Luckily, he still had a few lemons, with which he "so far qualified the ill taste of the spirit as to make it tolerable." It was not an experiment he repeated; when he was in Inverness, his usual base, or Edinburgh, he could get Punch made with brandy or rum, the same as in London.

By Burt's day, at least the idea of Punch had reached the Highlands, if not necessarily the precise thing itself. "When they choose to qualify [whiskey] for Punch," he observed, "they sometimes mix it with water and honey, or with milk and honey; at other times, the mixture is only the aqua vitae, sugar and butter; this they burn till the sugar and butter are dissolved." (Could this be another hint that "punch" was originally a word for any mixed drink in a bowl?) Indeed, when, at a country inn in the hills outside Inverness, the captain's servant was squeezing lemons for his master's Brandy Punch, the landlord asked him quite seriously "if those were apples he was squeezing." It would be a while before the lemon in any form entered the general run of Scottish country Punch-making; in 1773, Samuel Johnson, touring the Hebrides with Boswell, wrote to his beloved Mrs. Thrale that "their punch is made without lemons, or any substitute."

That's understandable, under the circumstances. Until the English built their military roads through the Highlands after the crushed rebellion of 1745, there weren't even footpaths through most of the region, let alone roads. Hardly less remote were large parts of the Irish countryside, where Punch nonetheless crept in as well. (That seems to have happened between the mid 1740s, when Isaac Butler, in the course of a longish ramble through Ulster, found the whiskey still being drunk in the old style, with mint and butter, and 1775, when Thomas Campbell encountered proper Whiskey Punch in Tipperary.[2]) Yet deprivation can teach as well as hinder. Once lemons did become readily available to whiskey-drinkers, there were certainly some who were happy to use them. At the turn of the nineteenth century, for example, the Edinburgh Infirmary was prescribing, in cases of dropsy, "a quart to four pints a day" of Whiskey Punch, "acidulated with lemon juice" (one might almost wish to be dropsical). And in their absence, there were those who

---

2 "After supper," he wrote to a friend, "I for the first time drank whisky punch, the taste of which is harsh and austere, and the smell worse than the taste. . . . The spirit was very fierce and wild, requiring not less than seven times its own quantity of water to tame and subdue it." Now, admittedly there was much bootlegging at the time, and the potheen was often less than debonair, but the last bit gives him away as a liar, a bigot or a milquetoast. Even if the whiskey he tried was pure alcohol, with it making up an eighth of the total volume, the Punch would have only been 25 proof; and in fact Campbell states that the stuff he had wasn't even the strongest whiskey available; if he was telling the truth about the dilution, the Punch would've been about the proof of a strong ale. But I digress.

cast about for substitutes: Captain Fancourt, who was stationed in Ireland around the same time, noted that Whiskey Punch was sometimes "acidulated with black currants when lemons were not at hand." But both groups put together still formed a small minority.

Most Whiskey Punch–drinkers, given the choice, preferred to do without the lemon juice. English Punch-drinkers had already established that spice was the fifth leg of the chair; nice when you had it, but nobody was going to call off a perfectly good Punch party for want of a little nutmeg. The Scots and Irish further determined that if your whiskey was good enough, you could saw off another leg. The scrupulous drew a lexical distinction: if it had lemon, it was Punch; if not, Toddy. Many used the terms interchangeably. That freedom of terminology was made easier by another learned lesson. Ireland and Scotland are not India or Indonesia or even England. The cold and the wet are constant for eight months of the year and intermittent the other four. Whiskey Punch, consequently, was almost always drunk at a temperature at which the cooling properties of the lemon juice were not needed or even desired. Acids become more corrosive as their temperature increases, and hot lemon juice consumed in the quantities one hears mentioned—quarts, gallons, firkins—ceases to be pleasant. The solution was to split the difference between Punch and Toddy—to use the acid-free but flavorful peel of the lemon and leave out the juice.

We don't know if it was an Irishman or a Scot who first established this procedure. It appeared on both sides of the Giant's Causeway at roughly the same time, in the last quarter of the eighteenth century. Procedures differed little, if at all, the only distinction between an Irish Whiskey Punch and a Scotch one being the nature of the whiskey. At first, that was no distinction at all, although by the turn of the nineteenth century, distillers in the two countries were starting to explore the divergent paths that they have followed since.

Eventually, this hot Whiskey Punch would spread from the Celtic lands to England, across the Atlantic and indeed to every corner of the earth where a lousy climate and poor heating make a

warming drink an object of utility. In England, it became something of a sporting-life favorite, embraced by such men as the actor
George Frederick Cooke, who could with a straight face lecture a
young colleague on the dangers of intemperance and dissipation
while drinking "jug after jug" of it. When King George IV, who was
scarcely less dissipated than Mr. Cooke, visited Ireland in 1821,
practically the first words out of his mouth to his Irish subjects
were, "I assure you, my dear friends, I have an Irish heart and will
this night give a proof of my affection towards you . . . by drinking
your health in a bumper of whisky-punch." While I'll bet he said
that to all the countries, he wasn't one to drink just anything—his
consumption was vast but not indiscriminate (see Regent's Punch),
and rumor had it he drank Irish Whiskey Punch even when he
wasn't sucking up to the subjects.

Even the pope himself learned to like it, according to Samuel
Ferguson's 1838 *Father Tom and the Pope, or A Night at the Vatican*,
which tells the story of Father Tom from County Leitrim and his
visit to "Room," where the pope "axed him to take pot look wid
him." Alas, Ferguson's priest was a creature of the imagination.
But few conceits in nineteenth-century fiction are as ludicrous as
the thought of sour, reactionary old Gregory XVI, the pontiff in
question, sitting down with an Irish country priest who produces a
bottle of good "*putteen*" from under his cassock and instructs his
host how to make Punch: "Now, your Holiness," says Father Tom
in Ferguson's imagination,

> this bein' the first time you ever dispinsed them chymicals . . .
> I'll jist make bould to lay doun one rule ov orthography . . .
> for conwhounding them. . . . Put in the sperits first . . . and
> then put in the sugar; and remember, every dhrop ov wather
> you put in after that, spoils the punch.

"Glory be to God!" cries the pope in stage-Irish (Gregory was born
Bartolomeo Alberto Cappellari), "I never knewn what dhrink was
afore."

The church was not amused, but everybody else was: Ferguson's satire was widely popular wherever English was spoken and stayed in print for the rest of the century; indeed, Father Tom's philosophy of Punch-making, and in particular the bit about the water, became axiomatic.

The church did, however, exact revenge of a sort, in the form of the charismatic Father Mathew, who in 1838 founded a total temperance society; within ten years, he had enrolled more than half the adult population of Ireland, in the process putting paid to the tumbler of Whiskey Punch as a national beverage. Here, anyway, are five ways to avoid taking the pledge.

BLACKWOOD'S HOT WHISKEY PUNCH

The so-called Scottish Enlightenment saw the land north
of the Tweed come into its own, intellectually anyway.
Characterized by a peculiarly Scottish mixture of deep and
daring thought and down-to-earth practicality, it was at full
boil from the beginning of the eighteenth century until the
French Revolution, at which point the Edinburgh intellectuals
had to pull in their horns lest they be thought seditious. But
the Scots are a stubborn people, and a number of them carried
right on with the speculating, philosophizing, criticizing and
whatever else it is intellectuals do when they're feeling their
oats. Among the manifestations of this low-key ferment was
one we have already come across more than once, Edinburgh's
Blackwood's Magazine—one of the greatest journals in the
history of publishing. Among the things that made it so were
the so-called *Noctes Ambrosianae*, or "Ambrosian Nights," a
lengthy series of lightly fictionalized dialogues between
various Scottish intellectuals who drink Punch at Ambrose's

Screeching hot. GREG BOEHM

tavern in Edinburgh and chew over the issues of the day. Written chiefly by John Wilson, at first with the assistance of the novelist James Hogg and our friends William "ODoherty" Maginn and John Gibson "Glasgow Punch" Lockhart and then without it, the series ran from 1822 to 1835. Collected, it fills five fat volumes. I can't pretend to have read through them all, but the stretches I've read abundantly display the Scottish Enlightenment's characteristic mixture of erudition and homeliness; free-thinking, muscular culture and good humor. And there's always Whiskey Punch, and it's always drunk hot.

Between the lively, informed conversation and the steady drinking without apparent inebriation, the nights at Ambrose's were taken by a generation of bright young men as the very model of modern social tippling, free from the brutishness and foolish high jinks that dominated the stereotypes (and often the reality) of gatherings high and low, and yet not stuffy or old-fashioned. That did nothing at all to hinder the popularity of Whiskey Punch.

This recipe is from another of Shelton Mackenzie's useful mixological footnotes, this one to the annotated 1854 New York edition of the *Noctes*. It tallies in detail and spirit with the practices depicted in many a passage in the dialogues. It most emphatically does not tally with another famous scene of Whiskey Punch–making, which first appeared in the pages of *Blackwood's*—that of Father Tom and the pope. Ferguson, an Irishman himself, should have known full well that at least some of the water goes in first when making Punch, if only to dissolve the sugar. On the other hand, if Father Tom could be faulted for his technique, I'm sure he would regard Mackenzie's formula, with its two parts water to one of whiskey, with the scorn and loathing due a particularly nasty heresy.

The mystery of making whisky-punch comes with practice.
The sugar should be first dissolved in a small quantity of
water, which must be what the Irish call "screeching hot."
Next throw in the whisky. Then add a thin shaving of fresh
lemon peel. Then add the rest of the water, so that the spirits
will be a third of the mixture. Lastly,—Drink! Lemon juice is
deleterious and should be eschewed.

SOURCE: R. Shelton Mackenzie, ed., *Noctes Ambrosianae*, 1854

SUGGESTED PROCEDURE

In a heatproof bowl, pot or jug, prepare an oleo-saccharum with the
peel of one lemon and 2 ounces demerara sugar. Set a quart and a
half of water to boil. Add 8 ounces or so of the boiling water to the
sugar (the quantity doesn't have to be exact), stirring well; this
should warm up the bowl as well as dissolve the sugar. Add a
750-milliliter bottle of Scotch or Irish whiskey and then the rest of
the water, or as much of it as you can tolerate. The Punch should be
kept warm, whether in a jug by the fireside, a bowl on a hot plate on
the sideboard, or a Crock-Pot wherever the extension cord reaches.

NOTES

Jerry Thomas, who has much to say about Whiskey Punch,
suggests to "steep the thin yellow shavings of lemon peel in
the whiskey." This is a fine idea, if you can plan forty-eight
hours ahead (don't leave them in longer than that; they'll get
bitter and spoil the whiskey).

The 2 ounces of sugar is a baseline; if the Punch lacks
unctuousness, adjust upward. I like a raw demerara for this.
As for the whiskey, Thomas gives us a rare brand
recommendation when he specifies Kinnahan's Lord
Lieutenant for his Irish Whiskey Punch. Unfortunately, "the
very Cream of Irish Whiskies," as it used to proclaim itself, is
no more. But like all Irish whiskeys of the time, it would have

been a thick, rich and smooth pure pot-still product. There are only a few of these left, but if you can get the Bushmills 10 or the Redbreast, you'll have a heavenly Punch on your hands. Otherwise, John Powers or Black Bush or any of the richer blends will do.

Thomas is particular when it comes to Scotch Whiskey Punch as well, calling for "Glenlivet or Islay, of the best quality." The Islay he stocked, Caol Ila, is still around and excellent; by "Glenlivet," he meant any one of a number of whiskeys from the region, Speyside, not just *the* Glenlivet—not that there's anything wrong with that Glenlivet. In any case, hot Whiskey Punch demands a pure malt whiskey. As a good Scot (on my mother's side), I'll add that it can be a vatted malt (or "blended malt," as they confusingly now must be called); it can be a young malt (indeed, it's better young); it can be a cheap malt. That doesn't matter—you're concerned with the pot-still body of the stuff rather than the nuances of flavor. Whatever's on sale will work fine, as will the bottle your boss regifted you with.

About the quantity of water that goes into hot Whiskey Punch, gentlemen may be allowed to differ. Personally, I'll keep Father Tom's rubicund visage in mind as I add the hot water, stopping when his scowl registers strong disapproval but not yet open disgust. That usually occurs when I've added a quart or so per 750-milliliter bottle of whiskey.

YIELD: up to 9 cups.

COLD SCOTCH OR IRISH
WHISKEY PUNCH

Irish whiskey and (especially) its Scotch cousin have a
persistent graininess that can render them tricky to mix with;
you can't simply plug them into your old rum- or brandy-
based Punch recipes and expect something delicious. Case
in point, this entry from the diary of Tennyson's friend
William Allingham: "After dinner T[ennyson] concocts an
experimental punch with whisky and claret—not successful."
I would think not, but had Tennyson mixed brandy and
claret, there would've been Punch Royal and smiles all
around. One must appreciate the poetic impulse, anyway.

The Irish, despite their poetic bent, agreed with their
Caledonian cousins on the subject of cold Whiskey Punch: the
best way to make it was to make hot Whiskey Punch and
leave it sitting around for a while. If you must add something,
both agreed, let it be a small proportion of the lemon juice.
Small, though, d'ye ken? Made thus—well, to quote the
character in the *Noctes Ambrosianae* through which John
Wilson channeled the crusty James Hogg, "it has a gran'
taste, and a maist seducin smell . . . the drink seems to be . . .
as innocent as the dew o' lauchin [i.e., laughing] lassie's lip, yet
it's just as dangerous, and leads insensibly on, by littles and
wees, to a state o' unconscious intoxication."

The formula, such as it is, is from Jerry Thomas. The Punch is
delicious.

THE ORIGINAL FORMULA

Cold Whiskey Punch

This beverage ought always to be made with boiling water,
and allowed to concoct and cool for a day or two before it is

put on the table. In this way, the materials get more intensely amalgamated than cold water and cold whiskey ever get.

SOURCE: Jerry Thomas, *Bar-Tenders Guide*, 1862

SUGGESTED PROCEDURE

Follow the same steps as for Blackwood's Hot Whiskey Punch (on previous page). Once the Punch is prepared, let it cool, strain it and refrigerate it in a sealed container. For Lemon Punch, as Thomas notes, "a small proportion of juice is added before the whiskey is poured in." Three ounces should do it. Serve in a bowl poured over a one-quart block of ice.

NOTES

Again, see Blackwood's Hot Whiskey Punch—although in this one you can probably get away with a blended Scotch, if it's a richish one. Once you're adding ice, the texture of the whiskey is less important. And I suggest you use all the water; cold Punch is meant to be refreshing.

YIELD: 9 cups.

American Whiskey Punch

In the early nineteenth century, Americans drank a fair amount of Scotch- and Irish-based Whiskey Punch, particularly in New York and Boston. As one might expect, they also made it out of their own peculiar kind of whiskey. There were, however, certain issues with it. During the Revolution, it had gotten us through. John Adams summed up the situation well in a letter he wrote to Abigail from Philadelphia in the difficult summer of 1777 (so difficult, he noted, that Punch was up to twenty shillings a bowl): "As to sugar, molasses, rum, &c., we must leave them off. Whiskey is used here instead of rum, and I don't see but it is just as good." Even after the war—well, let's just say that the republic was young and poor, and raw rye and corn whiskey cheap and plentiful and some things happened. Barrels of Pennsylvania rye and Kentucky corn traveled "smooth miles of turnpike way, / And *stumpy* roads, that crack the creaking wains," to quote "The Progress of Whiskey," a semicoherent parody of Thomas Gray's famous ode on the progress of poesy that appeared in the *United States Literary Gazette* in 1825, finally ending their journey "amid the odorous shade / Of New York's boundless cellars laid" or by being made into "rich streams of whiskey punch" for the social enjoyment of the golden youth of Boston.

But that was American Whiskey Punch's high point, at least as a communal drink. Before too many years had passed, if one were to broach the possibility of a festive bowl of it in polite company, one would meet with an answer such as this, from an 1835 short story: "Whiskey-punch . . . I thought was banished from all refined society." By then, in polite society, it was all about the Regent's Punch or the Punch à la Romaine (see Chapter XVII). In less polite society, both the whiskey and the bowl were out of favor, the former yielding to French brandy and Holland gin (drinking imported being an essential part of the front every sporting man must maintain) and the latter to the individual Punch made by the glass (for which see *Imbibe!*). In still less polite circles, well, then as now, you drinks what you can get.

By the time domestic whiskey became an acceptable tipple again for the kind of people who drank their Punches by the bowl, those people were no longer drinking their Punches by the bowl save on special occasions, and the Punches they were making then were complex affairs in which the whiskey played a supporting role at best (see Chapter XVIII for those). All of this is by way of explaining why early recipes for straight American Whiskey Punch are very rare indeed. This one, an expedient of desperation, comes from Frank Forester, the pioneering American sportswriter. Forester, however, was born Henry William Herbert, in England; that might have colored his perception of the quality of rye whiskey.

THE ORIGINAL FORMULA

It is well that a Sportsman, without being anything of an epicure, should, like an old campaigner, know a little of the art of the cuisine. . . . I commend him also to be his own liquor-bearer, as the spirits in country places are usually execrable, especially the rye-whiskey of Pennsylvania and the West.

If, however, he determine to take his chance in this matter . . . [t]he best receipt I know for cold punch, and that which I always use, is, to one tumbler of crushed sugar, one and a-half of spirit, six of water, the peel of two lemons, and the juice of one.

SOURCE: "Frank Forester" [Henry William Herbert], "A Few Memoranda and Brief Receipts for Sportsmen," 1849

In a three-quart bowl, prepare an oleo-saccharum with 8 ounces white sugar and the peel of two lemons. Add 1 ½ ounces lemon juice and 8 ounces water and stir until sugar is dissolved. Add 12 ounces cask-strength rye or bourbon, stir again and add between 3 and 6 cups of cold water, to taste. A quart-sized block of ice or enough cubes or pieces of it to fill the bowl past halfway are an excellent addition.

NOTES

More lemon juice is a fine addition: use up to 6 ounces, to taste. If you can't get cask-strength whiskey, use 16 ounces of 100-proof or 18 ounces of 80-proof and dock the water by 4 or 6 ounces accordingly.

YIELD: up to 9 cups.

CANADIAN PUNCH

Despite its undeniable richness of flavor, American whiskey has proven itself to be much more mixable than the Irish or especially Scotch variety. Take the following combination from Jerry Thomas, printed, as usual, without comment as to its origin. The idea of combining Scotch and pineapple gives me the shudders; rye and pineapple, however, makes for a wholly satisfying mixture.

I don't know if the "Canadian" this Punch is saddled with is intended to lay off any gaucheness the idea of a Rye Whiskey Punch might yet retain onto America's northern neighbor or if it's a reflection of the drink's true origins and of Canada's characteristic unpretentiousness and good sense. In either case, this is a dangerously alluring Punch, smooth, lightly fruity and endowed with uncommon powers of intoxication.

2 quarts of rye whiskey.

1 pint of Jamaica rum.

6 lemons, sliced.

1 pineapple, sliced.

4 quarts of water.

Sweeten to taste, and ice.

SOURCE: Jerry Thomas, *Bar-Tenders Guide*, 1862

SUGGESTED PROCEDURE

Infuse the lemons and the pineapple in the spirits for six hours without squeezing. Dissolve 12 ounces white sugar in 12 cups water, add the spirits—complete with fruit—and the rest of the water, refrigerate for a couple of hours, slip in a large block of ice and serve.

NOTES

The anonymous 1869 *Steward & Barkeeper's Manual* suggests a couple more lemons in this, and it's right. For the rye, by no means use Canadian whiskey unless it's explicitly labeled as a rye. The Canadian whiskey of today and the Canadian whiskey of 1862 are two very different things. It should be, if possible, cask strength; if not, add another 750-milliliter bottle of whiskey and dock the water by 3 cups. The rum should be one of the strong, aromatic members of the Pirate Juice class. A nice variation is to replace the final flood of water with soda or mineral water, in which case it will have to be added just before serving.

THE SPREAD EAGLE PUNCH

The Spread Eagle was of course the icon of the United States of America. It was also a stockjobber's term, going "spread eagle" on a stock being the same as buying it on margin. Jerry Thomas (whose recipe this is) being both a red-blooded American patriot and a degenerate stock-plunger, he was doubtless aware of both meanings and probably saw the irony there—what could be more American than going out on a long limb in the hope of getting something for nothing?

Just why either one should be commemorated by a mixture of Scotch and American whiskeys, I don't know; the 1869 *Steward & Barkeeper's Manual* has a "Bird of Freedom Punch" that combines Monongahela rye and New England rum (in a proportion of ten to one), which makes more sense (although some might call it a Canadian Punch). Yet this makes a better Punch. I can't say why it works, but it does. Mysteriously tasty.

THE ORIGINAL FORMULA

1 bottle of Islay whiskey.

1 bottle of Monongahela.

Lemon peel, sugar and—boiling water at discretion.

SOURCE: Jerry Thomas, *Bar-Tenders Guide*, 1862

SUGGESTED PROCEDURE

Follow the steps for Blackwood's Hot Whiskey Punch (page 190), but double all quantities.

NOTES

As long as you're using a nice Islay malt (go for one of the less peaty ones here, or it will be all you taste; Bruichladdich works splendidly), you should try to match it with a good

Monongahela—although nowadays the rye that was once made on the banks of that river is now made on the banks of the Kentucky and the Ohio. As always, the Rittenhouse Bonded is recommended.

As for that "discretion": to me, it suggests following the directions for Blackwood's Hot Whiskey Punch—thus, doubled, the peel of two lemons, at least 4 ounces demerara sugar and 3 quarts boiling water.

Personally, I like this one cold, so I make it the day before and serve it with a block of ice. And I have been known to double or even triple the amount of lemon peel.

YIELD: up to 18 cups.

XV

GIN PUNCH

G in Punch" is a combination of words that would have struck Jonathan Swift and his contemporaries not unlike the way "Crack Martini" strikes us today. King William's laudable attempt to strengthen English farmers hadn't turned out quite the way he planned. I won't get into the Gin Craze here; books have been written about it, and good ones (see, for example, Patrick Dillon's *Gin: The Much-Lamented Death of Madam Geneva*). Suffice it to say that by the second decade of the eighteenth century, "geneva" (the English mangling of the Dutch *jenever*), or "gin" for short, had become the intoxicant of choice—or rather, of necessity—for the scrabbling urban masses, just as destructive as crack but far more widely used. In this case, the Repression stage was fully warranted. A locally distilled knockoff of Dutch genever, geneva was nothing more than raw pot-still whiskey infused with something to hide the "nauseous," "gross" and "fetid" taste of the grain. The most conscientious distillers would use juniper berries for this, as did the Dutch. Everyone else used turpentine. The only thing to recommend it was its price: when arrack cost eighteen shillings a gallon, gin cost two.

Thus, the ludicrousness of "Gin Punch." Punch was high-church, gin the lowest of the low. And indeed, most gin-drinkers avoided the odious comparison by guzzling it in straight drams or, at best, tipping it into a mug of ale. But mixology is no respecter of boundaries, and by the 1730s, we start to see people making Punch with gin. Admittedly, they were not people of the best class: escaped convicts, Grub Street writers, Americans and the like. *The Fortunate Imposter*, an anonymous 1759 novel, locates it perfectly when it has its hero share a "twelve-penny bowl of hot *Gin-Punch*" with a "club of beggars." But the eighteenth century was a time of change, and as we have seen demonstrated so often in the story of Punch, time has a way of reconciling opposites. By the last quarter of the century, Gin Punch had ceased to be oxymoronic and had won a foothold in the citadel of acceptable drinks. It helped that with the Gin Craze having burned itself out, the hundreds upon hundreds of backroom distillers operating in the 1730s had been winnowed down to a much smaller number of large, technologically sophisticated players who made a product such that people could see good qualities in it other than cheapness. Indeed, the quality of the spirit had improved so much that some doctors took advantage of the widely touted diuretic properties of the juniper berry and prescribed Gin Punch to their patients. Another sign of progress: in 1776, James Boswell, then a respectable attorney, wrote in his diary, "I drank rather too much gin punch. It was a new liquor to me, and I liked it much."

Yet while Gin Punch was gaining acceptance, it was a tentative acceptance, and a conditional one. In part, it depended on what you powered it with. If by "gin" you meant the best grades of imported Hollands, the kind that often sold for the same price as old cognac, most were willing to overlook its lack of pedigree. If, though, it was

English gin you were talking about, which sold at a third to half the price, it might be of acceptable quality for medical use, but it was simply not genteel.

It is, however, an interesting phenomenon of English social history that the highest reaches of society often find ways to come together with the lowest against the middle ones, and Regency London was no exception. Slumming in low-class "gin palaces" was a popular diversion for the "Fancy"—those fashionable young sparks who devoted their leisure hours to cultivating pugilists and jockeys and betting on the results of their protégés' labors. The tastes they acquired in such establishments as the "sluicery," to which the aristocratic Corinthian Tom takes his equally well-bred friend Jerry Hawthorne in Pierce Egan's 1821 sporting-life classic *Life in London*—a nasty dive populated by broken-down old whores, street urchins and gin-soaked beggars—followed them to their more characteristic haunts: the club, the coffeehouse, the officers' mess. Even the most respectable inns at which the Fancy congregated, such as the ancient Blue Posts, learned to pride themselves on their Gin Punch. If there were still those agreeing with the young dandy caricatured in the *New Monthly Magazine* who pronounced Gin Punch "Vastly vulgar," Lord Byron, the most glamorous figure of his age, was not among them: according to his mistress, he wrote the last Cantos of *Don Juan* "with repeated glasses of Gin Punch at his side."

Up to this point—broadly, the last decade of the Georgian era, which ended with the death of George IV in 1830—Gin Punch, alias "Gin Twist,"[1] was made in the conventional manner: if cold, it took its ration of lemon juice, sugar and water much like any other; if hot, we can assume that it would have followed the trend with hot Punches in general and used the peel of the lemon but not its juice. In the 1830s, however, mixology kicked in with the introduction and immediate acceptance of the Garrick Club's take on the drink. When streamlined and downsized, this would become the John and

---

1 I suspect that the widespread popularity of this alternate name stems from an uneasiness with the combination of "gin" and "Punch."

then the Tom Collins, the drink that made gin an acceptable drink for the middle classes.

Here are three respectable ways of ginning.

HOLLAND GIN PUNCH

The perceived vulgarity of Gin Punch ensured that nothing like a recipe for it appeared during the eighteenth century, or if it did, it was tucked away so safely that I have been unable to find it. However, the sparse notices we do have for it give no indication that any extraordinary procedure was followed in its concoction.

THE ORIGINAL FORMULA

For Cold Holland Gin Punch, use the recipe for Major Bird's Brandy Punch, with the substitution of a good *corenwijn* or *oude genever* (a category that includes the grey-bottle Bols Genever) for the cognac.

For Hot Holland Gin Punch, use the recipe for Blackwood's Hot Whiskey Punch, with the same substitution for the usquebaugh.

SOURCE: The sources for early Gin Punch are so nebulous when it comes to details that they are not worth citing. Here, one must proceed by extrapolation.

NOTES

The American comedian Howard Paul left a detailed description of Charles Dickens's procedure in manufacturing hot Punch from "old gin" (which could be either Dutch or English; Dickens kept both in his cellar), "lumps of sugar" and "chips of lemon." Here Dickens omitted the flames found in the recipe he gave his friends, but he still made sure that "the mouth of the jug was closed by stuffing in the napkin, rolled up to do duty as a cork" and set by the fire. "And then the illustrious brewer," Paul concludes, watch in hand, timed the commingling of the work of his hand. In about six minutes the precious brew was ready to be reverently quaffed, and as he handed me, with a smile, a full tumbler, he kept his eye on my face, as if to watch my first impression.

Howard Paul was a lucky man.

GARRICK CLUB PUNCH

In a little series of meditations on various matters he published in 1835 as *The Original*, the English essayist Thomas Walker mentioned in passing how gratifying iced Punch was in summer. This prompted a substantial digression by the *London Quarterly*'s reviewer, to whom the world owes a debt of thanks. "Instead of icing punch," the reviewer writes, "the preferable mode is to mix it with a proportion of iced soda-water." And then he's off, touching on the Garrick Club—whose "gin punch . . . is one of the best things we know"; on Stephen Price, the club's American manager; on Thomas Hill, who was some sort of celebrity; and finally on Theodore Hook, one of the novelists and wits of the day and a man who was known to step high, wide and handsome in matters tipicular (he was Coleridge's partner-in-crime, you may recall, at their glass-smashing Punch party near Highgate). Hook, it seems, popped into the Garrick one warm afternoon "in that equivocal state of thirstiness which it requires something more than common to quench." He made his thirst known, and a recommendation was made: try the Gin Punch. He did. A jug was made "under the personal inspection of Mr. Price." He drank it. Five more were made, one after the other. He drank them, too. Then he shoved off under his own steam and made it to his dinner appointment. Let's see Jonathan Franzen pull that off.

We should focus on Mr. Price for a moment. He was an American, born the year England signed the colonies away. In 1808, the twenty-five-year-old Price was put in charge of running the Park Theatre in New York, the city's most fashionable theater. He would run it for the next eighteen years. Price was a betting man his whole life, a member in good standing of the so-called Sporting Fraternity. One of his most successful gambles was to import English actors to the New York stage at a time when Anglophobia ran high and loud (he began with the Whiskey Punch–loving Cooke). In 1826, after a most successful run, he decamped for London to take over the management of the renowned Theatre Royal, Drury Lane. There, he was less successful, lasting only two years. In 1831, though, when some well-funded theatrical types started the Garrick Club, they made him its manager. That's surprising. It's not just that, according to one who knew him, he was "not a highly educated man, nor the possessor of a very refined taste" or that he "unsparingly larded his conversation" with "coarse and highly objectionable epithets." He was also prickly, shrewd, brusque and imperious, to the point that Thackeray (a member) caricatured him in his *Book of Snobs* as the beastly "Captain Shindy." Hardly Garrick material, one would think.

On the other hand, he knew a trick with Gin Punch. In New York, he was so famous for drinking "gin and water" while complaining that "the glasses were too small and he had to fill them too often" that the tragedian James William Wallack eventually presented him with a special goblet that held over a quart. The H_2O in that "gin and water" probably wasn't the kind that just sits there. His Punch recipe, you see, which the humanitarian from the *Quarterly* was good enough to print, calls for "iced soda water." This was something new: while people had been experimenting with carbonated water and Punch since the 1780s, and iced Punch was by that point held in high regard, nobody seems to have put them together before (indeed soda water, a popular hangover cure, was seen as an antidote to Punch, not an accomplice).

We don't know if Price brought his formula with him from New York, but it's a good guess,[2] what with the American proclivity for iced drinks. Whoever first concocted it, it was a sensation: once outed in the popular *Quarterly*, it spread pretty much everywhere. And with good reason: Price's formula is utterly seductive, a bright, vastly refreshing tipple that bridges the gap between Punch and the modern long drink. Price himself didn't live to enjoy the acclaim he deserved: he was back in New York by 1838 and died two years later, but it would be another two decades before his innovation really caught on in his hometown, and then it would bear another man's name.

THE ORIGINAL FORMULA

Pour half a pint of gin on the outer peel of a lemon, then a little lemon juice, sugar, a glass of maraschino, about a pint and a quarter of water, and two bottles of iced soda water. The result will be three pints of the punch in question.

SOURCE: *London Quarterly*, **1835**

NOTES

That "gin" could mean either a Hollands or an Old Tom. I lean toward a Hollands, what with Price being a New Yorker and that being the gin in favor there, but then again Price was an Anglophile and, more importantly, by 1835 English gin was well on its way to dominance in the domestic market, despite a few dissenting voices. Either way, it's a damn tasty drink. (If you do go with Hollands, use an oude or the Bols Genever, not a corenwijn or jonge). The quantities here require a little precision wrangling. For the gin, you'll need 10 ounces

---

2 On the other hand, in an 1834 piece in the *New Monthly Magazine* we hear of one Raggett, at the Cocoa Tree (a popular coffeehouse), "who for no price will sell the secret" of his iced Gin Punch; one would like to know more about Mr. Raggett and his secret.

(remember, we're dealing with imperial quantities here). "A little lemon juice" is awfully vague; we'll get back to it in a minute. A glass—presumably a wineglass—of maraschino gives us another 2 ounces. A pint and a quarter of water comes to 25 ounces. Soda water bottles came in two sizes, 6 ounces and the more common 10 ounces; assuming the latter, two of those gives us another (imperial) pint. Total so far: 57 ounces, or 3 ounces shy of 3 imperial pints. So the lemon juice? Three ounces. Sugar? One ounce, more or less, of superfine will do. The *London Quarterly* be damned, I like a block of ice in mine, so I generally remove 10 to 15 ounces of the water to account for that and switch the rest to soda water—thus ending up with a quart of chilled soda providing the entire H_2O content of the drink.

In any case, it's best to begin by lightly muddling the lemon peel in the sugar and maraschino, and then add the gin and the water. Stir, add the ice if you're using it and pour in the soda water. Done.

YIELD: 7½ cups.

In his 1868 *Cooling Cups and Dainty Drinks*, William Terrington printed eight recipes for Gin Punch, including this one and three simple variations on it, the best of which is "Gin Punch a la Terrington," for which simply replace the maraschino with green Chartreuse. Indeed, many liqueurs can be substituted successfully for the maraschino here, with interesting results—or try, as Arnold James Cooley suggested in his 1846 recipe "cyclopaedia," a glass—2 ounces—of sherry (anything but a fino or Manzanilla). I also like to make it with green tea in place of half the soda water—so an American pint of each to 10 ounces gin, plus ice.

LIMMER'S GIN PUNCH

Limmer's Hotel. Where does one begin? In its heyday, which ran from about 1810 to 1850, this narrow old building at the corner of St. George and Conduit streets, just south of Hanover Square, was one of the hottest spots in London. Not everyone went there: it was chiefly a "resort for the sporting world . . . where you heard nothing but the language of the turf, and where men with not very clean hands used to make up their books," as Captain Gronow, the one-man archive of Regency and late-Georgian gossip, later recalled. Evidently the bookies rather set the tone for Limmer's standards of hygiene: according to Gronow, it was "the most dirty hotel in London." No matter; the clientele was frighteningly aristocratic—Byron was a regular, along with half the upper reaches of the army—and couldn't care less about such bourgeois values as cleanliness or comfort. The rooms were small, dark and unswept. The "coffee-room"—that is, the bar—was "gloomy." Its clock was the frequent target of the patrons' late-night pistol practice. The doorman had one leg. There was no closing time. That kind of place.

As long as the action was hot and the establishment kept the nouveaux riches and tradesmen out, which it did with an enthusiasm bordering on cruelty, it could count on upper-crust patronage. Particularly if John Collins (or Collin—accounts differ), the hotel's plump, cheerful yet dignified old headwaiter, was at hand to fetch a brimming glass of its famous Punch, which was based not on arrack, rum or brandy, or whiskey, but on "blue ruin"—gin.

I've written about Mr. Collins in *Imbibe!* and about the chilled, carbonated glasses of Gin Punch that traveled the world under his name. I'll concentrate here on what Mr. Collins was actually serving at Limmer's. This task is complicated somewhat by the fact that Collins seems to have known more than one way to make Punch, to judge by the compounds he's pushing in the brief sketches of him penned by his contemporaries. If he's offering "Sir Godfrey's mixture" to one, to another it's "Mr. Wombwell's mixture" and to yet another "the Prince of Wales' mixture," while a fourth is calling him "that elaborate compounder of whisky punch." About these we know nothing (well, the penultimate one is probably Regent's Punch, for which see Chapter XVII).

Everyone else, however, liked the Gin Punch, and indeed that's the mixture that ended up being associated with him. Unfortunately, authentic notices of it are surprisingly scarce, and it's difficult to pin down when he perfected it. Indeed, the composition of Mr. Collins's Gin Punch is one of the enduring mysteries of mixological history: was it the same as the bar drink that bore his name? Just gin, lemon juice and sugar, with soda water and ice? If so, what kind of gin was it? Most American bartenders, anyway, made it with Holland gin; we don't know what the English ones did, since they didn't write about it. Holland gin was certainly prized in England, often fetching the same kinds of prices that old cognac did.

There are, however, a couple of hints found in the press of the day that, combined with what we know about John Collinses and Gin Punch, might help us to resurrect it. What follows is of necessity rather close-grained, and since reading it is by no means necessary to the enjoyment of what proves itself to be one of the most delightful drinks ever concocted, a light, floral Punch that makes even the Garrick's seem coarse in comparison, if you are thirsty, I suggest you skip ahead.

One thing we can conclude is that the gin it was based on was in fact English. That deduction comes from "Wine, a Tale," a slight piece of fiction written by the prolific and then-popular novelist Catherine Gore, which appeared anonymously in

Tait's Edinburgh Magazine in 1833; in it the narrator, a junior officer in the navy, finds himself at the officers' mess of one of Her Majesty's regiments in the eastern Mediterranean. The company is sporty, the talk knowing, and soon "proposals" are made "for a bowl of 'Gin-Punch!'" One of the lieutenants, who happens to be both a lord and "a masterhand in the scientific brew," takes charge. The necessaries are assembled: Punch bowl, lemons, the usual. Then the spirits: "a bottle of Hodges' best . . . appeared in as orderly array as though we had been supping at Limmer's."

Mrs. Gore can be counted on to have gotten her details right, the behavior of the privileged being her bread and butter. She got her gin right, anyway, "Hodges full proof" being one of the dominant brands of the period, and one of the pioneering Old Tom gins—indeed, the category might have been named after Tom Chamberlain, Hodges's master distiller; so said *Notes & Queries*, anyway. The other key to Limmer's Gin Punch comes from an 1836 piece in the *New Sporting Magazine* titled "The Ascot Cup." It opens with a what-ho coterie of oh-so-fast Oxford boys discussing the races over "a huge jug of iced punch." On the table are bottles of "brandy, rum, gin, whiskey, Hollands &c." and "one large bottle of Capillaire." In its original French form, this was a syrup thickened with an infusion of maidenhair fern. In English hands, it was usually no more than a thick sugar syrup flavored lightly with orange-flower water. English or French, to our author its presence denotes "the experience of the worthy host with respect to the mysteries of Honest John Collins."

So. Is the original Limmer's Gin Punch nothing more than an Old Tom Punch, sweetened with capillaire and chilled with iced soda water? If it is, it goes a long way toward explaining the affection that Mr. Collins elicited from his regulars.

Proceed as for the Garrick Club Punch, but with Old Tom gin and using capillaire instead of the maraschino.

NOTES

To make capillaire (English style): stir 2 cups white sugar together with 1 cup water over low heat until sugar has dissolved. Remove from heat, add ⅛ ounce orange-flower water (the Lebanese Mymouné brand, available in Middle Eastern groceries, is excellent), stir and let cool. Bottle and keep refrigerated.

XVI

OXFORD PUNCH

People who spend a lot of time making drinks, whether for love or money, have a distinct tendency to get caught up in the idea of what I like to call "the mixologist's stone"—that one, talismanic extra ingredient that, when added to a drink, will transform it from adequate to ambrosial. The brine in the Martini, the maraschino-cherry yuck in the Manhattan, the Budweiser in the Margarita. The more unlikely the better. With it, the drink is perfect; without it, deformed. (For that matter, it doesn't even have to be an ingredient: it can be a technique (the "dry shake") or a tool or a size or shape of ice cube.) Punch-makers were no different. As the Punch Age progressed, the list of fetishized additions grew. Wine and milk and tea and porter, we've already seen. More than a few insisted on guava jelly. Others claimed a little butter in a jug of hot Punch was the very thing. One odd soul even insisted that you couldn't make good Punch unless you used water that had had rice boiled in it. While I suspect that most of these innovations were attempts to mitigate the consequences of using liquors of less than the first quality (a common theme underlying much mixological experimentation), they were nevertheless not unsuccessful. The Punches they produced were perfectly palatable, and often enough a good deal more than that (okay, I'm still wondering about the rice water). Yet mixologists did not rest. Mankind, after all, is curious and determined and will stride swingingly toward its own destruction.

Case in point: sometime around the end of the eighteenth century, one of the anonymous, unheralded geniuses that the mixological art throws off in such profusion took the bold step of adding calf's-foot jelly—basically, gelatin—to a ration of Punch, with the idea that (as an 1845 cookbook put it) "the jelly softens the mixture, and destroys the acrimony of the acid and sugar." It does. In fact, there is no drink in the pharmacopoeia more unctuous, more perfectly smooth and innocuous-seeming than Punch made thus. In my mind, it occupies a shelf in the same compartment that holds the rapier, the Colt revolver, the common house cat and the German Panther tank. It is a perfect killing machine. Here are two ways of letting it loose.

Oxford Punch

In 1827, an Oxford printer put out a little paperback pamphlet titled *Oxford Night Caps, being a Collection of Receipts for making Various Beverages used in the University*. Only thirty-four pages long, with forty "receipts," it was the first book ever published devoted entirely to mixed drinks. Its authorship has been attributed to one Richard Cook, born 1799, about whom I have been able to find nothing amusing or interesting. Whoever he was, Cook was an educated man, or at least good at faking it: the book omitted none of the footnotes, classical allusions and scraps of Greek and Latin then obligatory for a work of convivial literature. As with Jerry Thomas's *Bar-Tenders Guide*, for which it would to some degree serve as a model, the drinks it presented were a motley mix of the archaic and the up-to-date. Metheglin and Sack-Posset are included, but so are a number of the wine-based Cups that were beginning to replace Punch in polite society.

Yet there are also thirteen recipes for Punch, including this one. A glance at the formula reveals that this is no Sir-Toby-by-the-Fireside Punch, nothing that a country gent could whip up on the sideboard while talking dogs and horses with the squire from down the road. Where does one start? Along with Regent's Punch and Boston Club Punch, this is one of the most complicated recipes in this book. But anything drunk at Oxford in the glory days of mandatory Greek and Latin has got to be worth preserving. And who knows? One day, you might just have an occasion so special, a guest so honored, an anniversary so long in coming, that no ordinary drink will do. Anyone can spend money, but to assemble something like this, another of the high peaks of the Punch-maker's art, speaks of true love. (If you do make it, the gamesman in me suggests you display the recipe on a placard by the Punch bowl to, uh, satisfy the curious.)

THE ORIGINAL FORMULA

Extract the juice from the rind of three lemons, by rubbing loaf sugar on them. The peeling of two Seville oranges and two lemons, cut extremely thin. The juice of four Seville oranges and ten lemons. Six glasses of calves-foot jelly in a liquid state. The above to be put into a jug, and stirred well together. Pour two quarts of boiling water on the mixture, cover the jug closely, and place it near the fire for a quarter of an hour. Then strain the liquid through a sieve into a punch bowl or jug, sweeten it with a bottle of capillaire, and add half a pint of white wine, a pint of French brandy, a pint of Jamaica rum, and a bottle of orange shrub; the mixture to be stirred as the spirits are poured in. If not sufficiently sweet, add loaf sugar gradually in small quantities, or a spoonful or two of capillaire. To be served either hot or cold.* The Oxford Punch, when made with half the quantity of spirituous liquors and placed in an ice tub for a short time, is a pleasant summer beverage.

In making this Punch, limes are sometimes used instead of lemons, but they are by no means so wholesome.**

* Ignorant servants and waiters sometimes put oxalic acid into Punch to give it flavour; such a practice cannot be too severely censured.

** Arbuthnot, in his work on ailments, says "the West India dry gripes are occasioned by lime juice in Punch."

SOURCE: [Richard Cook], *Oxford Night Caps*, 1827

NOTES

With one or two modifications, the basic procedure here is sound. Begin with an oleo-saccharum of five lemons, two

Seville oranges and ½ cup white sugar; don't worry about including the peels in the initial jugging of the jelly and the juices—their work is done, and they may be discarded. For the jelly, mix two ¼-ounce packets of gelatin, bloomed in ½ cup cold water as directed on the packet, with 2 cups warm water, and use this in place of the "six [wine-]glasses" the recipe calls for. The wine can be anything, really, as long as it's French, white and reasonably dry. The brandy should be VSOP cognac—again, this is not an everyday recipe—and the rum a Planter's Best type or better. For the capillaire, see Limmer's Gin Punch, in Chapter XV. Clément, the makers of a very fine Martinique rhum agricole, also make and export a very fine orange shrub, which is nothing more than their rum infused with orange peels and a few subtle spices and sweetened with cane syrup; use 16 ounces of that and 8 ounces water. (If you can't find that, make an orange shrub by preparing an oleo-saccharum of 8 ounces demerara sugar and the peel of four Seville oranges, dissolving it in 8 ounces boiling water, adding 12 ounces VS-grade cognac and straining and bottling the result.) These last two ingredients should be added to taste. Remember that the pints here are probably 20-ounce imperial ones (the book came out only a year after the new measures were adopted, so it could go either way). When this is mixed, it should be bottled and promptly refrigerated. If serving it cold, you don't want to spoil the texture by adding ice.

The general quantity here amounts to a little less than a gallon and a half of liquid if Cook was using wine measure, or a little more if they were imperial. If you're going to go to all the trouble of assembling the ingredients, I suggest you double or triple the recipe and really do it up.

YIELD: at least 22 cups.

Punch Jelly

As Gary Regan observes in his modern classic *The Joy of Mixology*, Jell-O shots, although "looked upon by most people as an abomination created by young bartenders in the 1980s, . . . actually date back to at least the mid-1800s." An extension of an Oxford-style Punch with enough gelatin added to make it completely jellify, if that's a word, jellied Punch starts turning up in recipe books in the 1830s, although it may be rather older than that. While more of a curiosity than a full-fledged, working drink, it does have its conceivable uses. As Jerry Thomas noted in 1862, "This preparation is a very agreeable refreshment on a cold night." Careful, though: the professor also very rightly warns that it be used in moderation, as "the strength of the punch is so artfully concealed by its admixture with the gelatine, that many persons, particularly of the softer sex, have been tempted to partake so plentifully of it as to render them somewhat unfit for waltzing or quadrilling after supper." I would be particularly wary of the quadrilling.

THE ORIGINAL FORMULA

Make a good bowl of punch. . . . To every pint of punch add an ounce and a half of isinglass, dissolved in a quarter pint of water (about half a tumbler full); pour this into the punch whilst still quite hot, and then fill your moulds, taking care they are not disturbed until the jelly is completely set.

SOURCE: Jerry Thomas, *Bar-Tenders Guide*, 1862

NOTES

You can turn most any Punch into Punch Jelly, but you'll have to leave out some of the water, watch the citrus (acid keeps the gelatin from setting, so if it's a citrusy Punch, try using two-thirds of the normal quantity) and, as Mr. Regan suggests, add more sugar; sugars help the gelatin to set and give it flavor. For the gelatin, the regular calf's-foot kind works just fine and is a hell of a lot easier to find than isinglass. To incorporate it, for every pint of Punch the original recipe makes, omit 1 cup water from the recipe. Once you have prepared the punch base thus, dissolve as many ¼-ounce packets of gelatin in as many cups of hot water as you have omitted from the recipe (make sure to bloom them first in 2 ounces cold water each), stir to activate and then stir in the Punch. Pour it into a Jell-O mold and refrigerate.

I'm particularly fond of this when it's made with the more outré flavors of Punch, such as Islay Scotch or Batavia arrack. A Regent's Punch jelly, though, is truly divine.

XVII

REGENCY PUNCH

Punch not only tastes good, it's good for you—specifically, for your intellectual development:

> There is no stretch of imagination in pouring wine ready
> made from carafe, or barochio, or flask, into a glass—the
> operation is merely mechanical; whereas, among us punch
> drinkers, the necessity of a nightly manufacture of a
> most intricate kind, calls forth habits of industry and
> forethought—induces a taste for chemical experiment—
> improves us in hygrometry, and many other sciences,—to
> say nothing of the geographical reflections drawn forth by
> the pressure of the lemon, or the Colonial questions, which
> press upon every meditative mind on the appearance of
> white sugar.

Thus the wits of the *Noctes Ambrosianae* in 1829. I don't know if all that chemical experiment and geographical reflection made Punch-makers more intellectual in general, but it certainly did make their Punches more sophisticated. (Their hygrometry must've been top-notch, what with all that wrestling with the effects of atmospheric humidity on common loaf sugar.) By the end of the eighteenth century, Punch was evolving along strikingly similar lines to the ones the Cocktail is following today. On the one hand, there were the traditionalists: the arrack-drinkers and the Whiskey Punch men. They took their Punch strong and simple, with no funny business and no corner-cutting when it came to the ingredients, either in quantity or quality (in 1820, one New York tavern was so fanatic about what went into its Punch that it only made it with water from the Thames, imported specially from London; Cocktail geekery is nothing new).

On the other hand, there were the modernists, the experimenters. They thought nothing of subjecting the venerable old beverage to tropical fruits, liqueurs, fancy syrups, eaux-de-vie, raisins, berries, herbs and vegetables—"punch made of everything which extravagance could invent," as the decidedly skeptical author of the 1827 novel *The Guards* put it. To some degree, Punch had always been open to a little monkeying with the spirits, the spice, the acid and the sweetener. But modernist Punch-makers took the prismatic approach we've already seen applied on occasion, wherein a single ingredient—for example, the arrack—is treated instead as a subdividable class, and extended it beyond the simple matter of using a combination of brandy and rum for the spirits; lemons and oranges for the souring; nutmeg and cinnamon for the spice; or whey, wine or tea for some of the water. Rather than one or two spirits going into the Punch, there would be three, four, five. The task of sweetening it would be shared by liqueurs and syrups and tropical fruits. Some of those syrups and liqueurs would also do double duty as spices—indeed, more and more emphasis was placed on ingredients that bridged the categories, so that compounding a bowl of Punch became the equivalent of painting a rainbow.

As a part of this, the new school did something nobody but pirates had done before: they seriously attacked the water—the one native ingredient, the thing without which Punch was simply acidulated booze. In traditional Punch, the water simply lay there, providing dilution and nothing else. That would change. As we've seen with Gin Punch, the latest thing was to make that water sparkle, to put it to work. But even that was pedestrian compared to what came next. Why use water at all? Why not replace it with something truly exquisite? Why not use Champagne? Here are four Punches that explore the possibilities enabled by that daring suggestion.

CHAMPAGNE PUNCH

For Punch made with Champagne, we must look to the source of that sportiest of wines. The French have long viewed their neighbors across the Channel with the sort of bemused curiosity due to a minor laboratory experiment that has taken an unanticipated turn. They do things over there, and we're sure they have their reasons, but those are not immediately discernible by rational inquiry. Case in point, the French reaction to Punch: though Frenchmen were among the first to taste it, unlike the Germans or especially the Dutch, they maintained their distance. In 1735, for example, Noël-Antoine Pluche devoted a small section of his *Spectacle de la Nature*, a series of dialogues on natural history for the edification of the young, to what they were drinking in England. Their "liqueur favorite," the Prior informs his friends, is "le ponche," made from "two thirds eau-de-vie and one third water, with sugar, cinnamon, powdered cloves, toasted bread, often egg yolks and milk to thicken it all up."

"Eau-de-vie and milk," says the Chevalier, "there's a strange assortment!" At this, the Prior very sensibly points out that while they might interrogate the English for the way they mix their drinks, the English do the same to the French for the way they make their "ragouts."

Ah, the Count interjects. "But the thing most suspect to me about Punch . . . is the use of the eau-de-vie that's always its base, and which I consider pernicious." He has his reasons, which we don't need to get into. Suffice it for our purposes that they seem to have been shared by the broad run of his countrymen. Not until the end of the eighteenth century did Punch catch on in France. When it did, however, it settled right in. As Louis-Sebastian Mercier wrote in his landmark *Tableau de Paris* in 1788, "we adopted it before the most recent peace with England [i.e., 1783], and it is naturalized among us and served in the public cafés." Not, however, in its unaltered form: in Paris, men and women drank and socialized together, and social drinks had to appeal to both. According to Mercier, though, Parisian women initially rejected the new drink because of the "strong breath" that spirits leave. The solution was to make Punch not with spirits but with "vin de Champagne." Not even the Count could object to that.

At first, this Champagne Punch was controversial. The author of the 1780 *Descriptions des arts et métiers* notes with disapproval that "some gourmets, to better waste the good things in life, mix Champagne in with the arrack, half and half." Waste indeed—in France, Punch was initially a hot drink exclusively. Looking back on that grisly practice, "Turenne," the pseudonymous author of an 1866 French pamphlet on Punch-making, says, "do not speak to me of people who would heat sparkling wines. In every age there have been idiots and blasphemers."

By the time the French rose up and overthrew their kings, queens and courtiers (many of whom were afloat in—if not submerged by—Punch, as the author of a 1785 book of "anecdotes scandaleuses" of Versailles noted), Punch with Champagne appears to have found its footing as a cold drink. Fancy Punches would never be the same; just as gelatin proved to be the ultimate smoothing agent, Champagne was, and still is, the ultimate lightening one.

In this book, I've overused the vocabulary of delight. Here's yet another occasion where it must be quarried. This recipe for a plain Champagne Punch, unfortified by any spirits, is from New York, not Paris. But it's from Jerry Thomas, a member of that city's Sporting Fraternity in the very highest standing, and the world has never known greater devotees of

Champagne than the miscellaneous gamblers, actors, politicians, pugilists, writers and other players who made up that crowd. In short, he may be trusted on the subject. This light, fragrant concoction—as close as the classical art gets to the festive modern food-magazine style of Punch-making—is as pleasing to the palate as it is lovely to the eye.

THE ORIGINAL FORMULA

Champagne Punch. (Per bottle.)

1 quart bottle of wine.

¼ lb. of sugar.

1 orange sliced.

The juice of a lemon.

3 slices of pine-apple.

1 wine-glass of raspberry or strawberry syrup. Ornament with fruits in season, and serve in Champagne goblets.

This can be made in any quantity by observing the proportions of the ingredients as given above. Four bottles of wine make a gallon, and a gallon is generally sufficient for fifteen persons in a mixed party.

SOURCE: Jerry Thomas, *Bar-Tenders Guide*, 1862

NOTES

Dissolve the sugar—2 ounces will do—in the lemon juice first. Remember that a "wine-glass" is 2 ounces. The fruit slices should be thin. If Jerry Thomas was getting bottles of Champagne that contained a full quart, he was very special indeed; otherwise, they were the kind that were called a quart but held approximately 24 ounces. In other words, just use a normal bottle. Thomas and indeed most everybody making

Champagne Punch before the end of the nineteenth century would have used a Champagne that was considerably sweeter than a modern brut. Use the brut anyway. This Punch responds particularly well to being served from a refrigerated bowl. Otherwise, use a large block of ice. Dilution here is neither necessary nor desirable.

Punch à la Romaine, or Roman Punch

Simple Champagne Punch was only the beginning. Once the Parisians decided that they liked Punch, that they liked it with Champagne and that they liked it even better when there was just a little rum, brandy or kirschwasser in there, too, and maybe even a splash of one of the more delicate liqueurs, it didn't take them long to establish that they liked their Punch best of all when made by Italians, or at the very least with Italian know-how. The Italians in general and Neapolitans and Sicilians in particular had spent generations perfecting the art of making iced sherbets chilled with the snow that lingered year-round in sections of the Italian peninsula's mountainous spine—delicate, refreshing things that were between water and snow in texture and nectar and ambrosia in flavor. Italian confectioners had been established in Paris since the late 1600s; by the end of the next century, they had plenty of domestic competition, although there was still room for an enterprising young Neapolitan who knew his ice-making.

It was these "limonadiers," or lemonade sellers, who provided the first real haven for Punch in Paris. According to Mercier, by 1788 it had become one of their specialties.

I don't know who the first person was to cross one of the Italian-style "water-ices," which were only rarely alcoholic and then lightly so at most, with Champagne Punch, but it was a truly inspired mashup. It wasn't just a question of temperature: the limonadiers had learned to lighten and smooth out the texture of their ices with beaten-in meringue, and the addition of alcohol did nothing to harm that process.

The Parisians, anyway, must have believed one of the Italians was responsible for this new hybrid, for they named it Punch à

la Romaine—"Roman Punch."[1] In 1808, it was known
widely enough for a recipe to be included in a Swedish
cookbook. By 1810, Parisian cafés such as the Jardin Turc
and Tortoni's, run by a young Neapolitan, were doing
turnaway business in it. Anyone who visited the City of
Lights had to try the new Punch. There being no better way
to make something fashionable in London than to make it
fashionable in Paris, before long Roman Punch was well
enough known across the Channel for one satirist to score
capital against the notoriously dissipated prince regent by
having him exclaim, "Oh Roman Punch! Oh potent Curacoa! /
Oh Mareschino! O Mareschino! / Delicious drams!" That was
in 1813. It's possible, however, that the idea of the Punch-
flavored water ice came from Italy directly. When Byron
found the Venetians chilling their Punch only three years
later, he wrote to his friend Thomas Moore that they thought
this an English custom—that is, not a French one—and that
he would not disabuse them from that notion. Whatever its
real origin, though, the English considered it French and
argued about it accordingly. For some, it was the height of
refinement; for others, of decadence. Whichever it was,
everybody knew it—indeed, when one writer snarked on the
people of Bath for never having heard of it, as the *Album*
claimed in 1825, "several letters to the editors of the Bath
papers have been written, and one long pamphlet, stating that
the several authors had very often heard of Punch à la
Romaine, though only one asserted that he had ever tasted
it." Ouch.

Eventually, even the Americans came to learn of Roman
Punch, or at least the ones who lived in New York, at which
point a Londoner could no longer consider it truly fashionable.

---

1 One story of its origin that later circulated fairly extensively involved the pope's
private chef, the Empress Josephine, a Livonian prince and the prince regent. Romantic as it is, it is alas pure horseshit.

On both sides of the Atlantic, it settled into a comfortable existence as the sort of thing that would be laid before a cotillion of respectable people from good families in lieu of alcohol. Recipes multiplied, many straying far indeed from the exacting standards of the Italo-Parisian limonadiers. There are literally dozens from the first half of the nineteenth century, at all levels of complexity and strength. The variation in the latter has much to do, I suspect, with the fact that Jamaican rum is so very alluringly cheaper than French Champagne and enough more potent that if you give people a nice, slushy Punch made with it, sooner or later they're going to stop worrying that you're lowballing them on cost-per-guest.

I've provided two recipes: the easy way and the hard way. The easy way comes from P. C. Robert, a French chef and restaurateur (he founded the famous Tourne-Bride, in Romainville, just outside of Paris) who, when he was in the employ of the ambassador to England, must've made the stuff on a near-daily basis. The hard way comes from the immortal Charles Ranhofer, for over thirty years the head chef at Delmonico's, the greatest restaurant America has ever known. And hard it is: Ranhofer was the professional's professional, and his Punch à la Romaine is not something for a rakish young bachelor to whip together for a whist-party. It sure as hell is impressive, though. Oohs will be oohed, aahs aahed.

THE ORIGINAL FORMULA—THE EASY WAY (TRANSLATED)

Clarify a *livre* and a half [750 grams] sugar, add the [grated] zest of 2 lemons and 2 Seville oranges and the juice of 8 lemons. Add ½ liter of water to this mixture, pass it through a new, fine strainer and freeze it. Then beat the whites of 3 eggs into stiff peaks, which you will not incorporate into your Punch until the moment of service, adding then a glass of Champagne and a half-glass of rum. The compound being completed, serve this Punch in stemmed glasses.

SOURCE: P. C. Robert, *La grande cuisine simplifiée*, 1845 (for the original text, see the appendix)

NOTES

Modern sugar doesn't need clarifying. Stir 3 cups sugar and 1 pint water together over a low heat until sugar has dissolved. A *"verre"* (see the appendix), or "glass," was, as far as I can determine, 6 ounces. The rum should actually be a "rhum"— an old agricole one from Martinique (the Rhum J.M VSOP is a particular favorite). To freeze this, you'll need an ice-cream maker, which will set you back about thirty dollars.

YIELD: 6 cups.

THE ORIGINAL FORMULA—THE HARD WAY

(3515). Roman Punch (Punch à la Romaine).

This is made with one quart of lemon water ice (No. 3604) well worked in a freezer packed in ice; add to it a little citron peel or extract; the composition should be put in a rather large freezer to allow two Italian meringue egg-whites (No. 140) to be incorporated; it should first be added slowly in small quantities; working it well with the spatula to have it acquire much lightness, then add two gills of rum and a quarter of a bottleful of Champagne; work it well and detach from the sides of the freezer. The rum should be poured in gradually, as well as any kind of spirits in different punches; continue until sufficient be added to suit the taste. It is almost impossible to designate the exact quantity, that depending on the quality of the ingredients composing the punch; generally, the liquors are only put in just when serving. The punch should be sufficiently liquid to be drank without using spoons and as soon as served. Serve the punch in upright glasses provided with handles. This is sufficient for twelve persons.

SOURCE: Charles Ranhofer, *The Epicurean*, 1893

SUGGESTED PROCEDURE

Clearly, this will take a little explication. Let's take it in steps.

Step 1: Lemon Water Ice. Prepare an oleo-saccharum with 1½ cups superfine sugar and the peel of four lemons. Stir in 1 cup lemon juice, strain out the peels and add enough water to make 1 quart liquid. Put this in an ice-cream maker (see notes on page 230) and freeze loosely.

Step 2: Italian Meringue Egg Whites. In a nonreactive bowl, beat two egg whites to stiff peaks; reserve. Put ¾ cup sugar and 3 ounces water in a small pot and bring them to a low boil, stirring frequently, and heat it until it reaches 236–238 degrees F (the "small ball" stage); you'll need a candy thermometer for this. Pour this syrup in a slow, narrow stream into your egg whites, folding it in as you go. When it is all incorporated, stir some more until all is smooth.

Step 3: Assembly. Slowly incorporate the egg whites into the water ice while it's still in the ice-cream maker, stirring gently. Then slowly add 8 ounces rum and 6 to 8 ounces Champagne, also stirring. Your Punch is done. Serve in Champagne coupes.

NOTES

For the rum, you'll want at least a Planter's Best type, if not a Stiggins's Delight. Whatever you use, it should be rich and smoooooth.

REGENT'S PUNCH

There's something about the title that drives men a little off the rails. Prince of Wales. It sounds like you're really in charge of something, but in point of fact you're not. Your whole job is to wait until your father—or mother—either dies or becomes too feeble to wear the crown, and until then you will be eyed with deep suspicion by that parent and all who are allied to him or her. At the same time, you will be surrounded by people who will do everything in their power to make sure you get anything you want, with the expectation that one day they will be the ones giving some future Prince of Wales the fish-eye. It's a hell of a job. Some hold up pretty well; others are like George Augustus Frederick, first son of George III.

Sure, it couldn't have helped his disposition any that his father kept going mad, only to snap back into a precarious sanity just when it looked like the prince would get all the cake. Nobody likes to be teased. But did the prince have to be such a swine? The bigamy, the gluttony, the alcoholism, the pettiness and intrigue—an account of the Regency, when they finally let him run things in his father's place, and his later reign as George IV makes for pretty gamy reading. He did, though, have one redeeming quality: he had taste. He was unusually sound on art, on poetry, on architecture (although his rococo oriental-themed "Pavilion" at Brighton was a bit of a misstep), not so much on women, but definitely on food and drink. He knew his wines. He knew his brandies. And he definitely knew his Punches.

Regent's Punch, the formula he had made for himself and his guests on social occasions, was, as one might expect, on the elaborate side. Rather than the canonical five ingredients, it had ten. But while it was as rich and luxurious as one could imagine, it was also balanced and lively. Once people tried it, they wanted more—sometimes to their detriment. The formula's drawbacks were already well known in 1818, three years after it first appears in print. A satirical 1818 London "Diary of a Dandy" summarizes them neatly: "Saturday—rose at twelve, with a d——d headache. *Mem.* Not to drink the Regent's Punch after supper.—The green tea keeps one awake."

Unfortunately for the mixographer, with all "the mad delirious dizziness which follows the delightful excitation of mingled Champagne, green tea, and Eau de Garusse, in the Regent's punch," as John Gibson Lockhart quite accurately described its effects, nobody remembered to record for posterity the moment of the Punch's creation (and no, I don't know what "Eau de Garusse" is either). Captain Gronow recalled that the Punch was "made from a recipe by his *maitre d'hotel*, Mr Maddison," but it's possible that the prince regent himself had a hand in it; he was known to meddle with his potables.

Whoever invented it knew what he was about, although Regent's Punch was not groundbreaking per se, if one may speak of a mixed drink in such terms. The combination of arrack and tea dated to the reign of the prince's grandfather or great-grandfather, if not all the way back to East India Company days,[2] and it was in fact standard in the version of Punch that was causing such a sensation in Paris. The use of liqueurs and syrups was another Parisian limonadier's specialty. What Regent's Punch contributes to the art of mixing drinks isn't novelty, it's taste. Whoever first compounded it took the best ideas of the old English and

---

2 To cite one example among many, the 1756 novel *The Life and Memoirs of Mr. Ephraim Tristram Bates*, which influenced Sterne's *Tristram Shandy*, has people at one point drinking bottled "Arrack Punch made with Green-tea."

new French traditions and wove them together seamlessly into a complex, admittedly fancy Punch that was nonetheless heady and utterly intoxicating, without any of the technical challenges of Punch à la Romaine. It is another of the noble few that will be found relaxing in elegant leisure on Punch's version of Olympus.

Before long, like most appurtenances of the British high life, Regent's Punch was in common use in New York. Edgar Allan Poe's *Gentleman's Magazine* observed in 1839 that it was "long the fashionable tipple at the symposiums of the *elite*," and that was true whichever side of the Atlantic you were on. It didn't hurt that the Yankees had a Tory streak a mile wide and lapped up the royals and their doings like Devonshire cream.

Regent's Punch maintained some presence in the consciousness of the elegant drinker through the end of the century, making it into a number of the more modern bar guides, if by no means all. But even then, the formulae were degenerate, and like most drinks of its size and complexity, it quietly expired sometime between the Wright Brothers and Sarajevo. Oddly enough, one of its last redoubts was Albany, New York, where it was the traditional banquet-tipple of the state legislature. (Those were the days.)

The recipes for Regent's Punch are many and varied, a situation in which authenticity is difficult to establish. Fortunately, there are two that each have what is known in Qur'anic studies as an "isnad," a chain of oral transmission linking them to the Prophet, or in this case the Prince. One of them comes from William Terrington's 1869 *Cooling Cups and Dainty Drinks*, in which Terrington labels it "original." As he credits it to "P. Watier, Royal Lodge, 1820" and a Watier— J.-B., not P., but you can't have everything—had in fact been the prince's private chef and had for a time run a gambling club with a Madison (he was listed then as the prince's page, not maître d'hôtel), he may very well be correct. The other was published in 1845, in *Modern Cookery for Private Families* by Eliza Acton, who says she got it from "a person who made the punch daily for the prince's table, at Carlton palace, for six months" and that "it . . . may be relied on." Between these, which differ only in detail, we're about as close as mixology gets to a certified pedigree. Rather than my usual procedure, I'll recognize Regent's Punch as a special case and present both, followed by my attempt to harmonize them.

ORIGINAL FORMULA #1

Punch à la Regent, by P. Watier, Royal Lodge, 1820: original.

—Take 4 oz. of clarified sugar, thin peel of 1 lemon and 1 Seville orange, 1 bottle of dry Champagne, ½ bottle of white brandy, ½ gill of rum, ½ gill of arrack, ½ gill of pineapple syrup, 1 wine-glass of Maraschino; pour 1 quart of boiling water over 2 teaspoonfuls of green tea; let it stand five minutes; strain, and mix with other ingredients; pass through a sieve; let it remain in ice 30 minutes.

SOURCE: William J. Terrington, *Cooling Cups and Dainty Drinks*, 1869

ORIGINAL FORMULA #2

The Regent's, or George The Fourth's, Punch.

Pare as thin as possible the rinds of two China oranges, of two lemons, and of one Seville orange, and infuse them for an hour in half a pint of thin cold syrup; then add to them the juice of the fruit. Make a pint of strong green tea, sweeten it well with fine sugar, and when it is quite cold, add it to the fruit and syrup, with a glass of the best old Jamaica rum, a glass of brandy, one of arrack, one of pine-apple syrup, and two bottles of Champagne; pass the whole through a fine lawn sieve until it is perfectly clear, then bottle and put it into ice until dinner is served. We are indebted for this receipt to a person who made the punch daily for the prince's table, at Carlton palace, for six months; it has been in our possession some years, and may be relied on.

SOURCE: Eliza Acton, *Modern Cookery for Private Families*, 1845

When all is considered and thoroughly digested, we end up with something like this:

SUGGESTED PROCEDURE

Prepare an oleo-saccharum of the peel of two lemons, two small sweet oranges, one Seville orange and 4 ounces white sugar.

Make 1 pint green tea (using two tea bags or 2 teaspoons of loose tea). Let it steep five minutes and then strain it into the bowl with the oleo-saccharum, stirring until the sugar has dissolved.

Juice the lemons and the oranges into the bowl, stir well and then strain everything into a sealable gallon jug, pressing the peels and pulp well to extract every drop of essence.

Add 8 ounces VSOP-grade cognac, 2 ounces Jamaican rum, 2 ounces Batavia arrack and 2 ounces maraschino liqueur or pineapple syrup.

Cover the jug and refrigerate for an hour or two.

To serve, pour into a bowl and gently stir in two bottles of brut Champagne. Your punch is completed. Now smile.

NOTES

Terrington's "white brandy" is made only by Hennessy these days, and it is only available in France or in duty-free shops; if adventurous, you might want to try a good, smooth pisco. For the rum, we must assume that the prince had access to the oldest, mellowest London dock Jamaica; I like a mix of one part Smith & Cross and three parts of the nectarous Angostura 1919—here the rum must be suave as well as fragrant. If using maraschino, use Luxardo (the prince *loved* maraschino). The easiest way to make pineapple syrup is to prepare a rich simple syrup by stirring 4 cups demerara sugar into 2 cups water over low heat until the sugar is dissolved, letting this syrup cool, adding a pineapple cut up into half-inch chunks and letting it sit overnight. When strained, it will keep refrigerated for at least a week. If this Punch looks like it will be sitting around for a while, it's a good idea to refrigerate the bowl, or at least add a large block of ice. The historical record holds a great many variations, but many of them bear the marks of economy or expediency and can therefore be ignored. One ingredient that does come up early and often is "bloom raisins," which were made from sweet grapes from Málaga, Spain. These are steeped in the Punch and then strained out. Worth a try. Use a pound.

YIELD: 10 cups.

XVIII

AMERICAN FANCY PUNCH

America's early contributions to mixology have already been ably detailed by the likes of William Grimes, Gary Regan and Ted Haigh, and I took my own shot at it in *Imbibe!* In other words, I shall not dwell on them in detail. Besides, America's greatest innovation in the art of compounding Punch was to greatly extend James Ashley's work in applying the technologies of miniaturization and just-in-time production to the process, turning it from a large-bore social drink to an on-the-fly statement of individual desire—and, in the process, putting an end to its rule.

We did do one thing right, anyway. Even the most reactionary English bowl-scourer would have agreed that a tiff of iced Punch on a hot day was a welcome thing. It's unclear exactly when ice and Punch first met, but it probably happened long before the Tortonis and Mr. Maddisons did their work—England had a small but long-standing tradition of ice-cooled drinks. In 1666, for example, we find Pepys recording that metheglin is a "most brave drink cooled in ice." In England, however, ice was hard to get and expensive: private icehouses existed on the great estates, but in the metropolis, the water was too dirty and the freezing too spotty to support an extensive industry. In America, though, there was no shortage of ice whatsoever, at least not in New England and what was then the Northwest. Winters were long and cold, and the water was clean. It was only a matter of time that we began using it on a scale that only we could afford.

John Neal's satirical 1825 Revolutionary War novel, *Brother Jonathan*, has someone drinking "ice punch," but Neal wasn't born until 1793, and his book contains other imbiblical (to coin a word) anachronisms, so it must be taken with a very large grain of salt. Not so the 1806 advertisement from the New York *American Citizen* for a new ice company, which includes the (no doubt true) statement that "of latter years the Water in the Collect [the Lower Manhattan pond where ice was normally harvested] has been in a putrid state, to make the Ice unfit to be made use of in Liquors." This suggests that iced drinks had been in use for some time, and if so, it's inconceivable that Punch wasn't among them. At any rate, William Dunlap, in his *Thirty Years Ago, or The Memoirs of a Water Drinker* (1836), describes young sports at Cato's tavern drinking "iced punch" from a bowl, right around that same time. This, however, was one of the last appearances of the communal bowl in the wild; soon it would only be found in captivity: in clubhouses, meeting rooms and parlors, not in barrooms, lodgings and mess halls.

Once we had removed the bowl of Punch from its employment as a day-to-day drink, we started tinkering with it to fit its new role. For one thing, there was less impetus to restrict the strength at which it was brewed; special occasions grant special license. Instead of being artificial wines, American Punches began looking suspiciously like giant Sours, Fizzes and Cocktails. Whatever dilution was desired would come from melting ice, not additions of "the element." Another thing that goes with special occasions is special ingredients—luxury goods. Our Punches became wholly prismatic affairs, with fantastic assortments of rare liquors and fruits, lightened with Champagne and poured over lavish beds of diamond-pure cracked ice.

In New York City, the natural consequences of this tinkering were on display for all to see every January first, which was celebrated with the New Year's call. This was an old Dutch custom whereby gentlemen would go around to all their friends' houses on New Year's Day, salute their womenfolk, take a glass from the bowl that decorated the sideboard, and move on to the next. Invariably, with the strength of the Punches served, a significant proportion of the city's bourgeoisie would be drunk as boiled owls by the end of the day. The custom hung on, albeit somewhat precariously, well into the last half of the nineteenth century.

For one person, anyway, it would have been better had it died out a little sooner. In 1877, James Gordon Bennett Jr., publisher of the *New York Herald*, made his last New Year's call ever at the house of his fiancée, Miss May. It wasn't his first, or even his tenth, of the day, and for reasons that have never been otherwise explained, he made himself a little too much at home by whipping it out in front of the ladies and pissing into the living-room fireplace—or maybe it was the piano; accounts differ. Three days later, her brother horsewhipped him outside the Union Club. A duel was fought, down in Maryland. Three times they both fired; three times they both missed, perhaps deliberately. Their seconds decided that honor was satisfied, but soon afterward Bennett left for Paris, never to return. The New Year's call didn't last much after that—not because of the Bennett affair, although that didn't help, but because the city was getting just too damned big for drunk people to get around in safety.

Here are nine quick looks at Punch, American style, any one of which will make for a memorable New Year's Day.

Philadelphia Fish-House Punch

Having written about this, the most enduringly famous of American Punches, in both *Esquire Drinks* and *Imbibe!*, I wasn't planning to do so here. But writing a book about Punch without including it just didn't feel right. As I was pondering that, a reader of *Imbibe!* fortuitously sent me a newspaper article she had come across with the oldest recipe for this foundational American drink yet discovered. It dates from 1795, if we are to believe the Philadelphia *Telegraph*, which found it sandwiched between the leaves of a history of what is now America's oldest club in the library of a noted local bibliophile. It agrees in every major detail, anyway, with the one Jerry Thomas printed from Charles Godfrey Leland, a Philadelphia lawyer who was a member, or "citizen," of "the State in Schuylkill," the Philadelphia fishing club responsible for unleashing it upon the world.

THE ORIGINAL FORMULA

An interesting little volume, also, is the Memoirs of the Schuylkill Fishing Club. . . . Many original papers are sandwiched between the leaves, giving accounts of some of the club's jubilations, and containing a written recipe for punch, as follows:

To 1 pint of lemon or lime juice add

3 pints of mixture given below.

10 pints of water.

4 pounds of best loaf sugar.

When ice is put in use less water.

THE MIXTURE

½ pint Jamaica rum.

¼ pint Cognac brandy.

¼ pint best peach brandy.

The receipt is dated 1795.

SOURCE: Philadelphia *Telegraph*, 1880

NOTES

Begin by dissolving the sugar (1 pound should do, unless you like your Punch very sweet) in the lemon or lime juice (by Leland's day, lemon had become the orthodox souring). An oleo-saccharum is also not a bad idea here; use the peel of twelve lemons. In *Imbibe!* I spilled a fair amount of ink lamenting the loss of various old-time ingredients and coming up with kludges to work around their absence. Since then, we have been graced with such revenants as Batavia arrack, Hollands, Old Tom gin, real absinthe, crème de violette and one or two others that I'm forgetting. So I will not despair about the loss of peach brandy, an eau-de-vie of peaches distilled on the crushed pits and then left alone to slumber in oaken barrels. For many years, it was the most prized spirit in America, judging from the prices it brought. The last commercial distiller I know of to make it in any quantity was Lem Motlow. If you can't place the name, consult the label of a bottle of Jack Daniel's. He only stopped making it in the 1940s, so who knows, there might be a bottle of it floating around somewhere. Good luck. Or you can keep an eye on the microdistillers. There's already one version—Kuchan, from California—and it ain't bad. As for kludges: I like 3 ounces bonded applejack and 1 ounce good, imported peach liqueur. Serve iced; 7 pints of water should be enough.

YIELD: at least 25 cups.

Quoit Club Punch

The thirty members of the Richmond, Virginia, Quoit Club, founded in 1788, met every other Saturday from May until October "under the shade of some fine oaks," as one visitor recalled, at Buchanan's Spring, right outside of town. There they would throw the heavy, ringlike quoits at posts, eat barbecue and drink themselves silly on Mint Julep, Toddy and this, the club's Punch, which was prepared with great skill by Jasper Crouch, their black cook.

The club's most famous member was one of its founders, John Marshall, chief justice of the United States Supreme Court from 1801 until his death in 1835, the longest tenure in the court's history. For a great man, Marshall retained a sense of humor. As the story goes, on his watch the court cut down on the convivial tippling that had been such a part of colonial public life to the point that the justices only allowed themselves wine when the weather was wet. But, as Joseph Story, one of his fellow justices, used to recount,

> it does sometimes happen that the Chief Justice will say to me, when the cloth is removed, "Brother Story, step to the window and see if it does not look like rain." And if I tell him that the sun is shining brightly, Judge Marshall will sometimes reply, "All the better, for our jurisdiction extends over so large a territory that the doctrine of chances makes it certain that it must be raining somewhere."

Now *that's* legal reasoning.

The following recipe for the punch used I got from an old Virginia gentleman: lemons, brandy, rum, madeira, poured into a bowl one-third filled with ice (no water), and sweetened. This same recipe was used by the Richmond Light Infantry Blues, an organization that covered itself with glory during our Civil War. The Blues served this punch for years in a handsome India china bowl which held thirty-two gallons and which they greatly mourned when it was lost when the Spotswood Hotel burned on Christmas Eve, 1870.

SOURCE: Sallie E. Marshall Hardy, "John Marshall, Third Chief Justice of the United States, as Son, Brother, Husband and Friend" in *The Green Bag*, December 1896

SUGGESTED PROCEDURE

Prepare an oleo-saccharum of the peel of twelve lemons and 2 cups of light, fine-grained raw sugar. Add 16 ounces of strained lemon juice and stir until sugar has dissolved. Add one 750-milliliter bottle each of Jamaican rum, VSOP cognac and rainwater Madeira. Stir well and pour into Punch bowl filled a third of the way with ice cubes. Stir and let sit in cool place for twenty minutes before serving.

NOTES

Do not operate heavy machinery or make constitutional law after consuming this. For the rum, I like something in the Planter's Best line here, with just maybe a dollop of Pirate Juice to spark it up.

YIELD: 12 cups.

DANIEL WEBSTER'S PUNCH

In my mind, I can't divorce the Daniel Webster of history, the great Massachusetts senator, the orator, the statesman, from the Daniel Webster of the movies, the one played by Edward Arnold in William Dieterle's 1941 version of Stephen Vincent Benét's sardonic fable "The Devil and Daniel Webster." As played by Arnold, he's a bluff, jovial sort, a social man who knows how to get along with the people, and yet he has quiet, watchful eyes and the native shrewdness to know bullshit when he sees it, no matter how many flowers are growing out of it. Actually, in this case, fiction and history pretty much agree.

As part of that joviality, Webster did nothing to combat a reputation for liking to take a drink now and then. But while he might have forgotten himself from time to time, he seems to have been one of those drinkers who will sip from the glass and expound on the nectar within, only to set it quietly aside when the conversation has moved on. That makes me somewhat suspect the authenticity of this recipe for Punch, labeled as "Daniel Webster's" by the author of a New York bartender's book published in 1869, seventeen years after Webster's death. The anonymous mixographer adds the following introduction:

> If the god-like Daniel cared nothing for riches he did love a good punch, and he knew how to concoct a drink fit for gods. Sometime before his death, he gave his old life long friend, Major Brooks, of Boston, his benefaction and blessing, and left him, as the last earthly good he could bestow, the following recipe for what is now known here among the elect, as the Webster punch.

Well, perhaps. But there were other Webster Punches in circulation, including one whose reputed composition sounds suspiciously like Regent's Punch. Indeed, for a while there, in the middle of the century, the demand for a glass of Daniel Webster's Punch seems to have been a common way of playing "stump the bartender." Could it be that Webster was quite willing to let folks *think* he had a special way of making Punch, without going to all the trouble of actually having one? With that caveat, it must be admitted that this recipe makes just the kind of Punch that Webster, who was not averse to a little luxury in life, would have sipped with genuine enthusiasm.

THE ORIGINAL FORMULA

One bottle of pure old French brandy (smuggled direct preferred), one bottle sherry, one ditto old Jamaica rum, two ditto claret, one ditto Champagne, one dozen lemons, one pint strong tea, sugar, strawberries, and pineapple to suit the taste, plenty of ice, no water.

SOURCE: *Steward & Barkeeper's Manual*, 1869

SUGGESTED PROCEDURE

Prepare an oleo-saccharum of the peel of twelve lemons and 2 cups light raw sugar, such as Florida Crystals. Add 1 pint lemon juice and 1 pint black tea, made with 2 teaspoons loose black tea or two tea bags and steeped for ten minutes. Stir to dissolve sugar and strain into sealable two-gallon jug. Add one 750-milliliter bottle each of cognac, oloroso sherry and Jamaican rum; two 750-milliliter bottles of Bordeaux; 1 pineapple peeled, cored and cut into half-inch slices and a 1-pint box of cored strawberries. Refrigerate for an hour and serve by pouring into a two-gallon bowl three-quarters full of ice cubes and topping off with a bottle of chilled brut Champagne.

NOTES

For the cognac, use the best you can afford. An XO would not be out of place here. The oloroso sherry should be of the medium variety, but not too lush. For the rum, see the notes for Quoit Club Punch on page 244. The wine doesn't have to be from Bordeaux, but it does have to be dry, red and rich. Nutmeg on top of the finished Punch is a kindness.

Chatham Artillery Punch—
Original

One of the three recipes for bowl-sized Punches I included in *Imbibe!* was a version of this, formerly Savannah's favorite way of putting visitors in their place. The 1907 recipe I printed for it, while a good one, came with an acknowledgment that back when the Chatham Artillery first made it, "its vigor . . . was much greater than at present, experience having taught the rising generation to modify the receipt of their forefathers to conform to the weaker constitutions of their progeny." I always hate to print a weaker recipe when a stronger one exists or, with exceptions, a newer one when there's an older one.

I was therefore very pleased, some weeks after that book was published, to come across a little item in the *Augusta (Georgia) Chronicle* recounting the origins and original composition of this particular piece of ordnance. "Its history is this," the article explains:

> back in the fifties the Republican Blues, which were organized in 1808, visited Macon and were welcomed back by the Chatham Artillery. Mr. A. H. Luce, since dead, proposed to brew a new punch in honor of the Blues. Mr. William Davidson furnished the spirits.

Note that the Republican Blues here are the Savannah ones, not the Richmond ones with the gargantuan bowls of Quoit Club Punch. It must've been fun to be in one of those regiments, in peacetime, anyway. The Punch as originally made is utterly devastating. I can vouch for that, having now made it many times. To quote the *Chronicle*, "As a vanquisher of men its equal has never been found."

THE ORIGINAL FORMULA

The concoction was thus made: One of the horse buckets of ordinary size was filled with finely crushed ice; a quart of good brandy, whisky and rum each was poured into the ice, and sugar and lemon added. The bucket was filled to the brim with Champagne, and the whole stirred into delirious deliciousness. Rumor hath it every solitary man of the Blues was put under the table by this deceiving, diabolical and most delightful compound.

SOURCE: The *Augusta Chronicle*, quoted in the *San Antonio Light*, 1885

SUGGESTED PROCEDURE

Prepare an oleo-saccharum of the peel of twelve lemons and 2 cups light raw sugar, such as Florida Crystals. Add 1 pint lemon juice, stir to dissolve sugar and strain into an empty 750-milliliter bottle. Add water to fill any remaining space in bottle, seal and refrigerate. To serve, fill a horse bucket of ordinary size or a two-and-a-half-gallon Punch bowl with crushed or finely cracked ice, pour in bottled shrub and add one 750-milliliter bottle each of VSOP cognac, bourbon whiskey and Jamaican-style rum. Top off with three bottles of chilled brut Champagne. Stir. Then smile.

NOTES
There's little to say here beyond use good bourbon and real Champagne and make sure that the rum has some bouquet to it, but not too much—Planter's Best rather than Pirate Juice. Round up the usual suspects.

FRANK FORESTER'S PUNCH

To me there are few more poignant stories in the history of American letters than that of Frank Forester. In part, it has to do with the details of his life. Like me, he was a journeyman writer with a literary background, earning his living by doggedly pursuing a nonliterary genre. Like me, he liked good food, good drink and good company. But he died by his own hand, shunned by his editors, his friends and his family, in the house he never completed, in—worst of all—Newark.

But if I do not envy his fate, I do envy his skill. Henry William Herbert, to give his real name, was born in England to the clergyman son of a lord, educated at Eton and Cambridge, and exiled to America by his family when he couldn't pay his considerable debts. Once here, he supported himself by writing anything he could get paid for. He finally hit his stride when, as "Frank Forester," he took to writing about hunting and fishing. His best novels, *The Deerstalkers*, *My Shooting Box* and *The Warwick Woodlands*, are set in the parts of New Jersey and lower New York State that are now covered by malls, tract "homes," Outback Steakhouses and tight-meshed, strangling strands of blacktop. In his day, they were game-filled uplands, not virgin forest but not yet tainted either, and he captured their beauty as no one has. To read his description of the "defile through which the Ramapo, one of the loveliest streams eye ever looked upon, comes rippling with its crystal waters over bright pebbles, on its way to join the two kindred rivulets which form the fair Passaic" is to weep for what we have done. Today, the Ramapo meets the Passaic a half mile north of Route 80, near the Willowbrook Mall.

Perhaps Forester devoted himself too much to the bottle. Indeed, his works slosh with old Ferintosh Scotch whiskey,

good cognac, Holland gin, Jersey applejack and lots and lots
of fine Champagne, always described in loving detail. But
these potables were always consumed with a conviviality that,
by the end, he must have yearned for more than anything in
the world.

That conviviality is on full display here, as Forester's
recurring character Henry Archer makes a version of
Regent's Punch for the author's fictional alter ego and
namesake (both Englishmen) and Tom Draw, the Jerry
Thomas–like New Jersey tavern-keeper who served as the
token American in Forester's fantasy world of sport and
homosocial good cheer.

THE ORIGINAL FORMULA

"It is directly contrary to my rule, Frank, to drink before
a good day's shooting—and a good day I mean to have
to-morrow!—but I am thirsty, and the least thought chilly;
so here goes for a debauch! Tim, look in my box with the
clothes, and you will find two flasks of curaçao; bring them
down, and a dozen lemons, and some lump sugar—look alive!
and you, Tom, out with your best brandy; I'll make a jorum
that will open your eyes tight before you've done with it.
That's right, Tim; now get the soup tureen, the biggest one,
and see that it's clean. . . . [B]ring half-a-dozen of Champagne,
a bucket full of ice, and then go down into the kitchen, and
make two quarts of green tea, as strong as possible; and when
it's made set it to cool in the ice-house!"

In a few minutes all the ingredients were at hand; the rind,
peeled carefully from all the lemons, was deposited with
two tumblers full of finely powdered sugar in the bottom
of the tureen; thereupon were poured instantly three pints
of pale old Cognac; and these were left to steep, without
admixture, until Tim Matlock made his entrance with the

cold, strong, green tea; two quarts of this, strained clear, were added to the brandy, and then two flasks of curaçao!

Into this mixture a dozen lumps of clear ice were thrown, and the whole stirred up till the sugar was entirely suspended; then pop! Pop! went the long necks, and their creaming nectar was discharged into the bowl; and, by the body of Bacchus— as the Italians swear—and by his soul too, which he never steeped in such delicious nectar, what a drink that was, when it was completed!

SOURCE: Frank Forester, *The Warwick Woodlands*, 1851

NOTES

Given that a tumbler holds 8 ounces, the only remotely murky things here are the disposition of the peeled lemons and the size of the curaçao flasks. For the former, I say juice 'em, strain 'em and in with the juice. For the latter, well, I know the stuff came in little stoneware flasks, but their precise capacity has eluded me. But maraschino flasks contained a pint—probably a beverage pint, which is 12 ounces—so why not assume that curaçao flasks are the same and pitch in with a 750-milliliter bottle of Grand Marnier? It does no harm, anyway.

YIELD: 36 cups.

YALE COLLEGE PUNCH

In 2007: Trashcan Punch. In 1869: Yale College Punch.
Enough said.

THE ORIGINAL FORMULA

One quart bottle of brandy; 1 pint bottle of Champagne;
two bottles of soda water; 4 tablespoons of powdered sugar;
2 slices pineapple, cut up. Use Champagne goblets. Six Yale
students will get away with the above very cleverly.

SOURCE: *Steward & Barkeeper's Manual,* **1869**

SUGGESTED PROCEDURE

In a bowl, steep 2 half-inch slices of peeled, cored fresh pineapple in
a 750-milliliter bottle of VSOP cognac for an hour or two under
refrigeration. To serve, add 20 ounces soda water and 2 ounces superfine sugar, stirring until the sugar has dissolved, and then add 12
ounces cold Champagne.

NOTES

It bears repeating that a "quart" bottle of wine or spirits
was actually one-sixth of a gallon and a "pint" one-twelfth.
Personally, I hate leaving Champagne to sit around in the
bottle and go flat. When I make this, I pour the rest of the
bottle in.

YIELD: **8 cups.**

LIGHT GUARD PUNCH

The Michigan Light Guard, the Georgia Light Guard, the Lawrence Light Guard, the La Grange Light Guard, the Coldwater Light Guard—if there's one thing America had plenty of in the days before the Civil War, it was Light Guards. Every town that had any pretensions to high society organized one, with fancy uniforms and rich men's sons. But if there's one Light Guard that's probably responsible for this excellent, rather extravagant Punch, it would have to be the "Tigers"—the famous Light Guard of New York. A society outfit through and through, before the war they were tagged by city wits with the line "in peace . . . invincible, in war invisible." But after Fort Sumter, they were (as George Augustus Sala, the peerless observer of midcentury American life, noted) "not mere carpet knights, but distinguished as being among the earliest to volunteer in this monstrous war, on whose fatal fields they have left many a brave member of their corps." In which case, the anonymous so-and-so who rewrote Jerry Thomas's book in 1887 was probably correct when he pointed out, "This is sufficient for a mixed company of twenty, not twenty of the Light Guard."

THE ORIGINAL FORMULA

(For a party of twenty.)

3 bottles of Champagne.

1 bottle of pale sherry.

1 bottle of Cognac.

1 bottle of Sauterne.

1 pineapple, sliced.

4 lemons, sliced.

Sweeten to taste, mix in a punch-bowl, cool with a large lump of ice, and serve immediately.

SOURCE: Jerry Thomas, *Bar-Tenders Guide*, 1862

SUGGESTED PROCEDURE

Steep the lemons and the pineapple in the cognac for three or four hours in the refrigerator. When service is imminent, in a two-gallon Punch bowl dissolve 4 ounces superfine sugar in the sherry and Sauternes, incorporate the cognac and fruit, and add in the block of ice and Champagne (normally I would suggest constructing this in an iced bowl, but this Punch is strong enough that it could use a little dilution from the ice).

NOTES

The pineapple and lemon should both be in thin rings. As usual, it's difficult to prescribe for the sugar; the pineapple adds sweetness, but the Champagne soaks it up. I usually begin with 4 ounces and then adjust from there. For the Sauternes, see Captain Radcliffe's Punch in Chapter XI. For the sherry, use a fino or light amontillado, although white port is an interesting, if more lush, substitute.

USS *Richmond* Punch

The *Richmond* looked like a clipper ship with a stumpy little smokestack sticking up from the middle of its deck. She was a "screw sloop," one of the new, efficient propeller-driven steamboats that were beginning to replace the awkward side-wheel paddleboats of song and story. Christened in 1860, a year before Fort Sumter, she would become one of the Union Navy's most modern ships and consequently sailed wherever the shot was thickest. She had a hole punched in her side by the world's first ironclad warship, the CSS *Manassas*; she helped to take New Orleans; and she stormed Mobile Bay with Admiral Farragut, for which action twenty-seven of her sailors and three of her marines were awarded the Congressional Medal of Honor.

That was not the end of her career: in fact, she would serve until 1917, for a total of fifty-seven years. In 1870, she was flagship of the Mediterranean Squadron; in the 1880s, of the Asiatic Squadron, with ports of call in Yokohama and the like. By then, her half-rotten timbers were a haven to rats and bedbugs, and her stubby eleven-inch smoothbore iron guns were museum pieces, incapable of even denting the armor of the sleek, all-steel battleships of the day, with their turrets full of long, ten-inch rifled guns, a single shot from which could turn her to matchsticks. What kept her afloat?

I like to think it was the Punch. But alas the navy had been officially dry since 1862. So this noble beverage was probably not served on duty or even on board. Of course, that doesn't mean her officers couldn't have cooked up a bowl or two of this descendant of Punch Royal when relaxing ashore. I certainly would have: like its ship, it's a stubborn old-timer hanging on from an earlier age—rich, dark and leathery, and full of charm and worldly experience.

This celebrated punch is made from a stock, which can be kept in bottles, and at any time will produce an excellent punch by the addition of soda-water or Champagne and ice, and is very useful in that it can be prepared on the spur of the moment. In making the stock, care should be used that the tea should not be drawn long enough before using to become bitter. When the stock has been made it should be tightly bottled, and placed in a comparatively cool place. The following is the composition of the stock:

Jamaica rum, 1 quart,

Brandy, 1 quart,

Strong black tea, 1 quart,

Port wine, 1 quart,

Lemons, 12,

White sugar, 3 cups,

Curaçao, ½ pint.

Just before serving add 10 bottles of soda-water to 3 quarts of stock. Use plenty of ice.

SOURCE: Mary Louise Hoyt Barrol, *Around-the-World Cook Book*, 1913

SUGGESTED PROCEDURE

Prepare an oleo-saccharum with the peel of the lemons and the sugar. Stir in 18 ounces of strained lemon juice and the tea (made with 4 teaspoons of loose tea or four bags, infused for no more than five minutes). Add the liquors, strain, bottle and chill. To serve, pour into Punch bowl halfway full of ice cubes and add 1 liter chilled seltzer for every quart of stock.

NOTES

Regarding the rum, this Punch is tough enough to stand up to a full-on Pirate Juice or even a Batavia arrack (in honor of the *Richmond*'s epic Asian cruise); for the brandy, go with a VSOP cognac. A ruby port of not very distinguished pedigree will do fine. For the curaçao, however, you'll want Grand Marnier, or at least Gran Gala. Nutmeg over the top is very welcome here.

If laying your USS *Richmond* Punch down as a "stock" (a term of art in late American Punch-making for an aged mixture of everything but the water or Champagne), it's best to let the sediment settle for a couple of weeks and then siphon off the clear liquid.

BOSTON CLUB PUNCH

The Honest Rainmaker: The Life and Times of Colonel John R. Stingo is A. J. Liebling's great ode to the sporting life. A book-length debriefing of one James A. MacDonald, who as "Col. Stingo" wrote the racing column for the *Enquirer* (at the time a New York paper, not a national one), *The Honest Rainmaker* is a fire hose of old-school palaver, the kind they don't make anymore. Detailing fifty years' worth of wagers, scams, cons, schemes and benders, all executed with impeccable front despite restricted financing, the book out-Runyons Runyon at every turn.

Among the many literary gems the book offers is this awe-inspiring account of the prelunch libations of Dominick O'Malley, editor of the *New Orleans Item* and one of the young MacDonald's first bosses in the newspaper business, back around 1890. (The lunch itself, which Liebling goes on to recount in loving detail, is at Antoine's and on a scale commensurate with the aperitif. It begins with four dozen oysters, carrying on through things like "a red snapper flambee in absinthe," a salmi of woodcock and snipe, a chateaubriand, "*bleu,*" and a whole lot of other stuff too delicious to dwell on.)

Exactly how much Liebling embellished Stingo's recollections and how much truth there was in them in the first place are open questions. In this case, anyway, the details check out: Dominick O'Malley did edit the *Item*; the St. Charles still stood then; you'll find the Sazerac and the Silver Gin Fizz in any historically minded Cocktail book (including, of course, *Imbibe!*); the Boston Club, at the head of Carondelet Street, was indeed the most exclusive in the city; and while Hymen's remains untraced, Fabacher's Rathskeller, at Royal and Iberville, was a popular restaurant that, although it had no bar per se, still did a lively trade in drinks.

The Punch checks out, too, at least from the perspective of mixology. Although fearsomely complex, once assembly is completed, it reveals itself as an elegant, refined and most insinuating tipple that is entirely consistent with the state of the Punch-maker's art in the decades right before Prohibition. It's worth noting that the Boston Club itself (yes, it still exists) lacks the pure-blooded elegance it once had, judging by what it's currently passing off as Boston Club Punch, which is simply a large, watery Bourbon Sour with a few dashes of orange-flower water.

THE ORIGINAL FORMULA

Mr. O'Malley had abandoned his desk at the usual hour of twelve and betaken himself for prandial relaxation first to the bar of the St. Charles Hotel, where he had a three-bagger of Sazeracs, then to Hymen's bar on Common Street, where he increased his apéritif by four silver gin fizzes and after that over to Farbacher's saloon on Royal where he had a schooner or two of Boston Club punch. O'Malley was not of that sang-pur elegance which would have got him past the portal of the august Boston Club, the most revered in New Orleans, but he had bribed a fancy girl to wheedle the formula from the Boston Club bartender. It consisted of twelve bottles of Champagne, eight bottles of white wine, one and one half bottles raspberry syrup, one half bottle brandy, one half bottle kirschwasser, one quarter bottle Jamaica rum, one quarter bottle Curacao, two pineapples, two dozen oranges, two and one half lbs. sugar, seltzer and ice. This was enough to serve several persons.

SOURCE: A. J. Liebling, *The Honest Rainmaker*, 1952

SUGGESTED PROCEDURE

Prepare an oleo-saccharum of twenty-four oranges and 5 cups white sugar. Peel, core and dice the pineapples into half-inch chunks, add to the oleo-saccharum and muddle. Add the juice of the oranges and stir until sugar is dissolved. Strain the liquid into a three-gallon sealable container, pressing the pulp to extract as much of its essence as possible. Add 36 ounces organic raspberry syrup, 12 ounces cognac, 12 ounces kirschwasser, 6 ounces Jamaican rum, 6 ounces Grand Marnier and eight 750-milliliter bottles dry French white wine. Cover the jug and refrigerate for an hour or two. At this point, the Punch stock can also be bottled and kept refrigerated; if run through a fine filter after a few days, it will keep for a very long time indeed.

To serve, pour the stock into a very large Punch bowl over a very large block of ice and add a case of Champagne and 6 to 9 liters seltzer.

NOTES
The rum is here to provide bouquet and should be a full-on Pirate Juice; the cognac, VSOP.

The yield here is 120 cups. That's a lot of Punch. Indeed, I must confess that I have never made the full recipe. It can be easily scaled down, though, by following this formula: for every bottle of Champagne, add 3½ ounces sugar, the juice and rind of two oranges, one-sixth of a pineapple, 3 ounces raspberry syrup, 1 ounce each cognac and kirschwasser, ½ ounce each Jamaican rum and Grand Marnier, 1 pint white wine and a liter of seltzer.

FOUR ORIGINAL PUNCHES

The efflorescence of American Punch-making would prove to be brief: by the 1880s, in the new steam-powered, electric-lit, heavy-machinery America, occasions for gents to flit around the bowl like so many bearded hummingbirds were becoming scarce. The old leisurely slosh of club life, where Punch had been the order of the day for a century and a half, was on the wane. Rather than sideboards groaning under gargantuan bowls whose contents were curated by dedicated, one-drink specialists, clubhouses now featured full bars manned by expert, saloon-style barkeepers who turned out individual—and individualized—Cocktails in endless profusion. Drink what you like, but do it quick. Even the venerable Hoboken Turtle Club, once famous for the peculiar savoriness of its Champagne Punch, had taken to breakfasting on Cocktails by the pitcher (that way "you can't tell how many cocktails a man has drunk," as the club's bartender observed in 1893).

At the other great bastion of Punch-drinking, the splendid social function, it was also under siege. There the culprit wasn't the
short-and-potent Cocktail but rather the long-and-limp Claret Cup
and its ilk, early Victorian innovations based on "light" (i.e., unfortified) wines that were then iced, watered, flavored lightly with spirits and garnished like an Easter bonnet. As one etiquette guide
dictated in 1887, "Every lady should know how to mix cup, as it
is . . . preferable in its effects to the heavier article so common at
parties—punch." In England, this one had proved to be the deadlier
opponent; by 1850, Claret Cup, Champagne Cup and Badminton
(another member of the tribe) were the social drinks of choice. In
America, the Cup and Punch would both yield to the almighty
Cocktail.

Punch did survive, after a fashion, but it had to adapt to do so.
Labor-intensive techniques had to change, along with rare and exquisite ingredients (rising liquor taxes saw to that—once cognac cost
a hundred dollars a gallon rather than ten dollars, Brandy Punch
wasn't quite so attractive). Bottled, canned or frozen juices would
eventually replace fresh ones, just as they were doing everywhere,
and carbonated soft drinks would stand in for Champagne. By way
of compensation, twentieth-century Punch-makers borrowed the
fancy garnish from the Cup; if the Punch couldn't be exquisite, at
least it could be pretty. This situation prevailed until the end of the
century.

Fortunately, traditional Punch—*real* Punch—is beginning to
shake off its slumber and reclaim its kingdom. The Cocktail revolution of recent years has brought with it a renewed commitment to
doing things the old-fashioned way, without labor-saving shortcuts
or cheeseparing compromises. One by one, classes of drinks have
been pulled off the shelf, refurbished, restored and rejuvenated.
First it was the Gin Martini, then the Cocktail in general, the Sour,
the Fizz, the Julep. Now, it's Punch's turn. Walk into one of the
new, top-quality bars where the revolution is being propagated, and
there's a good chance you'll see a shelf of cheerful-looking bowls
and a few tables of people ladling themselves into soggy satori.

Death & Co., PDT and the Clover Club in New York; the Hawksmoor in London; Ten 01 in Portland, Oregon; Drink in Boston; Rickhouse in San Francisco—the list could go on, each bar with its own clever take on the now-ancient combination of strong and weak, sour, sweet and spicy.

Tempted as I am to close this volume by rounding up a bunch of formulae from these excellent establishments, I'll refrain: these days, top mixologists are churning out books like so many Grub Street alchemists, each encapsulating the philosophy, rituals and recipes of his or her bar. So I'll let the people behind those recipes write them up themselves. Instead, I'll close with four more or less original recipes of my own, each of which is included here because I have tested it on members of the tippling public many, many times and found it satisfactory—well, okay, not the last one, but that has peculiar reasons of its own.

BOMBAY GOVERNMENT PUNCH

Sometime back in 2003 or 2004, I took my first crack at writing a history of Punch, for Slow Food USA's newsletter, *The Snail*. Fortunately, one of the first books I consulted was Henry Yule and Arthur Burnell's 1886 classic of multicultural lexicography, *Hobson-Jobson: A Glossary of Colloquial Anglo-Indian Words and Phrases, and of Kindred Terms, Etymological, Historical, Geographical and Discursive*. For that article, as indeed for this book, it proved a peerless source, packed with illustrative historical quotations on—among many other things—Anglo-Indian drinking. It was there I first encountered the quote from the Order Book of the Bombay Government upon which the Bombay Presidency Punch described earlier is based. Lacking any convenient source of arrack, I applied its basic proportions sometimes to brandy, other times to rum and often to a mixture of both, of more brands than I could possibly recall. Over the years, I've inflicted the results on pretty much anybody I could lure within reach of a ladle, from the Culinary Historians of New York to the poker-playing foodies who attended the 2006 Foxwoods Food & Wine Festival, with a whole lot of friends and acquaintances in between. I haven't had a lot of complaints, which testifies to the soundness and flexibility of the East India Company's Punch-making.

THE ORIGINAL FORMULA

To prepare, first stir 2 cups demerara or turbinado sugar in 1 cup water over a low flame until the sugar has dissolved (about five minutes). Let this cool. Then squeeze twelve limes and combine the juice in a large bowl with 12 ounces of the sugar syrup and stir. Add two 750-milliliter bottles of 10 Cane rum—or one bottle of 10 Cane and one 750-milliliter bottle of

Hennessy Privilege VSOP cognac—and top off with 2 quarts water or, for a more stimulating concoction, cold black or green tea (use 2½ tablespoons loose tea or eight tea bags). Stir again and refrigerate. Half an hour before serving, add a large block of ice (this can be made by freezing 2 quarts of water in a bowl overnight), taste and adjust for sweetness, if necessary, with the additional syrup. Grate nutmeg over the top. Serves twenty, or ten journalists.

NOTES
Any decent cognac and/or rum (or, indeed, arrack) can be substituted for the Hennessy and the 10 Cane, although there is no pressing demand to do so. The yield here is technically 16 cups.

Plymouth Pilgrims' Punch

One of the most amusing things with which I have ever been associated is the Plymouth Cocktail Pilgrimage, an institution I cooked up with Simon Ford, then "brand ambassador" (as the drinks industry terms the person who goes around persuading bartenders and their ilk to drink a certain product) for Plymouth gin. Here's how it works: pick a city where a lot of fancy drinking has historically occurred. Identify its most famous bars, whether they're still there or not. Find the addresses for the ones that are gone. Figure out the signature Cocktails for each. Rent a bus. Round up fifty or so bartenders, journalists and Cocktail geeks. Drive them around in said bus, stopping only to have the appropriate drink at each location, whether that means standing on the sidewalk on Rodeo Drive across the street from the site of Romanoff's, strolling down the Strand in London sipping Limmer's Gin Punch out of a gallon-sized hip flask or getting chased out of Madison Square by the U.S. Park Service for clandestinely sipping Manhattan Cocktails there.

Now, one of the (few) problems with these pilgrimages is that bartenders dry out fast and require constant moistening. Yet while they must be provided with something to drink in between official Cocktails, that something can't be too alcoholic, and indeed should even be mildly stimulating. Here is our solution: a light, slightly caffeinated Plymouth Gin Punch I stitched together from several recipes found in William Terrington's 1869 landmark of Victorian mixology, *Cooling Cups and Dainty Drinks*. Each pilgrim, when he or she boards the bus, is issued an engraved hip flask full of it. If anyone should finish that flask—well, okay, they're bartenders. There are refills. Many, many refills.

Prepare an oleo-saccharum with the peel of three lemons and 2 ounces superfine sugar.

Add 1 cup fresh-squeezed lemon juice and stir until sugar has dissolved.

Add 4 ounces rich pineapple syrup, 1 ounce yellow Chartreuse and 1 liter Plymouth gin. Stir again.

Add 1 quart weak green tea (three tea bags, infused three minutes in 1 quart hot water and left to cool). When ready to serve, add 1 liter cold seltzer and a large block of ice.

YIELD: 14 cups.

NOTES

This recipe is for the original version, served in New York in 2007, where we called it the "Gowanus Club Punch" (there is no Gowanus Club, by the way). For every subsequent version, we replaced the yellow Chartreuse with a different liqueur and changed the name. Some others: for Los Angeles, it was the "Al Malaikah Shrine Punch," and the liqueur was Marie Brizard's Apry, an apricot brandy (a mainstay of Golden Age Hollywood mixology). For San Francisco, the "Sydney Ducks' Punch" (named after the Australian convicts who terrorized the city during the Gold Rush); for that, we used green Chartreuse, but we probably should have used Fernet-Branca. For New Orleans, we used Herbsaint, the local absinthe substitute, and called it the "Iberville Club Punch." Et cetera.

To make rich pineapple syrup, stir 4 cups demerara sugar and 2 cups water over a low flame until all sugar has dissolved, than let cool. Peel, core and dice a pineapple into one-inch cubes, put them in a bowl with the syrup and let sit at room temperature overnight (cover the bowl). Strain out the cubes, bottle the syrup and keep refrigerated.

Royal Hibernian Punch, Alias BarSmarts Punch

Another, rather more serious enterprise aimed at bartenders in which I participate is called BarSmarts, during which, under the aegis of the spirits giant Pernod Ricard, I get to travel around the country in the company of booze-business legends Andy Seymour, Paul Pacult, Steve Olson, Doug Frost and Dale DeGroff—my partners in the educational enterprise known as Beverage Alcohol Resource, or BAR—and certify bartenders' skills at mixing drinks. We roll into town, assemble a hundred or so bartenders, spend a few hours showing them some recent developments in mixology, and then ask them to make drinks for us, one at a time. To stand before Dale DeGroff and stir a Martini is not easy.

At least they get a taste of Punch first. One of those recent developments being Punch service, we like to give a quick lesson in how to do it in your bar. This is what we use as an example. It should be noted that traditionally, Irish Whiskey Punch was not adulterated with wine, even one so mellow and insinuating as a rainwater Madeira. More's the pity.

THE ORIGINAL FORMULA

Prepare an oleo-saccharum with the peel of three lemons and 6 ounces white sugar. Add 6 ounces strained lemon juice and stir until the sugar has dissolved. Add to this 12 ounces Sandeman Rainwater Madeira, stir and pour the Madeira shrub into a clean 750-milliliter bottle. Add enough water to the bottle to fill it, seal and refrigerate. Fill another clean 750-milliliter bottle with filtered water and refrigerate that, too.

To serve, pour the bottle of shrub, the bottle of water and one 750-milliliter bottle of Jameson 12 or Redbreast Irish whiskey into a gallon Punch bowl, add a 1½ quart block of ice and grate nutmeg over the top.

YIELD: 9½ cups.

QUICK & DIRTY PUNCH

Not everything has to be so complicated. Case in point. When I was appearing a few years back at the annual Southern Foodways Alliance conference at Oxford, Mississippi, the indispensable and indefatigable John T. Edge, the alliance's director, came up to me with a small mixological problem. The alliance had been donated a large amount of premixed sweet tea and a not-inconsiderable amount of bourbon. Did I know a tasty, traditional way of mixing them? Of course, the question was just John being polite; he knew full well what to do with both. But I was flattered to be consulted (as he suspected I would be) and came up with a Punch that breaks every single one of my core mixological principles save one, which is perhaps the most important one of them all: drink the best thing you can, given what's available. If you can get lemons and real tea, of course you're going to use those. But if it's a choice between commercial lemonade and iced tea and a campground full of folks stuck with Beam and Coke, why not cheat a little? Flexibility in the pursuit of intoxication is no vice.

THE ORIGINAL FORMULA

Combine in a bucket full of ice: 1½ quarts Newman's Own Lightly Sweetened Lemonade, 1½ quarts Newman's Own Iced Tea, 1.5 liters seltzer, 1.75 liters booze (something dark and flavorful; my favorite: 1 liter Jim Beam Black mixed with a 750-milliliter bottle of Wray & Nephew White Overproof rum). For that homemade look, add sliced lemons and grate nutmeg over the top. Ladle away.

YIELD: 26 cups.

NOTES

Other brands of lemonade and iced tea may be used, but try for the minimum number of ingredients in each. You can sour this Punch with fresh-squeezed lemon juice instead of lemonade (use about 14 ounces and add extra water), but that's really not what it's all about. Field conditions, people. If you use fruit-flavored tea, it will be all you can taste. The booze is up to you. Tequila? *Sí.* Bourbon or rye? Yep. Rum? You bet. Gin, vodka or ouzo? Not so much.

PERORATION

TO A FLY, TAKEN OUT OF A BOWL OF PUNCH.

PETER PINDAR, 1792

Ah! poor intoxicated little knave,
Now, senseless, floating on the fragrant wave—
Why not content the cakes alone to munch?
Dearly thou pay'st for buzzing round the bowl—
Lost to the world, thou busy, sweet lipp'd soul:
Thus death, as well as pleasure, dwells with Punch.

Now let me take thee out, and moralize.
Thus 'tis with Mortals as it is with Flies—
Forever hank'ring after Pleasure's cup:
Though Fate, with all his legions, be at hand,

The beasts the draught of Circe can't withstand,
But in goes ev'ry nose, they must, will sup.

Mad are the Passions as a colt untam'd!
When Prudence mounts their backs, to ride them mild
They fling, they snort, they foam, they rise inflam'd,
Insisting on their own soul will so wild!

Gadsbud! my buzzing friend, thou art not dead—
The Fates, so kind, have not yet snapp'd thy thread;
But now thou mov'st a leg, and now its brother,
And, kicking, lo! thou mov'st another.

And now thy little drunken eyes unclose,
And now thou feelest for thy little nose;
And, finding it, thou rubbest thy two hands,
Much as to say, "I'm glad I'm here again!"
And well thou may'st rejoice—'tis very plain
That near wert thou to Death's unsocial lands.

And now thou rollest on thy back about,
Happy to find thyself alive, no doubt;
Now turnest, on the table making rings;
Now crawling, forming a new track;
Now shaking the rich liquor from thy back;
Now flutt'ring nectar from thy silken wings!

Now standing on thy head, thy strength to find,
And poking out thy small, long legs behind;
And now thy pinions dost thou quickly ply,
Preparing soon to leave me—, Farewell, Fly!

Go, join thy brothers on yon sunny board,
And rapture to thy family afford;
There wilt thou find a mistress, or a wife,

That saw thee, drunk, drop senseless in the stream—
Who gave, perhaps, the wide-resounding scream,
And now sits groaning for thy precious life;
Yes, go, and carry comfort to thy friends,
And wisely tell them thy imprudence ends.

Let buns and sugar, for the future, charm;
These will delight, and feed, and work no harm;
While Punch, the grinning, merry imp of sin,
Invites th' unwary wand'rer to a kiss—
Smiles in his face, as tho he meant him bliss—
Then, like an aligator, drags him in!

BRITISH MUSEUM

A Brief Note on
Further Reading

As much as I would have liked to cap this book off with a full list of the hundreds of books, newspapers, magazines, pamphlets and other writings I consulted in writing it, to do so would have meant cutting a chapter of Punches. Given a choice between books and drinks, while I'd like to think that I would take the high road, alas I'll take the drink every time. Here, then, is the quick version:

Books, Google. The Internet, 2006–2010.

Okay, I exaggerate. But it's a plain fact that without Google Books (and, to a much lesser extent, the old Microsoft Live Search Books scans archived at Internet Archive), I might have written a Punch book, but not this one. The bones of the story would have been there, but in many spots the flesh would have been pretty damn meager. The ability to search through full-text versions of millions of eighteenth- and nineteenth-century books has meant that instead of one or two pieces of information to choose from, I often had ten or twenty, enough to distinguish the normative from the anomalous.

As many as possible of the primary sources I've drawn on are at least referred to by name and date. Here, though, are some suggestions for those who wish to read more deeply on some of the topics raised. For the early history of distillation, C. Anne Wilson's *Water of Life* (2006) is, although somewhat too speculative in spots, nonetheless quite enlightening. R. J. Forbes's 1948 *Short History of the Art of Distillation* remains the most definitive work on the subject. Anistatia Miller and Jared Brown's *Spirituous Journey* (two volumes, 2009 and 2010) has much of interest and has the advantage of accessibility. For other English drinkways, see A. D. Francis's excellent *The Wine Trade* (1972) and Peter Haydon's beer-centric *An Inebriated History of Britain* (2005).

For India and the East, any of the relevant journals, travel accounts and the like republished by the Hakluyt Society are well worth picking up, as indeed is any Hakluyt Society book no matter what part of the world it's dealing with. A good general history of the English East India Company is John Keay's 1991 *The Honourable Company*; would that there were a similar one of the mighty VOC, the Dutch East India Company. The fabulous *Nathaniel's Nutmeg*, by Giles Milton (1999), provides a riveting account of the contentious interaction between the two companies in the East. For Indian tippling, there is no better source than Satya Prakash Sangar's thorough *Food and Drink in Mughal India* (1999).

As for sailors, A. J. Pack's *Nelson's Blood* is the standard—and highly readable—account of rum-drinking in the Royal Navy (third edition, 1995). No better insight into eighteenth-century naval life may be gained than from Tobias Smollett's 1748 *Roderick Random*.

Roderick Random is also useful as a guide to London life at the time, as indeed are any of the novels of Smollett's contemporaries. In fact, to truly understand Punch and its milieu, I can recommend no better course of reading than Fielding's *Tom Jones*, Boswell's *Life of Johnson* (not a novel, but it reads like one), Richardson's *Clarissa*,

I suppose (I wish I liked that one more, insightful as it may be), and *Tristram Shandy*, if only because everyone should read that one.

For the Regency years and the early Victorian ones, nothing captures the social whirl better than the chatty reminiscences of Lord William Pitt Lennox, who knew everyone when he was young and talked about them all in amusing detail when he wasn't. Also most useful is John Timbs's *Clubs and Club Life in London* (several editions between 1872 and 1908; Google Books offers full access to at least two). These may and should of course be supplemented with a whole mess of Thackeray and Dickens.

Finally, the colonies. When they were indeed colonies, Dr. Alexander Hamilton wandered through them all, or at least most of them, and supped Punch where he went. The record of his 1744 trip has been published as his *Itinerarium*. When they were no longer colonies—well, much of the sporting life that sprang up then has been covered in *Imbibe!* But no better picture of it can be found than that in the novels of Frank Forester. *The Warwick Woods* is particularly recommended.

Sources for Rare Ingredients and Tools

Fortunately, Punch-making uses far fewer exotic ingredients and obscure tools than making Cocktails. For the liquors, the best place to go is DrinkUpNY.com, which carries Batavia arrack and other such goodies. Spices and exotic sugars can be obtained from New York's magnificent Kalustyan's (www.kalustyans.com). For ambergris, however, you'll have to send your treasure to New Zealand (www.ambergris.co.nz). The season for Seville oranges is short (December to February); when they're in season, try Melissas.com. I understand that they will freeze well, although I can never hang on to them long enough to try it.

On to the gear. Ladles are a problem; flea markets are your best bet there. I also have yet to find a truly elegant modern nutmeg grater, but perfectly adequate Le Creuset earthenware bowls and jugs may be obtained from Amazon.com (look for the stoneware

4⅝-quart mixing bowl and the three-quart Sangria pitcher). Ra Chand juicers can also be sourced through Amazon but are widely available elsewhere, for cheaper. Libbey 8089 two-ounce Georgia sherry glasses, my favorite style of Punch glass, can be found through Amazon.com.

Original Texts of Translated Recipes

For the completists.

PUNSCHGLÜHBOWLE

From *Bowlen und Punsche fur den Feld- und Manover-gebrauch der Deutschen Armee*, 1900

Man koche in einem geräumigen kochgeschirr zehn Liter leichten roten Landwein unter fortwährendem Umrühen mit fünf Liter Arrack, füge während des kochens ein Pfund Zucker bei und zerschneide vier Pomeranzen bezw. Apfelsinen, sowie zwei bis drei Citronen. Nachndem man besonders darauf geachtet hat, dass die Fruchtschieben von kernen befreit sind, lasse man die Fruchtscheiben mit der Mischung noch etwa fuenf minuten

kochen, giesse alsdann die kochende Mischung in eine Bowle um
und lasse dieselbe brennend servieren. Einer Berdünnung durch
einen Mehrzusatz von leichtem roten landwein steht nichts im
Wege.

PUNCH À LA ROMAINE (THE EASY WAY)

From P. C. Robert, *La grande cuisine simplifiée*, 1845

*Clarifiez une livre et demie de sucre, mettez-y le zeste de 2 citrons
et de 2 bigarades, exprimez le jus de 8 citrons; ajoutez à ce
mélange un demi-litre d'eau, passez le tout dans un tamis neuf
et faites prendre cette décoction à la glace; fouettez ensuite 3 blancs
d'œufs en neige, que vous n'incorporez dans votre punch qu'au
moment de le servir, en y ajoutant un verre de vin de Champagne
et u, demi-verre de rhum; l'amalgame étant bien fait, vous servez
ce punch dans des verres à pied.*

ACKNOWLEDGMENTS

First of all, I must acknowledge that sundry parts of this book have appeared, in altered form, in *Esquire, Saveur, The Malt Advocate, Bon Appétit, Wine & Spirits*, Slow Food USA's *Snail, Mixology* and the late, lamented *Gourmet*. I am very grateful to them all.

With every book I write I seem to need more help. The list of people who assisted me materially or spiritually in the preparation of this volume is absurdly long—far longer than a Punch-drinking man can accurately remember. If I have omitted your name here, you have my sincerest apologies, as does everyone to whom I still owe an email.

The number of people who have offered moral support and practical advice, shared hard-won morsels of information, offered venues for me to muse about Punch or supplied the necessary C_2H_5OH is truly humbling. Here are some of them: Dayan Abeyaratne (arrack! cashew fenny!), Eric Alperin, Stephan Berg, Cary Berger, Jeff Berry, Jacques "Van Der Hum" Bezuidenhout, the ever-helpful Greg

Boehm, Jared Brown, Tad "Joisey" Carducci, Fernando Castellon (our man in Lyons), Erick "Pac Man" Castro, Wayne Collins, Tony Conigliaro, Jason Crawley (and what a mistake it is to put those three together!), the ever-lovely Jill DeGroff, the indefatigable Philip "Mr. Genever" Duff, John T. Edge, H. Joseph "Thermometer" Ehrmann, Eric Ellestad, John Gertsen (thanks for the glassware, dude!), Ted Haigh, Robert Hess, the mysterious Allen Katz, Don Lee, Leonard Lopate (who is not averse to drinking a little Punch on the radio), Diego Loret de Mola, Lance Mayhew, Anistatia Miller, Rosalind Muggeridge of the Mount Vernon Hotel Museum (I want that bar!), Sean Muldoon and his shebeen full of sharks, Tal "Kopstoot" Nadari and all my good friends at Lucas Bols, Josey Packard, Linda Pellaccio of the Culinary Historians of New York, Jeff "Hennessexy" Pogash, Lis Riba (thanks for the Fish-House Punch recipe!), Debbie "the Rizz" Rizzo, Eric Seed, Tad "Old Tom" Seestedt, Daniel Shoemaker, Nick Strangeway, Lesley Townsend, Ann Tuennerman, Charles Vexenat, Charlotte Voissey, and the evil elf who keeps trying to get me to drink Fernet-Branca.

To the staffs of the New York Public Library, the British Library, the British Museum and New York University's Elmer Holmes Bobst Library, thank you. Without you, history doesn't get written. I should probably throw the staff of BookFinder.com in there, too.

Some poor souls have had to work with me while I was preoccupied with this project. To my partners in BAR, Dale "Marie" DeGroff, Doug "They're Going Down" Frost, Steve "Buzz" Olson, Paul "the Sexiest Man in Showbiz" Pacult, and Andy "Did He Just Say That?" Seymour, thank you, brave men. And to Aisha Sharpe, Willy Shine, and Leo "Lemonator" DeGroff, thank you, you rock! I say the same to my sometime partner-in-crime, Simon Ford. And also to Steve Walkerwicz, Suzanne Freedman, Shawn Kelley, Lora Piazza and Leslie Pariseau of BarSmarts. And my poor editors—Ross McCammon, Lew Bryson, James Rodewald, Beth Kracklauer, Noah Rothbaum, Tara Q. Thomas, Zoe Singer and Heather John. I swear I'll have it in in the morning. Okay, early afternoon. Would you believe end of the day? How many words again?

Many thanks are also due to the Associate Members of the North Gowanus Institute for Cranial Distempers. In ascending/ descending alphabetical order, they are: Hannah Clark, Patrick Watson, Melissa Clark, Mike Sweeney, Doug Dibbern, Cynthia Sweeney, Cheryl Donegan, Katherine Schulten, Mike Dulchin, Audrey Saunders, Sherwin Dunner, Bryony Romer, Linden Elstran, Julie Reiner, Susan Fedoroff, Michelle Pravda, St. John Frizzell, Zack Pelaccio, Tony Gerber, Garrett Oliver, Daniel Gercke, Nick Noyes, Vince Giordano, Lynn Nottage, Kenneth "Cagey" Goldsmith, Jessica Monaco, Paul "My Face Is a Mirror" Gustings, Valerie Meehan, Alex Halberstadt, Peter Meehan, Joltin' John Hodgman, Jim Meehan, Ana Jovancicevic, Laura McMillian, Shawn Kelley (Shawn's so nice she gets thanked twice), Chris McMillian, Steve Kelley, Joshua Mack, and the Piss-Artist Formerly Known as Gary Regan.

Janis Donnaud, my agent, is simply great. Thank you.

Marian Lizzi, my editor, somehow manages to stay funny and nice despite sometimes I am quite sure wanting to throttle me. Also, she's a hell of an editor. Thank you.

This project has caused my wife, Karen, and my daughter, Marina, to have to put up with more absence, preoccupation and stress-induced personality disorder than anyone should, especially people as sweet as they are. Here, where I need them the most, words fail me. Thank you.

Finally, I'd like to thank Kathie Lee for not wrecking my punch ladle.

INDEX

Page numbers in *italics* represent illustrations.